Western Theory in East Asian Contexts

Literatures, Cultures, Translation

Literatures, Cultures, Translation presents books that engage central issues in translation studies such as history, politics, and gender in and of literary translation, as well as books that open new avenues for study. Volumes in the series follow two main strands of inquiry: one strand brings a wider context to translation through an interdisciplinary interrogation, while the other hones in on the history and politics of the translation of seminal works in literary and intellectual history.

Series Editors
Brian James Baer, Kent State University, USA
Michelle Woods, The State University of New York, New Paltz, USA

Editorial Board
Paul Bandia, Professeur titulaire, Concordia University, Canada, and Senior Fellow, the W.E.B. Du Bois Institute for African American Research, Harvard University, USA
Susan Bassnett, Professor of Comparative Literature, Warwick University, UK.
Leo Tak-hung Chan, Lingnan University, Hong Kong, China
Michael Cronin, Dublin City University, Republic of Ireland
Edwin Gentzler, University of Massachusetts Amherst, USA
Carol Maier, Kent State University, USA
Denise Merkle, Moncton University, Canada
Michaela Wolf, University of Graz, Austria

Volumes in the Series
Translation and the Making of Modern Russian Literature, Brian James Baer
Interpreting in Nazi Concentration Camps, edited by Michaela Wolf
Exorcising Translation: Towards an Intercivilizational Turn, Douglas Robinson
Literary Translation and the Making of Originals, Karen Emmerich
The Translator on Stage, Geraldine Brodie
Transgender, Translation, Translingual Address, Douglas Robinson
Western Theory in East Asian Contexts: Translation and Transtextual Rewriting, Leo Tak-hung Chan
The Translator's Visibility: Scenes from Contemporary Latin American Fiction (forthcoming), Heather Cleary
The Relocation of Culture: Translations, Migrations, Borders (forthcoming), Simona Bertacco and Nicoletta Vallorani

Western Theory in East Asian Contexts

Translation and Transtextual Rewriting

Leo Tak-hung Chan

BLOOMSBURY ACADEMIC
NEW YORK • LONDON • OXFORD • NEW DELHI • SYDNEY

BLOOMSBURY ACADEMIC
Bloomsbury Publishing Inc
1385 Broadway, New York, NY 10018, USA
50 Bedford Square, London, WC1B 3DP, UK

BLOOMSBURY, BLOOMSBURY ACADEMIC and the Diana logo are trademarks of
Bloomsbury Publishing Plc

First published in the United States of America 2020

Copyright © Leo Tak-hung Chan, 2020

For legal purposes the Acknowledgments on p. ix constitute an extension of this copyright page.

Cover design by Daniel Benneworth-Gray
Cover image: A meeting of Japan, China, and the West,
Shiba Kokan, Late 18th century

All rights reserved. No part of this publication may be reproduced or transmitted in any form or by any means, electronic or mechanical, including photocopying, recording, or any information storage or retrieval system, without prior permission in writing from the publishers.

Bloomsbury Publishing Inc does not have any control over, or responsibility for, any third-party websites referred to or in this book. All internet addresses given in this book were correct at the time of going to press. The author and publisher regret any inconvenience caused if addresses have changed or sites have ceased to exist, but can accept no responsibility for any such changes.

Whilst every effort has been made to locate copyright holders the publishers would be grateful to hear from any person(s) not here acknowledged.

Library of Congress Cataloging-in-Publication Data
Names: Chan, Tak-hung Leo, 1954- author.
Title: Western theory in East Asian contexts: translation and transtextual rewriting / Leo Tak-hung Chan.
Description: New York: Bloomsbury Academic, 2020. | Series: Literatures, cultures, translation | Includes bibliographical references and index. | Summary: "A major contribution to translation and adaptation studies as well as to our understanding of East Asian culture and literature"– Provided by publisher.
Identifiers: LCCN 2020029929 (print) | LCCN 2020029930 (ebook) | ISBN 9781501327827 (paperback) | ISBN 9781501327834 (hardback) | ISBN 9781501327841 (epub) | ISBN 9781501327858 (pdf)
Subjects: LCSH: Translating and interpreting–East Asia. | East Asian literature–Translations–History and criticism. | Literature–Adaptations–History and criticism.
Classification: LCC P306.8.E27 C53 2020 (print) | LCC P306.8.E27 (ebook) | DDC 418/.02–dc23
LC record available at https://lccn.loc.gov/2020029929
LC ebook record available at https://lccn.loc.gov/2020029930

ISBN: HB: 978-1-5013-2783-4
PB: 978-1-5013-2782-7
ePDF: 978-1-5013-2785-8
eBook: 978-1-5013-2784-1

Typeset by Deanta Global Publishing Services, Chennai, India

To find out more about our authors and books visit www.bloomsbury.com and sign up for our newsletters.

To Sandy Jen Hai-hua

Contents

List of Illustrations	viii
Acknowledgments	ix
Introduction	1
1 The Transtextual Triad, Similar but Not the Same	10

Part I

2 Freely Rendered: Aesop's Fables in Nineteenth-Century China	37
3 A Higher Loyalty? The (Ab)uses of Aesthetic Theories of Translation	57

Part II

4 Adaptation Studies through a Translation Lens	75
5 Accommodation and Adaptation: The Case of East Asia	91
6 *Boys over Flowers*: Localization in a Web of (Re)adaptations	109

Part III

7 The Vicissitudes of *Imitatio*, Historically	131
8 "New Wine in Old Bottles": Two Sino-Japanese Traditions of Imitation	145
9 Receptive Transcreation: Simulating James Joyce's Narrative Style	162
10 The Aggregate Monkey: Parody and Pastiche in Japanese Manga	179
Conclusion	198
Bibliography	205
Index	227

Illustrations

Figures

5.1 "The Peony Lantern" with *Kundoku* Notations   100
8.1 A "Popular" Version of *Water Margin*: *Tsūzoku chūgi suikoden* (Chapter 1)   153
10.1 Sanzō, Monkey, Gojō, and Hakkai   192

Tables

4.1 Translation and Adaptation from a Semiotic Perspective (Adapted from Gottlieb 2005)   85
6.1 Names of Characters in the Japanese, Taiwanese, and Korean Versions   113
6.2 Names of Characters in *Let's Go Watch the Meteor Shower* (2009) and *Meteor Garden* (2018)   118
6.3 Major Taiwanese TV Adaptations of Japanese Manga and Novels   121
6.4 Major Korean TV Adaptations of Japanese Manga and Novels   122
8.1 Translations and Imitations of *Water Margin* in Edo Japan (Selected)   156
10.1 Categories of Imitations (Revised from Genette 1997)   181

Acknowledgments

For a book dealing with the twin subjects of Western theory and East Asian reality, it is only apposite that the main parties to be thanked should come from the two geographical regions at almost opposite ends of the world.

The major theoretical portions of the present book were presented at three CETRA Research Summer Schools, beginning with my Chair Professorial lectures in 2017, and then in the seminars that I conducted as regular staff in 2018 and 2019. I owe a great debt to the opportunities offered by the Center for Translation Studies at KU Leuven to learn through teaching. In fact, I was inducted into translation studies some twenty years ago there, through the most indefatigable of teachers, José Lambert, who commented extensively on my written work as supervisor at the time. Despite his hectic schedule divided between Belgium and Brazil last year, he also provided much insightful feedback on my manuscript right before it went to press. Special thanks go to Dirk Delabastita, Yves Gambier, and Luc van Doorslaer for their input on my theoretical framework; their views are apparent in the preceding pages. Luc's many kindnesses during my several trips to the Antwerp campus, too, will always be remembered.

Over to the East Asian side. The roots of my fascination with "East Asianness" go back to my postgraduate studies at Indiana University in the 1980s. Against the lively intellectual atmosphere fostered by the department faculty and students there, I was able to take advantage of the excellent Japanese language instruction and the wide-ranging courses on East Asian Studies. I recall with fondness the courses on modern Japanese literature that I took from Kenneth Yasuda, and on Japanese religions from Toyoaki Uehara. They were the subliminal driving forces behind this book.

More direct support came from Daniel Gallimore, my host during the semester that I spent in spring 2014 at Kwansei Gakuin University. I enjoyed tremendously the bi-weekly, one-on-one sessions in his office on Japanese literary and translation history from a Western Japanologist's perspective. It was Narita Shizuka, at the same university, who alerted me to the potentials of researching Japanese manga adaptations of classical Chinese literature. Among my other Japanese friends, my gratitude goes to Nana Sato-Rossberg, for her invitation to the First East Asian Translation Studies Conference in Norwich, where at a roundtable the central thesis of the present study had its inception, and to Emiko Okayama, who taught me much about Edo textual traditions and helped me avoid many a mistake in interpreting my research findings. My conclusion has benefited from the invaluable comments by Rebekah Clements, whose monograph on the cultural history of Japan in the early modern period has been a fountain of inspiration.

Among my Chinese colleagues, I would like to note the friendship of Hu Gengshen, Luo Xuanmin, and Tao Youlan, which has sustained me in recent years, especially as research without a pragmatic edge became less and less defensible. I also appreciate the invaluable assistance given by Ni Jindan, who allowed me to avail myself of her knowledge of premodern Sino-Japanese literary history. Her quick responses to my queries from Down Under are most appreciated.

Individual chapters of this book have been presented on various occasions over the past decade, although I would like to mention four of them in particular. One is the International Conference on "Globalization and Cultural Identity/Translation," held in Foguang University at Chiaohsi (Taiwan) in 2008, where I gave a keynote speech based on an early version of the chapter on Murakami Haruki. The other is Yeditepe University's International Conference on "Transferring Cultural Images: Parallels between Stereotyping and Globalizing," held in Istanbul in 2014. My keynote lecture on *Boys over Flowers* was warmly received by Joep Leerssen, who discerned striking Western parallels to the East Asian scenario I described. I thank him for his kind encouragement. In 2018, I gave two seminars, one on Murakami Haruki at the Center for Cross-cultural Studies, Fu-jen Catholic University, and the other on adaptation theory at the Department of Modern Languages, University of Exeter. I am thankful to Yang Chengshu and Ting Guo, respectively, for their invitations and the hospitality bestowed on me during my campus visits.

Portions of this book have been revised from previously published articles in *Perspectives, META, Linguistica Antverpiensia, Asian Cultural Studies*, and David Pollard's *Translation and Creation: Readings of Western Literature in Early Modern China, 1840–1918* (John Benjamins, 1998). In much the same way as the writers and artists discussed in this book transformed and revived earlier works, I have substantially rewritten these publications to bring the arguments in line with the central concerns of the present study.

For the impetus to embark on a project after decades of work on Chinese-English translation theory and history, I am indebted to Brian James Baer, whose acquaintance I made through my earlier St. Jerome monograph. When he first raised the possibility of my contributing a monograph to the "Literatures, Cultures, Translation" series, I had no idea it would take so long to materialize. The huge amount of time needed to peruse even the most rudimentary of references on my subject was something I could ill afford in the years when I played the double roles of department head and president of Hong Kong's translation society. The generous funding from the Hong Kong Research Grants Council, in the form of a Humanities and Social Sciences Prestigious Fellowship that gave me a full year's leave from Lingnan University in 2018–19, was thus a godsend, which enabled me to bring the project to completion.

I am grateful for the editorial assistance I have received since 2016 from Bloomsbury Academic. Other than Brian, I am also indebted to Michelle Woods, Joseph Gautham, Haaris Naqvi, Rachel Moore, Rachel Walker, and Amy Martin, whose expert guidance through the months of manuscript preparation ensured smooth sailing. The two reviewers' incisive criticisms encouraged me to revamp the original design of the book, and come up with something that I hope they can now find satisfying. Lin Qingyang, my doctoral student, deserves thanks for carefully proofreading several chapters; so does Vincci Leung, my research assistant of many years, who took care of administrative and clerical matters. Finally, like almost all my other scholarly endeavors, the present project bears witness to the unstinting support and sacrifice of Sandy, my loving wife of some thirty-five years. To her it is dedicated.

Introduction

Questions of how to define translation, how that definition changes across time, and whether it can be used to explain phenomena in different traditions, have continued to preoccupy scholars in the field. The present study begins with generic issues related to translation and, on that basis, moves on to discuss how concepts of translation can be integrated into the dynamics of culture. Understood broadly as transtextual rewriting, translation encompasses various forms of textual maneuvering that take place across languages and cultures, the most notable among them being adaptation and imitation, both belonging, with translation, to what appears to be the same "family." Often separately treated as different text-types, the three are in fact related through the bridging term of "free translation," the cross-writing strategy that does not work toward closely replicating the meaning of the original—in other words, refuting the principle of fidelity, the hallmark of what has been called the adequate translation. One needs to note that the trio should be understood not only as textual entities but, more appropriately, as discursive phenomena found in different traditions, both East and West, although in recent decades much rigorous theorization has taken place in the West, by scholars directly or indirectly associated with the discipline of translation studies. It thus behooves us to look at translation, adaptation, and imitation from institutional perspectives, to begin with.

Both translation studies and adaptation studies are young disciplines, but the alignment between the two is more than obvious if we trace the trajectories of their growth and institutionalization, which betrays what may be termed an attraction-repulsion syndrome. On the other hand, imitation studies constituted, for some time in the past, an arena for the study of intertextual relationships, although it has yet to recover from the stigmatization attached to the genre as a result of the valorization of originality as a key virtue in literary expression. The current view that imitation is a crucial facet of our postmodern condition may very well work in its favor. As of the present moment, one sees many translation scholars seeking shared ground even as certain adaptation scholars opt for a separate disciplinary identity, while re-establishing the link between translation and imitation studies seems to be a highly feasible endeavor, given the combined history the two forms have had for centuries. In any case, there is little doubt that, by bringing together the three big genres—as well as the concepts behind them—in scholarly investigation, new vistas can be opened up on cultural interaction in our rapidly globalizing context.

Having said this, however, we are still left with the problem of distinguishing between the three forms of transtextual rewriting that can be viewed through the prism of translation studies. The disparities between the three forms have been cited as the reason for generic segregation. But we would also like to note some crucial similarities. While the next chapter will elaborate closely the "similar but not the same" situation with regard to the transtextual triad, it will be useful to note the following at this point. With respect to the binarism of translation versus adaptation, there has long been a debate on which is the more inclusive term. Is adaptation part of translation, or is it the other way round? Given that the semantic coverage of the term "adaptation" has been continually enlarged over the years, one can return to etymological origins for some core meanings, and those of adjusting, accommodating, and modulating come to the fore. As for the semantic overlap between translation and imitation, perhaps "imitation" can be more strictly defined with reference to its root meanings of reproducing, duplicating, and remodeling. As will be discussed further in that chapter, such highlighting of some features reflects an "evolutionary" framework for understanding transtextual relationships. And when it is accepted that generic similarities can co-exist with generic differences, the boundaries between the three forms need not be frozen up; it is better that they remain fuzzy, yet definable though observable instances of actual use. Close and static definitions should be replaced with open, fluid ones, while value judgments (good versus bad, for instance) cease to be relevant. By abandoning the more restrictive definitions that "translation" has so far been given, it becomes possible to reformulate this word as the overarching term that encompasses marginal forms that hitherto "did not belong."[1]

The significance of all this for translation studies research cannot be overstressed. Under the impact of the contributions by an entire generation of translation scholars from the 1970s to the 1990s (e.g., Even-Zohar 1978; Toury 1980; Lambert 1991; Hermans 1999), translation has continued to expand its perimeters and is no longer understood in its narrower sense as a tool that facilitates communication with, or transmits information to, speakers of another language. A much broader conceptualization of translation by including in it textual phenomena that may be seen as "partially translational" will therefore expand the scope of enquiry to include more complex cultural

---

[1] With reference to the definitions attempted here, it must be added that popular vocabulary is often at odds with academic terminology as used in the present study. Perhaps nowhere is that seen more clearly than in the words "adaptation" and "imitation."

interactions that are taking place around us. Rather than isolating categories such as adaptation and imitation from translation, an attempt at integration will, as we shall show with reference to East Asian examples, prove useful in the analysis of a broad international context which had remained in the background when Western theories were advanced, debated, and consolidated. While the present study engages with terms that have almost become outdated—"free translation," "literal translation," and "fidelity," for instance, may be viewed as normative, philological categories that belong to another era[2]—the aim is nevertheless to revive their utility when redeployed to understand the varied manifestations of translation outside of the temporal and spatial contexts in which they were originally formulated. Such an approach can even pave the way for studies of other "new" phenomena or processes, like transformation, transcreation, and transculturation, in the future. It is precisely for this reason that, after the generic issues are dealt with in Chapter 1, we will move on to East Asia, in which the triangular model of analysis will be applied, with occasional comparisons with Western traditions. It is hoped that the Sino-Japanese case will reveal how a bolder conception of translation can enable better understanding of the issues involved in the writing of non-Western translation histories as well as reveal the strengths and limitations of Western views of what translation is.

Indeed the East Asian case illustrates very well how rewriting is practiced (if not yet theorized) in a different geo-cultural context. A concern with intra-regional dynamics, as seen in the textual inter-crossings between China and Japan, will inform the microscopic readings of individual works and the macroscopic surveys of entire traditions to follow. (One additional feature of this study is that some Sino-Western translations are also contrasted with Sino-Japanese ones.) Concrete examples of the three peripheral forms of translation, in particular, are analyzed to underscore the nature of transtextual interaction between China and Japan. Since a call was issued over a decade ago for research that counters Eurocentric paradigms, there has been unanimous agreement that a consideration of non-European cases will stimulate reflection on the applicability of theories developed in European contexts. Undoubtedly, very little research has been carried out on the bidirectional movement of texts between China and Japan outside of some departments of national literatures in the two countries, and only a few (e.g., Wakabayashi 2005a; Clements 2015) have attempted to work from a translation studies perspective. Western scholarship has so far devoted

---

[2] We may say the same of "equivalence," "domestication," "foreignization," and so on. It is perhaps time that these concepts should also be reviewed and renewed.

much less attention to translation involving two non-European languages than to that between European ones, or between a non-Western language and English, the present-day global lingua franca. As it is, intra-Asian translation traditions have often been sidelined even as the traditional East-West dichotomy attracts increasing interest. Hopefully, the present study will encourage serious thinking about mainstream models as well as demonstrate the advantages of a "trans" approach to rewritten texts by incorporating East Asian issues into a Western-based theoretical framework.

That a lacuna exists in the scholarship on Sino-Japanese transtextual relations from a translational perspective is a fact that bears reiterating. For a region that makes up over 20 percent of the global population, claims two of the world's largest economies, and boasts one of the longest written traditions in human history, the dearth of relevant research—in English as in the national languages—is nothing short of surprising. Other than a few monographs and doctoral theses (Pastreich 2011; Hedberg 2012) and one collected volume that is fast becoming dated (Salmon 1987, reprinted in 2013), studies of premodern rewriting practices involving Chinese texts by Japanese and Korean authors have been few and far between. As for the contemporary scene, there has been a recent flood of studies of the cultural interactions between China, Japan, and Korea as crystallized in the Japanese and Korean Waves (Cho 2011; Jung 2009; Chua and Iwabuchi 2008; Hillenbrand 2007; Iwabuchi 2004). Virtually none of these, however, deals exclusively with translations, and only a handful explore the adaptive and imitative dimensions of textual transfer in cross-cultural settings. Transtextual processes, as explicated with particular attention paid to their cultural implications, are little studied, except possibly the increasing concern with intermedial transformations that occur with texts in one medium reworked into those of another.[3]

The special nature of Chinese-Korean-Japanese transtextual rewriting, with its independent course of evolution outside of the West and a history as long as that of vernacular translations of Greek and Latin, is a challenging test-case for querying some posited universals in translation theory (see Chesterman 2014). Putting aside the question of whether untranslated Chinese texts with added notations as read by Japanese and Koreans are indeed "translations," there is overwhelming evidence that translation had been practiced in East Asia ever since there were diplomatic and religious

---

[3] For long, literary adaptations and imitations have constituted the bulk of texts "moved" between China and Japan. However, with the contemporary dominance of media like TV and film for re-presenting texts, there has been a shift of research interest from the verbal to the visual (or verbal-cum-visual).

activities involving speakers without knowledge of each other's languages. It goes without saying that understanding the textual relationship between East Asian countries will throw new light on "universalist" approaches to translation that can be critiqued for its lack of due respect for particularism—or regionalism, for that matter. Institutional compartmentalization is again a cause for the unsatisfactory situation: it is readily obvious that research on East Asian intertextualities has traditionally been undertaken either in departments of national literatures (like Departments of Chinese, Japanese, and Korean) in the three countries, or in comparative literature departments, where East-West comparisons occupy center stage. Since, in numerical terms, translation studies departments are still smaller, one has yet to see how translation theories and methodologies can be more extensively deployed.

Much has been said of a dialogue between East and West in translation theory, but are we seeking convergences rather than divergences, analogues and not antitheses? If, in answer to calls for theoretical enlargement (Tymozcko 2007), translation is to be reconceptualized through examining practices past and present in diverse geo-cultural sites, undoubtedly significant challenges will be presented by the East Asian case, with its distinctive regional characteristics. The difficulties are compounded by a narrow definition of what translation is, as we have explained above. Ultimately, we must ask: What if the traditional boundaries within which the concept of translation has been confined were to be replaced by a more fluid and flexible notion that includes not only adaptation and imitation, but also transcreation, versioning, remediation, transposition, localization, and so on—even "transmesis" (Beebee 2012)? No doubt, in the light of its Latin etymon *transferro* (meaning "to transfer" or "to carry across"), translation should be allied to all the "trans" processes like transfusion, transmutation, transplantation and, of course, transfer.[4] The current study presents a case in which translation and adaptation and imitation are merged rather than made to fall within neatly separate compartments, with implications for understanding models at variance with those from European contexts. There happens to be an abundance of the "free" forms in traditional and even modern East Asia, including adaptations of Chinese narratives in Japan and Korea, imitation and spin-offs by Japanese authors who recast borrowed

---

[4] Transfer studies has evolved significantly in recent years: from its early beginnings in France and Germany, to acceptance by the US and Canadian academia; it is now an influential interdisciplinary field (see Espagne and Werner 1988; D'hulst 2018). Its affinity with the approach adopted in this book can be seen in the shared concern with the transformation of transferred cultural artefacts through adaptation, imitation, and other re-semanticization processes.

material, contemporary parodies of canonical novels from China, and so on. Put simply, there have been more of these forms of "translation" than of "faithful" or "literal" translations, more of "translation improper" than of "translation proper" (to use Roman Jakobson's terminology). What do we make of such a scenario? Can East Asian translation realities sit comfortably with Western theory?

A useful starting point for the exploratory trip we are taking is Joseph R. Allen's idea of the "Babel fallacy" in East Asia (Allen 2019). He raises the point that the notion of translation—as an interlingual operation involving the rendering of a source text into a target text on terms of equivalence—is a Western one, advocated in the first place by theorists whose primary focus is on its prototypical form. While translation of this kind was indeed practiced in premodern times in China, Japan, and Korea, it never assumed the centrality imputed to it by scholars eager to transplant Western models.[5] Instead, the peripheral forms, whether free or adaptive or imitative, were more pervasive in earlier times, especially in the literary sphere. This can be easily understood given the centrifugal force exerted by the cultural center that was China. It should be said that it was in the nonliterary fields (like religion, science, and technology) that translation of the prototypical sort dominated, as it still does today in pragmatic domains where fidelity remains the golden principle to be followed. The idea of faithfully translating literature (out of respect for the original author) is very much a modern Western product, which entered East Asia along with the incursion of the West on other fronts from the nineteenth century onward. Of course, the institutionalization of translation studies as a discipline in the past few decades has also played its part in endorsing the fidelity approach, with teachers often castigating renditions by students that deviate more or less substantially from their originals.

At the same time, however, an open and inclusive model has also been advocated by a certain sector of the community of Western translation scholars, in hopes that a range of derivative or rewritten texts can be studied under it. This includes those that are not even labeled as translations, although adaptations and imitations remain examples par excellence. While noting that an expanded definition could spell the end of translation studies as an autonomous discipline, Dirk Delabastita (2008) still averred that translation studies can be empowered through the reconceptualization. He envisions "translation" as "part of a general, interlingually based and intertextually inspired model of discourse, all of which it informs rather than simply

---

[5] It ought to be added that while adaptive and imitative forms of translation were favored by premodern Japanese and Korean rewriters, in the case of China the two forms were practiced intralingually, with earlier works in the literary tradition adapted and imitated.

disappearing into it" (2008: 245). In a way that corroborates the method adopted in the present study, he suggests how this model makes possible the consideration of non-Western variants of translation, allowing us to see the dissonance between East and West. In contrast, under the limelight of the closed model of translation, which posits an "exclusive, binary and unidirectional relationship" between the source and target texts (2008: 239), scholars may have to struggle to find instances which are comparable to those in the West, if only to show that other parts of the world have not fared so badly after all.

The fact is that only under a broadened conception of translation can we properly assess translation in East Asia. Its true face reveals itself easily if sufficient emphasis is placed on peripheral, marginal, and variant forms. Given the predominance of China in the regional linguistic, geographical, and cultural arena over the course of millennia (and, in a way, extending into the present), this simple fact has to be recognized in order for deductions to be accurately made on intra-regional relationships of any kind in East Asia.[6] Therein lies the fundamental cause for differences between the translation histories and practices between East Asia and Europe. The importation of some core ideas and predispositions from the West, while making us more perspicacious observers, can also result in our placing different emphases when approaching premodern East Asian translation history. For future research on theory, it would be important to probe further into emic East Asian perceptions of the various forms of transtextual rewriting under the umbrella of "translation," as well as the impact of the imposition of an etic framework on a different region of the world, especially with regard to its past. This can very well pave the way, eventually, for an "inter-continental turn" in translation studies.

Structurally, the present study is organized around the three forms of transtextual rewriting theorized in Chapter 1 but dealt with separately in the three main parts of the book. In Part I ("Free Translation"), two cases that feature the uses of this method are examined: nineteenth-century Chinese translations of Aesop's fables and late twentieth-century renditions of Murakami Haruki's novels by Lin Shaohua. Many reasons have been adduced for the liberal renderings of the original texts. They range from practical to ideological causes: from the translators' linguistic deficiencies, to cultural incommensurability, and to the influence of an ingrained tradition of thinking about language use in translation. This part ends with some reflections on

---

[6] This is not an attempt to replace a Eurocentric with a Sinocentric approach to translation. "China-at-the-center" is a reality that every culture in the East Asian region has to contend with, including China itself.

how the fidelity rule has been tempered within Sino-Japanese as well as Sino-English translations. Especially worth noting is Lin's deployment of a semiclassical Chinese prose style to (as he argued) enhance the beauty—and, consequently, the receptivity—of the original Japanese texts. Such stylistic manipulation happens to be quite widely practiced, judging by the body of theory that has accrued around it, and its deployment in the contemporary translations of premodern Japanese literature into semiclassical Chinese is worth examining from the perspective of how one language is viewed by users of another.

In the next two parts the arguments follow similar trajectories, with Western theories and traditions setting the stage for the analyses of Sino-Japanese examples. Occasional cases of Sino-English adaptations and imitations are brought in for comparison purposes. Chapter 4 of Part II ("Adaptive Translation") examines the interface between translation and adaptation, with scholars of both fields looking at each other across a theoretical divide. On the whole, translation studies scholars have been more inclined to see the perceived gap between the two as bridgeable, and some have proposed that reconciliation can be achieved through the sharing of methodologies and terminologies. In the next chapter, adaptive translations from East Asia are reviewed with a focus on the accommodation strategies adopted by the rewriters. It is argued that adaptations have for long occupied a central position in the Sinosphere, practiced primarily in the periphery and circumscribed by China's central geopolitical position. To show how the prioritizing of Chinese cultural contexts is something that impacts the adaptive process, Chapter 6 analyzes a number of Chinese TV adaptations of a Japanese manga that were immensely successful with audiences in Mainland China, Taiwan, and Hong Kong. Although this is a case that has intermedial and re-adaptive dimensions, accommodation strategies still sound the dominant note, when much that is Japanese is removed from the Mainland and Taiwanese versions and Sinicization is the dominant strategy. The examples cited bear out an interesting aspect of the modus operandi of Sino-Japanese adaptation.

Part III ("Imitative Translation") opens with a brief survey of the evolving discourse on imitation in the West, from antiquity to twentieth-century modernism. The stress on the "family link" between translation and imitation, often brushed aside in modern theories of translation, is the most fascinating part of this history. In contrast, we have in the next chapter two traditions of imitation in Japan, one of poetry and the other of fiction, both representing responses to original canonical texts in Chinese. Those of the latter are well exemplified by the deluge of early modern imitations of a classical Chinese novel, widely read by the urban population. For a much-needed contrast, three imitations of James Joyce's *Ulysses* in Hong Kong in the 1960s are discussed in Chapter 9; they exemplify a more conventional approach to a non-Asian fictional masterwork. They throw into sharp relief imitation as a form of apprenticeship—in this case, also homage to Joyce, the stream of consciousness master. Our final chapter looks at some late twentieth-century manga imitations of another well-known Chinese novel. Rewritings of classical Chinese fiction are a common occurrence in Japanese literary history, but what is special here is the radical approach adopted by the manga artists, which betrays a "revisionist" attitude toward the Chinese classical canon. Of special interest is the rather playful stance of the new versions, which deviate substantially in plot and style from the original text.

A full treatment of the transcultural processes at work in translated, adapted, and imitated texts in East Asia is beyond the scope of the present study. Most notably, Sino-Korean transtextual relationships merit in-depth study, if only to add a more nuanced description of what happened in the Chinese cultural sphere. Unfortunately that will have to be left to someone with a thorough grasp of Korean translation history and culture, as well as mastery of the Korean language. But the triadic, syncretic approach adopted here will, hopefully, go a long way toward showing the contours of intercultural dynamics in the region, which only emerge when adaptations and imitations are viewed through a translation lens. It may be well-nigh impossible to exhaustively showcase the possibilities offered by a transnational and transcultural approach to the study of rewriting practices. Yet this project will have been worthwhile if questions can be raised as to how the study of intra-Asian transtextual rewriting forces us to interrogate the relevance and applicability of Western theory.

1

The Transtextual Triad, Similar but Not the Same

Any consideration of the interrelated triad of translation, adaptation, and imitation must begin with a fourth term: original composition. To look for the origin of the opposition of the three transtextual genres against a relative latecomer on the scene of literary history, the eighteenth century is a valid and convenient starting point. Before that time, more books were ready to clearly display their lineage—or linkage to previous works—but with the advent of the Enlightenment (and then Romantic) notions of authorship, values of "originality" came to assume a more prominent position along with the glorification of individual talent. This was, of course, part and parcel of the steady historical progression from literature as communal to literature as originating with an individual author. The flip side of this is that the creative use of others' ideas came to be almost universally denounced, with evident consequences for the evaluation of derivative genres, among them the three categories that are at the center of the present study. In our century, originality has been given a much-needed boost through the implementation of laws on copyright protection. It could be said that current laws in this area, while useful as a weapon against plagiarism, make things more difficult for creative borrowing in its various manifestations, as in the writing of parody. Even the contracts giving translators the legal permission to translate, contracts that they have to obtain from the publisher, ironically work against the entire profession by affirming the secondary and subordinate position of translations with respect to original texts, reinforcing the notion of original and exclusive authorship.

Wedded to the idea of originality is that of autonomy. A construct "in which the meaning was perfectly explicit in itself, without reference to any other text, whether oral or written" (Angélil-Carter 2000: 27), the autonomous text is the original text. Shelly Angélil-Carter has added: "Originality and autonomy as values are based on an ideology which tends towards individualism and competition, rather than community and co-operation … [and toward] analysis rather than synthesis" (2000: 27). Yet both have come under attack in the past half-century or so. Thomas McFarland (1985) has interpreted the post-Romantic revolt in terms of what he calls the "originality paradox," one founded on the conflicting claims of individual expression and the cultural past. Harold Bloom's theory of the "anxiety of influence" (1973) indirectly enables transtextual rewriting to return to its rightful place: poets can seek to overcome their belatedness with respect to other poets in the tradition, even to emulate the achievements of their predecessors. The value of derivative works is to be decided without any reference to originality. To Northrop Frye, "poetry can only be made out of other poems; novels out of other novels" (1957: 97). The question now is whether originality is even necessary, an argument that is further strengthened by a generation of deconstructionist thinkers who argue that texts are split within themselves.

Among the most prominent of these thinkers is Gérard Genette, whose view of a transtextual perfusion informs the present study of the three "free" forms of translation. According to him, "Thus does Borges's utopia come to be accomplished, the utopia of Literature in a perpetual state of transfusion, a transtextual perfusion, constantly present to itself in its totality and as a Totality all of whose authors are but one" (Genette 1997: 400). What all the studies of intertextuality drive home is this: if all texts exist in relation to a web of other texts, then the concept of autonomy evaporates, as does the quest for originality. Further discussion of poststructuralist views need not detain us here: in the ensuing discussion reference will be made to many who have spoken directly or indirectly on the subject of textual alterations, modifications, and transformations. What concerns us here is the enlarged understanding of translation that transtextual studies makes possible.[1] Translations are like adaptations because, whether the translator wants to alter the original or not, a translation cannot but be changed from its source. Translations are also like imitations because, even when the translator does not copy, borrow, or steal, a translation will of necessity be imitative of another text. In the final analysis, all texts are figments of Genette's "Utopia of Literature."

Patrick Cattrysse has compared the relationship between translation and adaptation to one between siblings, similar yet not the same (Cattrysse 2018). But I would also characterize the relationship between the triad in the present discussion using the same metaphor. Because of the comparability as well as discrepancy between the three genres of this book, I will begin with definitions of the three terms with reference to a number of disciplinary perspectives beyond the field of translation studies, in particular, cultural studies, literary

---

[1] What Julia Kristeva says shows that it is important to study the translated text in relation to other texts: "[The text] is a permutation of texts, an intertextuality. In the space of one text several utterances, taken from other texts, cross and neutralize themselves" (Nöth 1990: 323).

criticism, theater/film studies, and intellectual history. Three-way comparisons will be made to clarify the murky boundaries between the trio. Through the contrastive approach, we will be in a position to see the distinctiveness of each, while appreciating why adaptation and imitation, the two peripheral categories, can be subsumed under the rubric of translation. Central to this chapter are ways in which adaptive and imitative practices allow us to better understand translations that contravene the cardinal principle of fidelity.[2]

What Is (Free) Translation?

One might as well begin with a quotation from Andrew Chesterman in which he gives an expanded definition of translation. He alerts us to the fact that translation need not be defined solely with reference to faithfulness:

> In fact it seems that the only necessary and sufficient condition for a text to be appropriately called "a translation" is that there must be some perceived relation between target text and source text. This condition is met if (a) the translator claims that such a relation exists, and (b) the receivers of the text (intersubjectively) accept that such a relation exists. The claim of translation status is obviously the stronger, the larger the proportion of receivers who agree. If receivers disagree, all we can say is that the translation status of the text in question is in doubt, as it would be if the (majority of the) receivers disagreed with the translator's claim. (Chesterman 2017: 169)

In other words, it is the claimed relationship, not the faithful replication, that counts. The dominance of linguistic approaches to translation in the West has led to prejudice against free translation, but Brian Baer has noted how perceptions have changed over the years: "liberated from traditional models that construct translation as an exercise in message transfer ... translated literature is no longer defined by the now philosophically untenable concepts of fidelity or equivalence" (2014: 334). In fact, almost ironically, the liberal method was even the primary mode at certain historical junctures, like that of late nineteenth- and early twentieth-century China. The fidelity paradigm

---

[2] A range of terms are used in the present study to denote forms of translation that are antithetical to free translation; namely, "faithful translation," "literal translation," "verbatim translation," "close translation," "text-bound translation," depending on the context of discussion. The theoretical nomenclature is, of course, "prototypical translation," or "translation proper" (á la Roman Jakobson).

there only earned legitimacy as the result of theory and practice in the 1930s, when men of letters like Lu Xun made strenuous efforts to introduce foreign literature through "faithful" translations. Going beyond the aim of learning from foreign models of writing, Lu believed that extreme literalism makes possible the enrichment of the Chinese language; for him, close adherence to the source text allows foreign lexicon and syntax to be absorbed into Chinese.

However, there may be some sense that free translation has "returned" as an object worthy of theoretical investigation due to the mushrooming of interest in film adaptation since the late twentieth century. Admittedly, film adaptation scholars have recently revoked the principle of fidelity, first by looking at the difficulties of remaining faithful to the written source text, be it a Jane Austen novel or a Shakespeare play, and then by exploring why infidelity should be the norm rather than the exception (e.g., Dicecco 2015; Starr 2006; Stam 2000). But then the impossibility of attaining equivalence has also garnered attention from translation theorists. They have approached the subject from perspectives that are descriptive (Hermans 1985), polysytemic (Even-Zohar 1978), and cultural (Bassnett and Lefevere 1998). Of course, free translation, while similar to adaptation, nevertheless needs to be distinguished from it. The indiscriminate use of the term "adaptation" to the point that it can be applied to any text that uses but alters a prior text is the cause of some confusion in theorizing about free translations.[3] It is therefore necessary to examine free or adaptive translation as a method or genre of its own, keeping some distance from the more slipshod and less theoretically rigorous use of "adaptation" in general parlance.

While our focus is on literary translations, free translation is also extensively used as a method in rendering nonliterary texts. It can be used not just on materials of an operative or vocative nature (à la Karl Bühler and Katharina Reiss) like advertisements or speeches, but even on science and technology texts, for these can be translated quite "unfaithfully," according to specific circumstances and readerships. It also has been used to denote a wider range of transtextual rewritings than the ones examined in the present study. Huang Zhonglian (2002) lists a dozen examples in the first chapter of his book on "translation variation" (2002; see also Xu 2000), including the following:

1. the Chinese recasting of the Indian Naga (snake-God) legend;
2. the condensed translations in China's World Literary Masterpieces series;

---

[3] It has also led to the virtual elimination of the category of imitation, which extensively modifies the text on which it is based. Of this more will be said below.

3. the monk-poet Su Manshu's rendition of Goethe's poem on Shakuntala in the form of Chinese regulated poetry;
4. Evan King's translation of the Chinese novel *Rickshaw Boy*, in which he replaces the tragic ending with a note of optimism;
5. adjustments made by the United Nations interpreter Jean Herbert in his conference interpreting assignments (according to his own account);
6. the three Japanese translations of Lin Yutang's novel *Moment in Peking* (*Jinghua yanyun*) in which the attacks on the Japanese are deleted; and
7. the 1951 Russian translation of *Robinson Crusoe*, shortened for a teenage readership (Huang 2002: 3–10).

There is indeed ample room for such "translation variations," although, as Huang correctly points out, in Chinese translation studies circles, such adaptive translations have for long been ignored, and viewed as not worthy of consideration because of their disregard for the paramount principle of fidelity (2002: 11–21). For many contemporary translation scholars, too, they run afoul of the rule that translation should fulfill its primary purpose of communication by conveying the original message as accurately as possible to an audience without the linguistic competence to access the source text.

Nevertheless, in the present study we will not deal with the full range of "translation variations" noted by Huang. A variety of alterations are at the translator's disposal in handling their originals, and some of them can be treated from the perspective of censorship, others from a reception point of view, and still others from considerations of effective interlingual transfer. It is hoped that more conceptually rigorous definitions of adaptation and imitation will enable us to differentiate between the varied "unfaithful" forms of translation. Leaving the problematic differentiation between adaptation and imitation for discussion later in this chapter, I would like to stress here the importance of more closely defining "adaptation" so that it does not become a designation for *all* derivative texts that differ from the sources on which they are based. Naturally, one can opt for all-inclusivity, taking into account a great number of modes of adaptive translation (e.g., condensed, partial, expanded, elaborated), strategies of adaptation (e.g., addition, deletion, substitution, camouflage, rewording), and degrees of adaptation (e.g., intensive, restrained, minimal, wide, narrow).[4] But adaptation is not co-extensive with free translation. In choosing to use adaptation in its

---

[4] Huang cites eleven subgenres of adaptive translation (2002: 30–1) and seven adaptive strategies (2002: 19), each of them having a corresponding Chinese term. However, he generally emphasizes the full vs. partial distinction, with the difference between translation and adaptation defined accordingly.

restricted sense for understanding certain ways in which fidelity is practiced, we believe it has the advantage of giving us a firmer grasp of the varied applications of the method and genre that is called "free translation."

As noted above, in the move away from the fidelity principle in translation, the ideas of the poststructuralists regarding textual transformation are highly relevant.[5] One can cite those of leading textualists like Roland Barthes ("a text is made from multiple writings" [1977: 48]) and Umberto Eco ("intertextual collage" [1985: 3]), but it is Gérard Genette whose ideas of transtextuality have been widely applied in the field of translation. In *Palimpsests: Literature to the Second Degree* (1997), he discusses several categories of transtextuality. Among these, "intertextuality" ("all that which puts one text in relation, manifest or secret, with other texts") can be applied to translation in general,[6] whereas "hypertextuality" ("a successor text modifying a precursor text") characterizes the modus operandi of free, adaptive, and imitative translations—all of them being "hypertexts." The extent to which difference, rather than equivalence, has moved to the center of translation studies through the intervention of poststructuralist thinkers is shown clearly by Jacques Derrida, who not only introduced the concept of "différance" but also pronounced that "for the notion of translation we would have to substitute a notion of transformation" (1981: 26). The early linguists' optimism about the possibility of achieving accuracy in cross-lingual transfer has been slowly displaced by the doubts and skepticism about faithfulness enunciated by a more recent generation of thinkers.

Actually, "normal" translations can "falsify" the original more than free, adaptive, and imitative renderings, even reinterpretations and modernizations. The first step in the direction of subverting literalism or fidelity, and enlarging the definition of translation, can be said to have been taken by Susan Bassnett and André Lefevere (1990), who spearheaded the cultural turn in translation studies in the early 1990s. They gave the green light for extending the use of the liberal method in their endorsement of the concept of rewriting. For Lefevere, "translation is a rewriting of an original text" (1992: xi). Since then, the interest in researching forms of rewriting, from transtextual, transcultural, and translingual perspectives, has increased exponentially and now constitutes a sizeable portion of

---

[5] Palmer and Boyd (2011) give a succinct account of the impact of poststructuralist notions of intertextuality on film adaptation scholarship and the resultant shift away from a concern with fidelity, which allows for the reading of Hitchcock as an original *auteur* despite his recurrent use of literary source texts (2011: 1–9).

[6] Genette treats intertextuality as a smaller category than transtextuality. He defines it "in a restrictive sense, as a relationship of co-presence between two texts or among several texts: that is to say, eidetically and typically as the actual presence of one text within another (1997: 1–2).

translation scholarship. Along similar lines, Lawrence Venuti has ventured the provocative view that "all translations are adaptive" (Venuti 2011). The most recent advocate for including various forms of transtextual rewriting is, however, Edwin Gentzler, for whom versions, abridgements, stagings, films, adaptations, novelizations, pre-visions, and sequels (2017: 168)—as well as tradaptations, transfigurations, creative interference, and furtherings (175)—could well form part of the repertoire worthy of study by translation scholars. While the present study will limit itself primarily to a consideration of rewritings involving verbal transfer, Gentzler's study (2017) of the full range of post-translation rewritings—some of which will fall under our adaptation category, others our imitation category—is evidence of the opportunities offered by texts that adhere to their originals only loosely.

How Adaptation Is Viewed

Theater and film scholars have engaged seriously with issues of defining adaptation, the former mainly in cross-cultural terms, the latter primarily in intermedial contexts. To begin with, we can note the discussions by Catherine Diamond, who has compared the generic characteristics of translation and adaptation (and, to a lesser extent, imitation) in her thesis on the Little Theater Movement in Taiwan. She proceeds with a definition of adaptation based on four attributes, noting that (a) the adapted text is goal-oriented and constrained by the target system; (b) the source text should be an artistic work, featuring legendary or historical material; (c) the audience is informed that the text is an adapted one; and (d) there is a crucial shift in intention from the source to the target text (1993: 111). She proposes a taxonomy of four categories of adaptations:

1. Generic (or intersemiotic) adaptation, such as films made from novels.
2. Diachronic (or modernizing or updating) adaptation, in which a new context in the present replaces the one in the original.
3. Ideological adaptation, in which previous work is rewritten to convey a specific message (for example, a political one through attacking the regime for its failings).
4. Cross-cultural adaptation of texts, as in intercultural theater. (This is not distinguished from linguistic adaptation, which also belongs to this category.)

Diamond then moves on to contrast adaptation with translation. For her, translation is "the initial stage of adaptation [and it] introduces both conscious and inadvertent changes into a text" (1993: 131), and it is always an interpretation that represents the text in a new linguistic context. According to her, because translation implies an adherence to faithfully rendering the original, it should not be beholden to the same standards of evaluation applied to adaptation. As a whole, from her perspective of theater adaptation, Diamond sees adaptation as a superior mode, and translation as just part of the adaptation process which brings a foreign play to the local audience (131).

While holding a less than laudatory view of translation, Diamond emphasizes the many contributions of adaptation. She claims that it downplays the alienness of the original, so that what is foreign becomes familiar. It also reconfigures the source text with reference to target social, cultural, and aesthetic values, and localizes the text to ensure easy reception by the target audience (1993: 137–9). "Assimilation" is the key word in her approach, while faithfulness deserves little attention. The value of an adaptation is found in its ability to apply premises from the source to the target culture, allowing the audience to gain new insights and, as it secures popular acceptance and recognition, serving ulterior purposes that may be both personal and political in nature. Nevertheless, in spite of her enthusiasm about her own subject, especially about how adaptations can facilitate intercultural exchange, she notes that the slant toward the recipients might mean that the adapted cultural imports will close the door to alternatives instead of opening up the world. Such self-reflectivity is indeed indispensable to a fair evaluation of the genre.

In striking contrast to Diamond, translation scholars studying drama adaptation have approached the topic differently. As a detailed account will be given in Chapter 4, only representative cases are noted here. To begin with, much significant work has been done on adaptive translations in Canadian theater. In Edwin Gentzler's account (2017: 169–72), the word "tradaptation" was first introduced in connection with Michel Garneau's 1978 Québécois translation of Shakespeare's *Macbeth*, which was altered to reflect the linguistic and cultural needs of those living in Quebec and pushing for independence from Canada. The tradaptor's relocation of the original *Macbeth* from the Scottish countryside to rural Quebec makes possible the successful transfer of content from Shakespeare's play, allowing it to communicate effectively in the "local" language with a late twentieth-century audience. In the wake of Garneau (who also rewrote other plays by Shakespeare), a swathe of canonical French and English plays was turned out by other tradaptors, while Garneau's tradaptations were made accessible to audiences the world over when performed outside Canada through the efforts of Robert Lepage. The extensive changes made to the originals, together with the insertion of a political message embedded in them, make it incumbent upon us—according to Gentzler—to consider tradaptations as a new form of "rewritten translation" or "refracted translation" (2017: 170-1). He agrees with Yves Gambier (2003) that the definition of translation should be enlarged in light of theoretical and practical innovations made in the areas of drama adaptations and accepts the new perspective proffered by tradaptation as a form combining translation with adaptation.

On the other hand, in its early days film adaptation studies shared theoretical premises with translation studies, although more recently the two have moved somewhat apart with regard to some foundational principles. As a discipline, film studies became established largely through the research of George Bluestone (1957) and others on films based on novels. But as it gradually assumed disciplinary independence, it has also shifted its focus to a range of intermedial adaptations beyond the novel-to-film category. The first generation of critics had worked on the notion of equivalence between the novel and the film—the source and target texts, respectively. They analyzed the adapted film with reference to its faithfulness to the original, in the mode of so-called "fidelity criticism," much as an older school of translation criticism had evaluated translated works. But this practice was eventually faulted by scholars like James Naremore (2000) for its theoretical inadequacies, and it is now generally accepted that the adherence to textual fidelity is hardly conducive to the exploration of hidden potentials in movie adaptations. With such a shift went the early link between film adaptation and translation theory.

Despite such divergences of concern, the terms used to describe "losses and gains" in film adaptation studies are still applicable to the analysis of translations. Robert Stam's list of tropes used in adaptation, like "actualization, reading, critique, dialogization, cannibalization, transmutation, transfiguration, incarnation, transmogrification, transcoding, performance, signifying, rewriting and detournement" (qtd. Jameson 2011: 215) are usable in the description of translations. Other concepts, for instance, "commentary," "transposition," "remediation," "cross-referencing," "analogue" and so on, could also be utilized to enrich the explication of translated texts. It may even be said that, while film adaptation studies borrowed from translation studies in its beginning stages, the direction can be reversed if adaptation strategies become research tools for scholars working on transtextual modifications that have occurred to translations. Recent moves to address the analogies and differences between adaptation and translation, together with the deepening of interest in the crossovers between the two forms of rewriting, signal the possibilities for methodological "cross-fertilization" at a higher level than that of source-target compatibility. In the context of such emerging research trends, the inadequacy of fidelity as a cardinal principle becomes even more transparent, and the path is opened for the adaptive translation to take up a more central position.

There is one problem, however, with such an outlook on possible connections between the two fields. Adaptation, as defined by film scholars, often appears to be an impossibly broad field that embraces a wide assortment of intertextual, intercultural, and intermedial forms. But when textual reworkings—on verbal, visual, kinetic, and other levels—are extensively carried over to the translation field, translation studies may be little different from intertextual studies. The openness of intertextual studies means it can turn translation into merely one of its subareas of study. Indeed, there are signs of such a position: artistic forms from theater and dance, to opera, songs, and video games, have been taken up as objects of study. While overlapping concerns justify the adoption of methodologies in neighboring fields, it remains important to see that, while certain translations are clearly adaptive, not all adaptations are translational. Even when translation scholars engage with derived forms appearing in other media, it is important that they privilege a translational approach over one that is simply intermedial or vaguely intertextual. It is for this reason that the present study is against the idea of "anything goes." To highlight this point, Parts II and III of the present book are entitled "adaptive translation" and "imitative translation."

We can end the present section by noting the linked (and then delinked) fortunes of translation and adaptation in Western literary history. They are linked, of course, because of the considerable overlapping between the methods of *free translation* and adaptation. A number of theorists (e.g., Walter Benjamin, Corinne Lhermitte, Patrick Cattrysse) have also mentioned the "kinship" between the two. The closeness between the two can be seen, for example, in the *belles infidèles* tradition in seventeenth-century France, where one blended into the other. In being thus connected, they suffered similar fates with the advent of the Romantic Movement, which fueled what may be called the "birth of the author." This, together with the emergence of the concept of "originality" and the appearance of ideas of ownership and individualization later, dealt liberalism in second-order rewritings a heavy blow. Translations that are not strictly literal are debased on comparison with original compositions, and only faithful ones have value since they make the original available in other languages, however imperfect. This has led to over a century of worship of fidelity and what Steven Yao has called "the fetishization of semantic content" (2002: 232), which has largely reigned until the present. As altered copies of the original, adaptations naturally suffered a worse fate, until a reversal occurred principally as a result of its increasing valence in spheres of artistic activity like theater and film. In fact, it may be said that a consequence of the epistemological revolution of the

Enlightenment is the drawing of stricter boundaries between translation and adaptation, and these intensified over time, as each became bent on finding its own niche in the face of serious stigmatization. The metaphors of sibling resemblance and dissimilarity, deployed to figure the relationship between the two, capture very well the dialectic of difference and similarity that undergirds the history of Western thinking about the pair.

Why Imitation Is Important

Unlike adaptation, the definition of which affects the drawing of disciplinary boundaries, imitation is not a "rival" of translation, and attempts at defining it are related simply to its acceptance (as creative) or rejection (as expropriative). Howard Weinbrot considers imitation as an "outgrowth of the theory of free translation" (1966: 434), which captures neatly the relationship between the two, although this statement can apply to adaptation as well. The dictum that informs imitation theory comes from Horace: *Nec verbum verbo curabis reddere, fidus / Interpres* (as a true translator you will take care not to render word for word), although Horace was actually talking about free translation. As with adaptation, there is, of course, a wide spectrum of imitative forms used by the "faithful" imitator, who wants to represent closely some aspects of the original work at one end, and the "creative" imitator, who reworks to his/her liking a selected model at the other. If we look back at its history since antiquity, we can see distinct periods of praise and disparagement, although the latter tendency has generally been strong in our time, especially where it is placed in opposition to authenticity. The judgment that imitations are secondhand, copied, and unoriginal has haunted it ever since Plato connected it with falsehoods, in both literary and real-life contexts.

Interestingly, it is in the realm of translation that imitation was practiced with fervor several centuries ago, and vigorously theorized by John Dryden—he once noted that "imitation of an author is the most advantageous way for a translator to show himself" (Dryden 1680)—as well as other Augustans of that era. Nonetheless, as was the case with adaptations, with the reign of Romantic aesthetics and its valorization of the imagination, imitation fell out of favor. Add to that the dominance of realism in the nineteenth century, and imitations could not but be belittled by artists and writers who cared only for art that was authentic, unique, and singular. Valuable artwork, it was believed, should be differentiable from objects that were copied. As we thrived in the age of modern technology, in the confrontation of what Miles Orvell (1989) has called "the culture of imitation" with "the culture of authenticity" (in America), the latter easily gained the upper hand.

Yet, with the ascendancy of postmodernism, a revised view of imitation came to the forefront. Along with the reconceptualization of the roles of the author, the reader, and especially the text by a generation of postmodern theorists, questions began to be raised as to what the authentic really entails, even whether it can be said to exist. Using examples from contemporary music and painting, Lena Henningsen points out: "a work can, in fact, be regarded as authentic, even if it has been transmitted in a form other than the *original form* as created by its author" (2010: 23; italics in the original). The opposition between the imitative and the authentic is being rendered irrelevant. At the same time, plagiarism can also be delinked from imitation: imitators creatively rework prior texts; plagiarists do not. Even more powerful is Jean Baudrillard's exposition of the loss of "the real" due to the reliance of our society on models and maps as substitutes. As Baudrillard puts it, "It is no longer a question of imitation, nor duplication, nor even parody. It is a question of substituting the signs of the real for the real" (1994: 2). In an era characterized by total obliteration of authenticity, imitation has taken on new life. The impact of this development is now felt by researchers in many disciplines, including theater scholars, literary critics, historians, and, not least, translation theorists.

A survey of contemporary views on imitation could begin once again with Catherine Diamond's negative evaluation. For her, "imitation," intrinsically linked to "appropriation," has pejorative connotations, while "adaptation" is a neutral term (1993: 153). In tandem with her assessment of translation, imitation is seen as inferior and not conducive to creativity, paling beside adaptation as a derived form. Furthermore, Diamond thinks that imitations can occur only within the same art system, thus excluding transtextual activities across genres and media. As described earlier, recent institutional developments have steered researchers toward studying inter-connections between works in different semiotic systems. Indeed, the interest in intermediality has been one of the fastest growing areas of humanities research, and the opening up of imitation studies is something to look forward to. Reflecting the long-standing castigation of imitation, Diamond denounces imitation because of its link to plagiarism. Her negative stance stands in contrast to an earlier tradition of thinkers whose leading spokesman is Ben Jonson, for whom imitation is a legitimate means of refashioning classical works to suit contemporary needs. It is doubtful, too, whether appropriation is simply "borrowing" or "stealing" from another work without understanding of what is borrowed or stolen. Neither should it be faulted on account of the failure of the resultant product to be integrated into the new context.

For the viewpoint of literary historians, one may note an example in which the worth of imitations has been affirmed. In her study of the nineteenth-century Spanish realist novel, which came into being via imitations of French precedents, Elisa Martí-López narrates how they served as a crucial catalyst. To her, imitation underwent a sustained period of suppression due to the Romantic Movement, but the practice of imitation was galvanized in Spain by the conflict between two ideologies—the Neoclassical belief in imitation as the foundation of all creative practices versus the nativist (Schlegelian) belief in the cultural distinctiveness of a nation. In this light, the birth of the Spanish novel through imitative appropriations of the French model shows the productive borrowing of the foreign for use in a native context (2002: 58). This process, entailing the use of an Otherness to construct one's identity, is also a translational one: George Steiner's famous four-stage "hermeneutic motion" (i.e., trust, aggression, incorporation, and compensation) (1975) is relevant as a description of not just the process of translation, but also that of imitation. Looking at the Spanish imitations of two French novels, Martí-López notes how imitation can successfully eliminate foreignness through analogical transference. It thus becomes a kind of "free translation" because it allows for an unrestricted number of changes to the source texts, especially as they pertain to the foreign elements in the original.

As a contrast to the perspectives of theater and literary critics, we can look at the contribution by translation theorists. Like Diamond and Martí-López, Georges Bastin and Hugo Vandal-Sirois also align imitation with appropriation. In the latter part of an article on adaptation, they classify imitation as a kind of appropriation; in their formulation, appropriation figures as a higher-level category within which imitations, transcreations, and so on fall. They highlight one aspect of the phenomenon of appropriations—namely, in appropriations "any link between the source and the target texts is voluntarily eluded" (Bastin and Vandal-Sirois 2012: 35). This underscores how radically the element of infidelity is conceived in this case. The two authors go on, in the same article, to discuss at length the nature of imitations, justifying the use of the word "appropriation" as an equivalent of "imitation." This use of terminology was of course first proposed by Julie Sanders in *Adaptation and Appropriation* (2006). There she devotes attention to what she considers two separate categories of derivative works: adaptation (which "signals a relationship with an informing source text or original") versus appropriation (which "frequently affects a more decisive journey away from the informing source into a wholly new cultural product and domain") (2006: 26). It should be added that her distinction is consistent with our contrastive definitions of adaptation and imitation, to be enunciated below.

How do we understand the relationship between imitation and translation? From one angle at least, in its appropriative role, imitation bears similarities to domesticated translation. In the context of the present discussion, both are also forms of mediation between the indigenous and the foreign. But the proverbial saying that "mediocre writers imitate, great writers plagiarize" may point to one reason why writers would not want to have anything to do with imitation, while granting a certain degree of legitimacy, albeit small, to acts of translation. Translation researchers of a more conventional bent also harbor misgivings about imitations: only tangentially linked to their originals, they inevitably fall short of meeting the equivalence standards to which translations aspire. As forms of literary rewriting, of course, the two forms are similar in that both make available the transfer of foreign literary models, modes, and conventions, and both are forces of literary innovation, contributing to the evolution of literary forms in the target culture. As far as the degree of imported "newness" allowed is concerned, imitations may be as strong an agent of change as translations, depending on how imitators use the freedom they have to depart drastically from indigenous modes of expression.

In the transplantation of outside literary models, therefore, imitations make a special kind of contribution. Besides the case already discussed above with reference to Martí-López's book, which shows imitations bringing about changes in the literary system, we will also look at the history of the introduction of stream of consciousness fiction to China (in Chapter 9). It is a fact of modern Chinese literary history that the translations of Joyce's novels (and those of others) came after the imitations, which were used by authors (especially those keen on borrowing Western techniques) to learn their craft of original composition. Collectively, the (domesticating) stream of consciousness imitations helped lodge the foreign literary model in Chinese soil more quickly than the translations (however domesticating), and they facilitated the absorption of the foreign genre by the Chinese readership. While there is more than one way of introducing foreign literature, imitative translations can be more expedient than the faithful but more "constrained" literal translations. The transplantation of the stream of consciousness novel to China in the twentieth century nicely parallels that of the French realist novel to Spain in the nineteenth century: the transmission of the new genre followed similar trajectories, with imitations preceding the translations and setting the stage for local, original productions.[7]

---

[7] Imitation may even be seen as a form of (unstructured) quotation or (incidental) allusion, or at least a partial translation. One often sees that only parts of the original are retained—not the 100 percent aimed at by the "ideal translation."

Distinguishing Adaptation from Imitation

Some early definitions of adaptation and imitation present them in almost the same terms, betraying a lack of differentiation. For Raymond Barry and A. J. Wright, adaptation is "the recasting of a literary work from one form to another" (1966: 5). M. H. Abrams sees imitation as a means of indicating "the relation of one literary work to another literary work which served as its model" (1999: 123). These conceptualizations are little different from the contemporary use of adaptation as an overarching term for all transformational rewritings. Of course, there are obvious similarities between adaptations and imitations because both are forms of derivative literature, or (as in the present study) of creative and re-creative translation. But it is possible to see the differences between the two as a matter of *degree*, measurable in terms of the engagement that the translator has with the text, his perception of himself as a writer/reader, and his projection of an intended readership. Another way to make more precise distinctions is by returning to everyday usages. As the dictionaries have it, to "adapt" is to "change [something] to make it suitable for a new purpose or situation" whereas to "imitate" is to "copy what [others] do or produce."[8] The present study proposes to look into all these considerations and redefine the dyad within a difference-within-similarity schema, to arrive at new definitions in a paradigm of textual evolution. The following have been put forward as contrasts between the two forms.

Nature of Reception. In Barthesian terms, there is "writerly" reception as opposed to "readerly" reception. The view of adaptations as having "result[ed] from a clear orientation towards a group of recipients of the text" (Malmkjaer 2000: 2) contrasts with Ben Jonson's famous adage that the imitator is "able to convert the substance, or riches of another poet, to his own use" (Jonson 1985: 585). Malmkjaer's focus is on the readerly aspects; Jonson's, on the writerly element. While this distinction is far from conclusive, it remains true that, whereas the alterations are often made in an adaptation so that it is more palatable to the target audience, the modifications in an imitation are signs of the imitator's effort to "try out" some aspects of another (foreign) writer's compositional technique.

Degree of Explicitness. An adaptation contains more explicit textual links to the source than an imitation, where fewer such references are typically made. In other words, there is more specificity in the transtextual operations of an

---

[8] According to *Collins COBUILD English Dictionary*.

adaptation than in an imitation, in which the deployment and rearrangement of discursive fragments are mostly identified. In a different context, Michael Worton and Judith Still have expressed this view; for them, "to imitate is necessarily to generalize" (1991: 14).[9] In light of this, it may be useful to distinguish between the two in terms of whether the use of a prior text is "signaled" or "unsignaled." Although there are examples of adaptations being unsignaled, there is a greater tendency for imitations not to reveal their sources. In fact, even when an adaptation contains extensive modifications to the base text, it may still boldly announce its provenance. On the contrary, even while replicating an original, the imitator may not acknowledge the connection at all.

Number of Linkages. Genette, who coins the word "mimotext" for an imitation, takes the extreme view that one adapts a source text, but imitates an entire genre (1997: 81). In the majority of cases, indeed, an adaptation references one text only, while an imitation may borrow from several. In discussing the "sources" for Hitchcock's movies, B. Barton Palmer and David Boyd also see adaptation as "any text that borrows centrally and substantially from *another* text (including, most often, taking over its identity in some fashion)" (2011: 2–3; italics added). For them, even though all texts exist in a web of intertextual linkages in the Kristevan universe, an adaptation exhibits a more sustained engagement with one source. Thus, an adaptation forges a link with one rather than many texts, while an imitation, in invoking several sources, often ends up with complex intertextual modalities.

Extent of Modification. Phyllis Frus and Christy Williams's collected volume (2010) gathers together a dozen articles on derived texts. All of them have so significantly altered their sources that the term "adaptation" ceases to be an appropriate designation. In their Introduction, the two editors discuss how seriously the hypotexts are reinterpreted so that the word "transformation" should be seen as a more suitable nomenclature.[10] However, though Frus and Williams have not hesitated to use the word "imitate" in their article (2010: 8–9), the word "transformation" is simply synonymous with what we call "imitation." In particular, to say that transformations are "inspired by" (rather than just "based on") other texts (2010: 5) implies that they are the

---

[9] Genette has also said that imitation can only be done "indirectly" and "*to imitate is to generalize*" (1997: 85; emphasis in the original).
[10] While "transformation" can highlight the process of textual change, it does not seem to have the specificity required of a generic term; it serves better in describing the rhetorical rather than the ontological aspect of transtextual activity.

same as imitations. It makes sense, therefore, to consider both adaptation and imitation as forms of free translation, in contradistinction to literal renditions.[11]

A final point of clarification was made by none other than Genette. He cited Joyce's *Ulysses* and Virgil's *Aeneid*, both derived from the *Odyssey*, as different examples of transformation, but they can actually serve to differentiate the two forms discussed here:

> The transformation that leads from the *Odyssey* to *Ulysses* can be described (very roughly) as a *simple* or *direct* transformation, one which consists in transposing the action of the *Odyssey* to twentieth-century Dublin. The transformation that leads from the same *Odyssey* to the *Aeneid* is more complex and indirect. . . . Virgil does not transpose the action of the *Odyssey* from Ogygia to Carthage and from Ithaca to Latium. Instead, he tells an entirely different story: the adventures of Aeneas, not those of Ulysses. He does so by drawing inspiration from the generic—i.e., at once formal and thematic—model established by Homer in the *Odyssey* (and in fact also in the *Iliad*): that is, following the hallowed formula, by *imitating* Homer. (1997: 6; emphasis in the original)

Notably, Genette did not call the first, direct type of transformation an "adaptation" (though he did consider the second type an "imitation"). But the truth of the matter is that adaptation does not even figure as a generic or technical category in *Palimpsests*. While he expatiated at length in his book on all the subcategories of literature, from parody to pastiche, from travesty to caricature, and from transposition to forgery, "adaptation" hardly ever showed up. As critics have noted, there are problems, gaps, and inconsistencies with his structural approach, but as this quotation shows, he did pinpoint very precisely the difference between the two modes. Adaptations involve "saying the same thing differently," while imitations entail "saying another thing similarly" (1997: 6). Incidentally, the Chinese rewritten versions of Joyce's *Ulysses*, to be discussed later, happens to yield the most interesting results when read as an imitation, and not an adaptation, of the modernist masterpiece.

---

[11] My only question concerns Frus and Williams's emphasis on the hermeneutic shift in the derived works. Many texts analyzed in their anthology may exemplify this aspect of imitation, but since there are innumerable instances of imitations (e.g., fan fiction) that bear not even the loosest of connections to the purported originals with respect to subject matter, the reinterpretation element may not be as crucial as it is with adaptations.

The Evolutionary Framework

That adaptations and imitations are similar yet different is crucial to their reconceptualization as forms of textual evolution. In the humanities, a recurrent concern is with adaptation as a transtextual activity that occurs as texts move between locales, and as a transcultural process that takes cultural artefacts from one cultural body to another. Yet adaptation is also a keenly researched subject in the sciences. It is, first and foremost, a biological activity, and its importance has been enunciated most rigorously by none other than Charles Darwin, whose theory of evolution posits a process of natural selection through which organisms become better adapted to their surroundings in order to survive. Human beings thus become what they are through accommodating themselves to their environment, just as innumerable species in the natural world come into being through genetic variation. Given such a theory, the analysis of adaptability figures as a central task in the scientific revolution launched even before Darwin and others, and adaptive evolutionism, by which organisms are matched to their ecology, is just another term for Darwinian evolution.

Once we depart from the traditional focus on translation proper and on interlingual transfer, as supported by fidelity and equivalence theories, ideas about evolutionary change become eminently relevant to translation. Luc van Doorslaer (2018) has recently argued for the need for a broadened definition of translation so that forms of "unfaithful" rendering can be brought within its fold. To spur the effort at remapping the discipline, according to van Doorslaer, it is necessary to theorize the changes and alterations in the act of transfer on dimensions other than that of the purely linguistic. What if "the fuzzy conceptual borders and interactions" (2018: 222) that translation studies shares with neighboring disciplines are to be understood within a common framework of textual evolution? What if translation is viewed as an encompassing term covering all the evolutionary phenomena, including adaptations and imitations? Variations are seen in the traits inherited by the offspring, and these allow them to survive in the new ecology. These are analogous to the alterations made to the source text that allow them to be better received in the target culture. The weight of much traditional translation theory has fallen on a belief in the primacy of the original text, resulting in an aversion to modes of free, adaptive, and imitative translation. In theorizing adaptation in evolutionary terms, I propose a different solution as to how to tackle the foreign, the alien, and the untranslatable, and to understand how, through an array of strategies, the text can adjust to the receptor environment. As texts, therefore, adaptations can be seen as ecologically determined; like ecologists, scholars dealing with translation in the adaptive mode can unravel the relationship of textual organisms to a changed environment.

Adaptation is effective in the transplantation of concepts and theories from one place to another, and the subject has been dealt with by translation scholars. At the level of concepts, Sebnem Susam-Saraeva (2006) has studied the transmission of feminist ideas across linguistic and cultural borders in her history of cultural adjustment and transfer. The history of almost all adaptations is one of textual evolution, involving both cultural adjustment and accommodation. Anna Malinowska has emphasized the role of "textual practices . . . for understanding the process of cultural exchange" (2014: 25) through the content adjustments in translations of popular or genre fiction, such as the *Fifty Shades* novels from Britain to non-Anglo-American contexts.[12] Adaptation is indispensable because only through "surgical" modifications can the linguistic and cultural gaps between source and target contexts be bridged. Malinowska explains successful transfer with reference to the "adaptability of . . . phenomena to new environmental settings and the capabilities of the latter to incorporate the migrating objects of difference" (2014: 27). Adaptive translations make for safe passage into the target environment.

While adaptations can be understood ecologically, imitations can be viewed genetically. Genetic study, a fledging branch of translation research, began as a subfield of literary criticism, representing the European response to Anglo-American intentionalism in the genesis of literary works. Textual scholarship on how texts come into being is carried out by looking at materials like author's notes, prior drafts (termed *avant-textes*), and variant versions of the published product, where these are available. Possibilities for "doing" genetic criticism of translated texts have recently been explored by Jeremy Munday (2013; 2014). Drawing inspiration from him, Chinese researchers have unearthed archival information about how eminent translators went about their work (e.g., David Hawkes translating *Dream of the Red Chamber*), with the aim of chronicling the birth of translation masterworks (like *The Story of the Stone*, a translation of *Dream*) (see Fan 2016). Imitative translations can be similarly studied. They are, after all, textual progenies drawing textual properties from "father texts," which they re-use in a different context. Such a process of textual evolution is observable, of course, in adaptive translations too, but imitative translations lend themselves more readily to such analyses. They provide materials for studying what characteristics of the original text are retained, and what altered, in the process whereby a text is passed

---

[12] Significantly, she draws particular attention to the modifications in the translations that are caused by differences in ethical and sexual mores.

on from one "generation" to another. As the branch of biology that studies heredity and variations, genetics can contribute to a more precise definition of imitations.

With this as the basis, one can see from a fresh perspective how imitations come into existence, for instance, by hypothesizing the possible links that unsignaled imitations have to the imitated texts. Hypotexts thus become texts of origin that can explain the hypertexts' *genos*, a Greek word that means both "birth" and "family." The concept of *genos* is also traceable back to Aristotle, who said that the myriad things of the world are produced either by nature, by chance, or by art (in *Metaphysics*). Rather than created by nature or chance, imitations are products of art—they are engendered offspring with their own familial and ancestral ties. An apt metaphor for sui generis literary works is divine providence, for they are God-given, as described in the Biblical account of creation. By contrast, without elaborating on Darwin's quarrel with the creationists in the Origins Controversy, one can easily understand that, in transtextual rewriting, the roots of a derived text are to be found in another text (or texts), and not in any act of original creation that produces texts of the first-order. What is more, imitations evince divergences from their sources. The study of these differences entails the detailed cataloging and analysis of individual textual features. Metaphorically, these are genes, the parts of cells inherited from a parent. As in the genetic sciences, such studies help build a genealogy that shows the continuities with, and the disjunctions from, the forebears, in an evolutionary history of second-order works.

However, in such an approach it is generally the similarities that carry greater significance than the differences. In adapted works, it is the other way round: it is the modifications that are of interest because of their interpretive significance. To continue with the Darwinian analogies, the transfer of preexisting textual elements can be compared with the inheritance of traits from one's father, parents, or ancestors. The sequence of imitations of the same predecessor text can be likened to an evolving genealogy. Although it is problematic to say that all imitations are traceable to a common ancestor, as in Darwinian theory, it is possible to understand all the imitations derived from a common source (e.g., the Japanese manga imitations of the Chinese novel, *Journey to the West*; see Chapter 10) as constituting a distinct lineage. Especially worth noting, in the context of translation studies, is that features are transmitted not from the indigenous cultural tradition, but from an alien one. It is said that the mobilization of foreign cultural matter "not only refer[s] to the transfer of past material, but also means the *selection* and interpretation processes of how to standardize the cultural present in the process of production" (Härter 2014: 56; emphasis added). In the case of imitative transfer, the process involves procreation rather than production. It is human, rather than natural or divine, selection that ensures the preservation of characteristic features in a new generation.

That being said, imitations must not be seen as downright uncreative; textual mutation is a complex phenomenon. Viewing imitative works as lacking in originality has had a history of its own that lasted for two centuries in the West. According to Lena Henningsen, the "dogma of creativity" (2010: 18) reached a peak with the German Romantics' conception of the artist as a genius, and the imitative mode was maligned. The debatable dichotomy between authenticity and imitation, as well as the groundless equation of imitation with plagiarism, has ended up reinforcing the view that imitations are compositions of a lower order. This, however, contrasts glaringly with the evolutionary view, in which the latecomers could be seen as an improvement on its forbears.[13] Henningsen highlights three aspects of originality in imitations: combination, intentionality, and novelty (2010: 20-2). Although the imitator can theoretically borrow from the imitated text in any way (even to the extent of forgery and copying), creative ones can skillfully blend new materials with the old, allowing them to mutually illuminate each other.[14] Authenticity has long been upheld as a criterion against which imitations are unfairly judged, but unlike the case of non-textual imitations (like technological innovations), such a yardstick falls short since the later product should not be evaluated in the same terms as the source it is based on.

A final word on definitions. Defining translation, adaptation, and imitation as forms of textual evolution helps clarify some boundaries which are fuzzy. Such fuzziness has partly been due to the enlargement of the meanings of the terms themselves, especially as used in common parlance. This has come to the point where one sees a contradiction between the meanings of specialized terms in academic discourse and the accrual of extended meanings as those same terms are used in everyday life. While this situation applies to all three terms in question, it is perhaps especially so with "adaptation," which has become almost synonymous with "change" in ordinary usage. We can take a hint from Andrew Chesterman's suggestion that working definitions can be used until necessary modifications are made in line with emerging, new "landscapes" (Chesterman, et al. 2003: 199). The foregoing proposal is an attempt to redefine the relationship of translation to adaptations and imitations, seeking

---

[13] One should note here, of course, that developmental or progressivist histories have been as much critiqued as the cult of originality, as shown in Dipesh Chakrabarty's critique of Western historicism at the heart of colonialism (2000).

[14] By using the pastiche, which brings forth a hybridized product (in an act analogous to cross-breeding or artificial selection), the imitator can (re)produce works with artistic distinction from which newness is not altogether absent.

greater definitional clarity despite difficulties in delineating disciplinary turfs. From an evolutionary perspective, "translation" becomes an umbrella term, under which adaptation and imitation can be subsumed. There is a possibility that such a schema can be applied to other forms of rewriting, but that falls outside the scope of the present study, in which we strive to draw links between the three genres that go under what Doorslaer calls the "paradigm of change" (2018)—all carried out in opposition to the widely held "fidelity principle."

On Classifications and Methodologies

Before we move on to explain our methodological approach, interesting comparisons can be made between the tripartition of the present study and a rather similar classification by Karen Thornber. "Transculturation" is the term she uses to analyze the manifold ways in which former (semi-) colonies of Japan—China, Korea, Taiwan, occupied Manchuria—crossed linguistic, geographical, and national frontiers and engage with their colonizer in contact zones in the first half of the twentieth century. It is of three kinds: (a) interpretive transculturation, which involves cross-cultural literary interpretation; (b) interlingual transculturation, within which both translation and adaptation are subsumed; and (c) intertextual transculturation, denoting the process by which texts are linked through the deployment of similar themes, plots, characters, and even titles. The third type is further subdivided into passive and dynamic ones. The former is used for works sharing textual features (for instance, when they deploy a shared convention) by coincidence; the latter, for those in which an author makes active use of a precursor text (for example, through allusions).

The parallels between Thornber's model and ours are obvious.[15] Imitations fall within her third category; indeed she discusses how issues of creativity and influence (2009: 214–15) affect the way we look at intertextual transculturations.[16] She also notes the overlap between translation and adaptation, with an acknowledgement that the boundary between the two is "diaphanous" (2009: 138). Her definition of "adaptation"—"rewriting

---

[15] A more detailed analysis of transculturation as a process occurring to texts crossing borders is given in Chapter 5.
[16] Thornber's category of intertextual transculturation is perhaps not completely co-extensive with our class of imitations. Given the imitators' often explicitly stated motivations, an element of agency (and not happenstance) is quite pronounced in the imitations, and so they can only be dynamic, not passive, transculturations.

loosely into another language" (2009: 4)—is virtually identical with ours: she points out how adaptors negotiate with their source texts and justify the changes made in paratextual materials. There are examples in her book, too, of the motivations for textual alterations; among these is the attitude of Korean and Chinese authors toward their colonizer, with the result that "whereas Chinese adaptations [of Japanese texts] tend to amend depictions of China by attacking Japanese literary creations, Korean adaptations contrast Japan unfavorably with Korea" (2009: 161). Other than the addition of the first (interpretive) category, her taxonomy roughly corresponds to our triadic scheme.

That makes it particularly enlightening, when we see that her classificatory system and ours exhibit subtle methodological differences. First, Thornber emphasizes the cultural implications of textual contacts between the three countries in the East Asian literary sphere from around 1895 to 1945. The linguistic dimension, however, is also foregrounded in the present study: the transtextual rewriters are seen to be responding to texts in another language. For instance, Ezra Pound's brazen reproductions of classical Chinese poetry were done in response to the Chinese texts in question, and the language component is crucial to his re-creations on the basis of Ernest Fenollosa's notes. Second, Thornber's analysis takes the reader beyond the merely textual, as she includes in her accounts of transculturation "events" as well. Literary figures traveling abroad and meeting their counterparts are described in some detail, building up to a picture of cross-national friendships and networks. Third, although Thornber's "interpretive" category is viable as one kind of rewriting, it signals different concerns than ours. The critics she mentions often do not focus their attention on the linguistic properties of the text; even where they deploy close reading skills, what they have written is a far cry from translation, adaptation, or imitation. Despite our two slightly different approaches, however, Thornber's insightful classification works very well with the body of intra-East Asian rewritings she examined, and her rightly placed emphasis on the cultural impact of transtextual rewriting (seen in the way it "refracts" the interweaving of textual material) mirrors that of the present project.

Of course, our attempt at a working redefinition of the relationship between the three forms creates methodological problems not easily resolvable. After all, translation, adaptation, and imitation, as strategies of rewriting and as transtextual genres, are similar but not the same. Differences are meaningful, but so are similarities. Anil Bhatti has theorized about similarity in a recent article, and he sees the overlapping of objects of study in this way:

> Similarity can't work without difference, but difference has always worked without Similarity. . . . Overlaps lead us, both in everyday life

as well as in reflective theoretical thinking, to the conclusion: things are a little bit similar, but not quite identical. The thought of Similarity only works when you say: it's not just identical; it's similar. Furthermore, Similarity allows us to introduce the uncertainty principle into our analysis. Uncertainty means that every category of thought has blurred borders, not a sharp edge. (Bhatti 2014: 18)

Bhatti's harsh criticism of the makeshift polarities, simple dichotomizations, and clear-cut borderlines that are imposed on the "world of things" is relevant to our study of the transtextual triad. It is precisely the similarities and the overlapping that will continue to haunt scholars exploring a transdisciplinary field involving the three siblings—or triplets.

The greatest methodological challenge is presented by the overlapping between adaptation and imitation. Many publications show that researchers treat imitations (in our categorization) as adaptations. Ezra Pound's rewriting of classical Chinese works is a case in point: his *Cathay* poems have often been designated "adaptations" rather than "imitations," but in view of their departures from the originals, which are so drastic that the Chinese subtext is not even recognizable, they are analyzed as imitations in our scheme. It is understandable, of course, why many Poundian scholars have a preference for "adaptation." Also, in Lhermitte's categorical separation of adaptation from imitation (2004: para. 1) and her treatment of some well-known imitators as adaptors, we see the degree to which the two are troublingly inseparable yet separate. In the East Asian scene, some examples are found in Claudine Salmon's collected volume *Literary Migrations* (1987), where the term "adaptation" is indiscriminately used for all forms of rewriting based on antecedent texts, without any sensitivity to those (i.e., the imitations) that are more extensively modified. Judging from these instances of use, it seems that adaptation, as a more neutral term, has found much easier acceptance by critics and is the preferred terminological choice when talking about second-order writings that are intended to be unfaithful to the originals from which they are derived. This, unfortunately, means that imitation can only be a subcategory of adaptations.[17]

Given the extensive overlap between the three transtextual modes, it is perhaps beneficial to see them existing in a spectrum, where one "fades" into the other at the edges. In this light, one can conceive of "free translation" as coterminous with "adaptation," and of "free adaptation" as synonymous with

---

[17] If, as Lhermitte has noted, the word *adaptatio* first appeared in the thirteenth century (2004: para. 3), then *imitatio* has had a much more illustrious lineage, its roots traceable back to Aristotle.

imitation. At one end of this continuum, therefore, we find extreme literalism (or word-for-word) translation, while the most liberal imitative rewriting of a prior text—which may even be invoked without reference, or deliberately concealed—stands at the other end.[18] The link between what Genette calls the hypotext and its hypertext becomes more and more tenuous as one moves from translation, through adaptation, to imitation, witnessing an intensifying degree of transformation, distortion, and infidelity. Individual case studies in the chapters that follow will bear out the usefulness of this approach, where the instances of transtextual practice that occupy the gray areas are allotted spaces in this taxonomic system, so that a particular *perspective*—one of three—can be deployed in the analysis. That means, in effect, that a certain text could be treated under a different category than the one given in this book, although by placing it where it is, we can spotlight characteristic traits—to use an evolutionary term—with reference to the theoretical framework aforementioned. For example, the Japanese manga based on *Journey to the West* will be treated as imitations, because they are better understood as such, even though they can also go into our adaptation chapter. In this way, the methodologies and the classificatory system will be mutually reinforcing.

This takes us to Chapter 2, which focuses squarely on "free translation" by analyzing the different ways in which three nineteenth-century translations of Aesop's fables freely depart from the English version used as their source text.

---

[18] In a similar vein, Paola Gentile and Luc van Doorslaer have observed that "the differences between the studied objects in translation and adaptation studies are usually gradual, not essential" (2019: 1).

Part I

2

Freely Rendered

Aesop's Fables in Nineteenth-Century China

Among the many reasons why free translation becomes a preferred method is a lack of competence in translating from a foreign knowledge, and such was the case of translations into Chinese from Western languages at the end of the nineteenth century.[1] The use of intermediary texts like an earlier translation (most often from Japan), or a collaborator who explained the source text or rendered it orally into Chinese, was a practice quite common in the days when, in eager pursuit of Western knowledge and know-how, translations of Western written materials were undertaken with great fervor. While the government, with the establishment of the Translation Bureau in the Office of Foreign Affairs (Zongli yamen) in Shanghai in 1861, could depend on trained personnel to translate official documents and books on practical subjects like science and technology, at the nongovernmental level translation expertise was in short supply, since overseas study was as yet unheard of, and only a minority had acquired bilingual facility at institutions like the School of Combined Learning (Tongwen guan), a language school founded in Beijing in 1862. Apart from the abundance of errors discernible in these translations of Western works into Chinese, the failure to capture faithfully the meaning of the original texts was ubiquitous. This was particularly rampant in the case of literary translations that appeared when China fully engaged with the West at the end of her last dynasty, the Qing (1644–1911).

The present chapter will look at three Chinese translations of Aesop's fables from roughly this period as examples of free translation in a specific historical context, focusing on the cultural changes introduced for various reasons into the text. Note should be taken of the fact that the fable is viewed by some as literary, and by others as folkloristic, and it is also a subcategory

---

[1] Before the High Fever of nineteenth- to twentieth-century translations, there were also two other periods in Chinese history in which translation was attempted on a large scale, involving: first, Sanskrit Buddhist texts from India (in the ninth century); and second, Latin religious and scientific texts from Europe (in the seventeenth century). But the nature and magnitude of the "third wave" far superseded the two earlier ones.

of children's literature. But then it is the element of oral transmission—fables are usually relayed by word of mouth, and often read aloud by parents to their children—that often gives rise to the many free renditions when they travel to diverse linguistic destinations. Spearheaded by Scandinavian scholars (e.g., Puurtinen 1991; Klingberg, Owig, and Amor 1978), translated children's literature has been amply studied (Alvstad 2019; Lathey 2016; O'Sullivan 2012; Van Coillie and Verschueren 2006), and some of their findings are relevant to the translated fable. Separate treatment has also been given to folktales in translation: with reference to examples from Europe and South Africa, Judith Inggs (2019) notes the substantial overlap between folktales and children's literature. In fact, studies specifically of how the translations deviate from the source texts is more the rule than the exception.

Readership considerations, too, are crucial to translated fables. If considered more closely, the fable, like all children's stories, should be regarded as more than just reading material for children. The worldwide success of Antoine de Saint-Exupéry's *The Little Prince* (1943) is a case in point, showing that fables are read as much by adults as by children. That is why the literary, as much as the oral, elements in the translations demand attention. As seen in our case-study, certain alterations to Aesop's text were made in deference to adults. This explains the use of the Chinese literary language rather than the vernacular, as well as the allegorical treatment given to the fables—the latter more evident at the end of the century than in the earlier ones. Thus, the greater latitude in the translation of fables in general, as well as the specific need to make accommodations at a special point in Chinese history, are key factors in affecting the form Aesop's fables took in nineteenth-century China. Taken as a whole, liberalism rather than literalism was the rule. The translations were carefully adjusted to the expectations of receptors at the time.

In general, it is quite futile to attempt to apply standards of textual fidelity or equivalence to the analysis of the translated fable. Instead, the liberal strategies of translated fables are perhaps best understood through the application of a functionalist model, in which the fable is seen to be adjusting in various ways to the receiving culture and the targeted readers. While translations of individual Aesop's fables were first undertaken as early as the sixteenth century by Jesuit missionaries like Matteo Ricci (1552-1610), Nicolas Trigault (1577-1628), and Giulio Aleni (1582-1649), it was only in the nineteenth century that "complete" translations of Aesop's fables appeared. All the translations in this period evince significant departures from the original, maintaining much distance from the English translation that served as the source text. They also bear a kinship to one another, so there is more resemblance among the contemporaneous translations than affinity to the English text being translated—not to mention the original

Greek work. Then, too, the translators worked upon the understanding that the reader would not be able to compare the source and target texts, and this was obviously another cause for utilizing the liberties. In point of fact, the first close, literal translation of Aesop using the Greek source text (by Zhou Qiming) did not appear until 1955.

Our focus will be on three translations from 1840 to 1903, which happen to illustrate very well the nature and function of free translation in an earlier period in China. They are Robert Thom's *Yishi yuyan* (abbreviated as T); Zhang Chishan's *Haiguo miaoyu* (Z); and Lin Shu, Yan Peinan, and Yan Ju's *Yisuo yuyan* (L).[2] Two English translations will be cited for comparison purposes—Lloyd W. Daly's version, *Aesop without Morals: The Famous Fables, and a Life of Aesop* (1961), and S. A. Handford's *Aesop's Fables* (H) (1954). As Yan Ruifang has pointed out, the three translations represent a second stage in the Christian transmission of Aesop's tales to China, after the initial phase involving the early Jesuit missionaries of the seventeenth century (2011: 1–2).[3] Viewed in terms of the history of fable translation in China, we can make two pertinent observations. First, previously there was a much longer period during which many more translations were undertaken of Buddhist fables in medieval times. Second, later in the twentieth century, many eminent Chinese translators engaged in translating non-Chinese fables and retranslating Aesop's fables from the source language, and these are far more faithful and source-oriented. As unfaithful renditions, the three translations under consideration evidently responded to the changing cultural and political situation in the target country rather than to contemporary perceptions of the source country. The end-products are noticeably Sinicized. By focusing on the "textemes of change" in the translations, we will explore how the goals of individual translators shaped the fables of Aesop as they were transplanted to Chinese soil.

Yishi yuyan and Cultural Accommodation

Other than the translations of a few fables by the Protestant missionary and magazine editor William Milne (1785–1822), there were only isolated

---

[2] In the citations given in parentheses in this article, the number after the abbreviation is the number of the entry being discussed. With the exception of the three translations that are the focus of this chapter, all other literary works are referred to by their commonly used English translated titles.
[3] For a chronology of the major events connected with the translation of Aesop's fables from 1581 to1904, see Yan (2011: 183–5).

Chinese versions of Aesop until *Yishi yuyan* came along. Eighty-two tales are included in this nineteenth-century translation by the English diplomat Robert Thom (1807–46), and he was assisted by his Chinese teacher, a certain "Mun Mooy Seen-shang" (Mr. Unenlightened) who taught Chinese to foreigners in the Canton area (Ge 1992a: 96).[4] Yan Ruifang estimated that Thom did the translation shortly after his arrival at Macau in 1835 (2011: 4). As opposed to the other two translations to be discussed, it was meant as a primer for English learners of Mandarin Chinese and Cantonese, with transcriptions in both dialects appearing in the right column, one above the other. One extant version shows that the text is divided into three columns. The Chinese translation is in the middle, with the transcriptions to the right and the back-translation into English to the left (given first in readable prose, then word-for-word) (Yan 2011: Fig. 1). Also, Thom evidently aimed to use the translation to introduce Chinese culture, in addition to the dialects, to foreign learners. Nevertheless, it was censored and listed in the Index Expurgatorius, according to Zhou Zuoren (see Zhou 1982: 194–7). Herbert Giles described the reception of the collection in this way:

> In every case save one these efforts [to translate European works into Chinese] have been rejected by the Chinese on the ground of inferior style. The exception was a translation of Aesop's fables . . . by Robert Thom. . . . This work attracted much attention among the people generally; so much so that the officials took alarm and made strenuous efforts to suppress it. (Giles 1935: 429)

The suggestion has been made that the translation was censored because of its veiled attacks on Qing government officials, but it is also likely that the censorship was due to a general fear of the pernicious influence of Western culture as such. The translated text contains no direct criticism of Chinese officialdom; it is even possible that the fear of proscription led the translator to tone down the exogenous elements.[5]

---

[4] Robert Thom was British Consul in Ningbo and a compiler of language texts. Ge Baoquan (1992a) describes at some length the background to the 1840 translation. According to Samuel Couling, Thom's published works include a translation, *The Lasting Resentment of Miss Wang Keaou Lwan* (1839), *Chinese and English Vocabulary* (1842), and *The Chinese Speaker* (1846) (1917: 554). As far as we know, Thom also wrote an article on "The Dreams of the Red Chamber" for the Ningbo-based *The Chinese Speaker*.

[5] According to Yao Dadui, it was "Mun Mooy Seen-shang" who did the Chinese translation making use of Roger L'Estrange's 1669 English version, *Fables of Aesop and Other Eminent Mythologists, with Morals and Reflections*. Thom then back-translated this version into English while the two sets of transcriptions were added (Yao 2018: 171). He did not give evidence for such a division of duties, however. For another discussion of the background to Thom's translation as well as its transmission, see Wang (2008).

One distinguishing fact about Thom's translation is that it was initiated by the source-language speaker, like the previous Jesuit translations, but unlike those that followed. In the nineteenth century, this was not an unusual phenomenon: Westerners like Timothy Richard (1845–1919) and Young J. Allen (1836–1907) translated foreign works into Chinese, with some assistance from the target-language speakers. Thom gave his intentions as follows:

> I have proposed this little work, with no intention to attract men's praise for the beauty of my composition; for alas! my fellow-countrymen of England, as well as those of all other Foreign countries whatever—who feel anxious to thread the mazes of Chinese Literature—are only beating about the door as it were, trying in vain to find an entrance! … [Morrison's dictionary] merely communicates to the Student the meaning of each particular character, and no more! Thus, as regards the formation of chapters and sentences, we are without any work to which we may refer as to a standard . . . how then under such circumstances, can we hope to wield the pen and compose with classic elegance? (qtd. Bridgman and Coleman 1840: 202)

For Thom, the translation is more than just a means of introducing Chinese words and expressions to the language learner. Its aim is not only to present the lexical items that an elementary learner needs to acquire to master the Chinese language, but to show the beauty of classical Chinese prose and how it can be written. This preface shows Thom quite eager to showcase Chinese literary culture as a means of enabling Westerners to understand China better.

Through history, of course, Aesop's fables have been used as a language textbook in the West. In England, for example, they had been used in this way in grammar schools until the eighteenth century. If the translation was indeed meant as a learner's text, then the extensive cultural adaptations would have been introduced by the translator in order to introduce Chinese culture to the Western reader. However, considering the directionality of the translation (from English into Chinese), we have a rather singular case of acculturation here. The normal situation, where the culture-specific elements of a source text are replaced in an attempt to "naturalize" the text for the target reader, becomes reversed. In *Yishi yuyan,* through the acculturation strategies, the translator actually "exoticizes" a familiar text for the English reader-learner, inculcating elements of a foreign (Chinese) culture. Of course, when the same translation was read by the Chinese readers—which indeed was made possible by the many reprints of the translations in popular journals like the *Wanguo gongbao* launched by Allen in 1868—the tales turned out to be well Sinicized. For the Chinese readers, it was an acculturated text; for the English readers, it was a foreignized one—at least more so than the English translation.

Shi Zhecun considers Thom's translation to be the most literal of the four nineteenth-century renditions of Aesop's fables he collected in his anthology (Shi 1991: 262), but this statement needs to be properly qualified. There is abundant tampering with the original text, seen in the changes of proper names and the introduction of a new time frame in several of the tales to give them an almost mythological flavor. The famous tale of "The Hare and the Tortoise" (T5) is removed to the times of Emperor Yu, of the ancient but largely legendary Xia dynasty. The story of the lion and the boar fighting over the dead body of a lamb until both are exhausted and a wolf comes along to carry off the carcass (T2) is attributed to *The Classic of Mountains and Seas*, a quasi-geographical account of prehistoric China. "The Brick Barrel and the Metal Barrel" (T17) is narrated against the backdrop of Emperor Yu taming the floods, a mythical event familiar to Chinese readers; the two barrels are even said to be floating down the rivers Si and Huai, in present-day Anhui and Jiangsu. "The Wolf Devouring the Lamb" describes how "both birds and animals could speak" in the times of Pan Gu, creator of the universe in Chinese mythology (T1). Real place names like Emei Mountain (in present-day Sichuan) (T13) mix with fictitious place names like "the Village of Nonsense" (T6) in the translation.

Time and again Chinese deities are substituted for Greek gods and goddesses from the original text. Although generally Aesop's fables take on an almost timeless, universal quality, many of them feature a pantheon of Greek gods that invariably binds the narratives to Western contexts. Greek deities like Aphrodite, Hermes, Athena, Tiresias, and Apollo are featured in Aesop's fables, yet all of them have disappeared in Thom's translation. There Yama, the ruler of hell in Chinese belief and a key figure in Buddhist lore, appears to the old man who would rather die than live (T18). In "The Frogs' Plea," the Greek god Zeus in the original is recast as Emperor of the North, who dispatches a snake to a community of frogs pleading for a ruler (T28; cf. H42). A charioteer cries out for help from the Amida Buddha when the wheels of his carriage get mired in the mud (T34). On this list of acculturation items there is also the story of the cat-turned-beauty who chases after a mouse planted in its bed by a fun-loving Chang'e, the female Chinese immortal who lives on the moon (T40). On the whole, *Yishi yuyan* is a case showing considerable freedom in translation, and Thom seems to be interested in mythologizing Aesop's tales, imbuing the animals with the aura of legendary creatures and transposing the stories to earlier historical periods.

Thom's acculturation strategy is also seen in his translation of proverbial expressions. Many Aesopic fables have given rise to metaphorical proverbs in English, like "the lion's share," "sour grapes," and "cry wolf," just like similar ones in the Chinese tradition. But in most cases, these are found in the final sentence—the epimythium—which contains the "message," usually a wise saying with a proverbial ring. One can readily appreciate the tremendous difficulties these textemes presented to the translator. On the whole, Thom skillfully inserted Chinese proverbial expressions so that the text reads "Chinese," and the most successful instances involve the use of functionally equivalent proverbs, although new aphorisms coined by the translator using the linguistic structures at his command also can create the desired effect. Here are a few of the old Chinese proverbs that find their way into the Chinese translation:

1. "The mantis seizes the cicada, not knowing that behind them lurks the oriole." This is the proverbial equivalent to the truism expressed near the end of the story about the two cocks fighting over their prey (T6).
2. "When the snipe and the clam are engaged in a bitter tussle, a fisherman reaps the profit" (T2). In expressing the idea of third-party profit, Thom resorts to the proverb originating in a story from *Strategies of the Warring States*. There the diplomat Su Dai advises the Duke of Zhao not to launch an attack on his own State of Yan, since it will be a third state (Qin) that stands to gain when that happens.
3. "Mountains may be moved but it is hard to alter a person's nature" (T40)—a proverb based on a popular folktale.
4. "Better be a cock's beak than a bull's rump." The Chinese saying is generally ascribed to the politician Su Qin, who prefers to be a minister of a small state rather than a minor official in a large one (T38).
5. "When the lips are lost the teeth will be exposed to the cold." Appearing in the story of the father exhorting his sons at his deathbed to stick together by showing them the strength of a bunch of wooden sticks tied together (T19, cf. H175). This Chinese proverb comes from two ancient classics, *Zhuangzi* and *The Spring and Autumn Annals*.

The use of analogous Chinese proverbs is more than an easy solution to an intractable problem; it is in keeping with Thom's attempt at mythologizing Aesop's fables. Not only are they short, memorable, and self-explanatory, but they also bear the sign of antiquity, thus working in tandem with the repeated references to Chinese legends in the text. The effect is to exoticize the text to the English reader. The inclusion of Chinese proverbs in the translation is perhaps also justified pedagogically: they need to be introduced to the learners, who were seeking to master the language. Apparently, it is this pedagogical motive which, in line with Thom's argument in the preface, justifies all the alterations in the text, though one can argue whether this in itself is *sufficient* justification.

Thom's translation invites comparison with the earlier Jesuit translations, also initiated by source-language users and translated freely. But the latter were bolstered by a proselytizing motive—an attempt at introducing Western religion to the Chinese reader through the syncretic blending of native and non-native beliefs. Christian discourse is interpolated in those translations, which were intended to serve the Jesuits' mission in China. Notable examples are the translations by Matteo Ricci in *Ten Essays on Eccentrics* and by Nicholas Trigault in *Selectae Esopi Fabulae*.[6] However, Thom's translation worked in exactly the opposite direction, for it aimed to introduce Chinese cultural and linguistic items to Western readers with only a modicum of knowledge about China. While it also ended up introducing the Greek fables to Chinese readers as well, from the beginning Thom's enterprise was conceived differently than the Jesuits'. The concerns of a missionary contrasted with those of a diplomat, and the respective intended audiences were different.

Questions raised with regard to the uses of acculturation in Thom's translation need to be framed differently from usual. For one thing, acculturation does not always serve to domesticate a text, since the target readers do not necessarily come from the target-language community. Translating out of one's mother tongue for readers who are learning the target language presents a rather special and unique scenario, especially as translation into one's first language is now generally encouraged, while today's foreign language learners are invariably advised to use authentic texts rather than translations. While most scholars would say that "Mun Mooy Seen-shang" was responsible for polishing Thom's Chinese, the question of how the collaboration with a Chinese mediator affected the outcome is worth further exploration. As the nineteenth century wore on, when Chinese translators themselves took up the task on their own, acculturation did become no more than a means of accommodating a translated text to (Chinese) readers. Principally, however, it is functional considerations that have led to the retention or erasure of the Otherness of the exogenous text. Questions can be raised, too, as to whether the well-adapted translation can be a replacement for the original, and why liberalism was the rule of thumb in nineteenth-century Chinese translations. These take us to the two other translations of the fables.

---

[6] Pre-Qing translations have been analyzed at some length by Ge Baoquan (Ge 1992b).

Haiguo miaoyu and Generic Assimilation

Ge Baoquan was right in pointing out that *Haiguo miaoyu* (literally, Marvelous Fables of the Seabound Country) was edited, and not translated, by Zhang Chishan, whose name appears on the title page (Ge 1992a: 103). Since some of Aesop's fables in this translation were almost copied word for word from Thom's *Yishi yuyan* (36 out of the total of 70, according to Yan Ruifang [2011]) and another version called *Yishapu yuyan* (published in the 1840s by the Anglo-Chinese College in Hong Kong), we are quite unsure of what part Zhang played as a translator. The collection may be considered as an edited work, or a downright case of plagiarism. Also, apart from the fables copied from Thom, *Haiguo miaoyu* seems to contain others which had appeared earlier, but which cannot now be traced. It may have included non-Aesopic fables as well, and Yan believes that some tales were probably copied from imitations of Aesop appearing in the newspapers and magazines of the time (Yan 2011: 8).[7] There are many postclassical references in the text; these may have been inserted into the later versions of the Aesopic fables. The collection is best seen as a hybrid text where translated and imitated texts were blended and then all of them attributed to Aesop.

In his preface Zhang Chishan says that, since harsh admonitions will not readily be heeded, the best way of inducing people to take the moral path is through an indirect method. To him Aesop's fables are an "ancient bell" (a conventional Chinese metaphor for moral exhortation), which wake people up from their slumbers, since the messages are obliquely presented through the stories:

> [This book] tenders advice with good intentions; it admonishes through allegorical means; it reminds one of the basic virtues; it leads one on the path to enlightenment. On reading it, one is filled with pleasure and can discover concealed meanings. To put it simply: "By penetrating into the depths of human experience, it becomes a remarkable piece of writing."
> ... Its intended goal is to encourage people to mend their ways, pursue honesty and goodness, and return to a state of innocence.

To the nineteenth-century reader familiar with prefaces to the official and semiofficial histories, his preface would have sounded familiar. What is

---

[7] One interesting imitation was Chen Chunsheng's *Dongfang yisuo* (1906), which Yao Dadui discussed at some length (2018: 173–7). It replaces Aesop with the Han dynasty court jester Dongfang Shuo (c.160 BCE–c.93 BCE), who tells didactic stories in a vein similar to Aesop's, although they are based on ancient Chinese sources.

more, Zhang's preface is couched in language similar to that used in the prefaces to short story collections in premodern China, which is the genre most closely resembling Aesop's fables. In fact, *Haiguo miaoyu* adopts an adorned classical Chinese prose, replete with parallel sentence structures and classical allusions. The preface similarly uses this elevated style to invoke a range of moral imperatives. Ethical injunctions are of course a common feature in the works by Chinese historians and short story writers in the premodern era, and Zhang similarly used them to justify his collection.

While there is no knowing the extent of Zhang's actual contribution as a translator, it is clear that, unlike Thom, the translation evinces little attempt to "acculturate" Greek cultural references. It is also less strongly Sinicized than Thom's as a whole. For example, "Venus" is transliterated into Chinese as "Weinasi" (Z35), with an added explanation that she is "the goddess of beauty in ancient Rome"; in Thom's translation, she is transformed into Chang'e, as we have noted earlier. In the story about the Greek priest whose two daughters ask him, respectively, to pray for sunshine and rain (Z33), Zhang's version identifies the priest as Greek, unlike Lin Shu's Aesop translation later, which gives no hint of his nationality. Some of the tales purportedly take place in India (Z36), Persia (Z8), and even America (Z38). The woman acrobat who walks on a tightrope (Z2) is reputedly Italian. There is also the satiric fable of the two stupid religious devotees who go to "the Sunday temple" (obviously one of the early Chinese translations for the Christian church) (Z21). Thus, on the whole, there is much less departure from the original Aesop text, whether Zhang had used it or not.

However, to a smaller degree, signs of acculturation are still visible. In "Death Wish" (Z13), Yama—the King of Hell—sends a "ghost" to talk to the old man who wants to die. While a multitude of Greek gods appear in the original, there is no mention of ghosts there. Even more non-Aesopic is the conversation between the old man and the ghost that ensues, in which the man is persuaded to renounce his suicidal wish. Another instance is the myth about beasts and birds waging an unending battle against each other in the days before the Great Deluge of ancient China (Z47)—one entirely fabricated. Chinese folk sayings and proverbs, too, are scattered throughout the text, as in Thom's rendition. As a result, there is a curious admixture of things non-Chinese with things Chinese, and this contrasts markedly with the more consistent acculturation strategies in Thom's translation. Fable after fable, the collection displays a blend of the exotic-Western with the indigenous-Chinese. This is shown in the following list of foreign proper names retained in the translation, juxtaposed against those that have been Sinicized:

Exotic Elements	Sinicized Elements
Europe (Story 1)	Pan Gu the Creator (12)
Italy (2)	Yama (13)
Persia (8)	Ghost-messenger (13)
Church (21)	Amida Buddha (40)
Greece (33)	Rotten Confucian (43)
Roman Empire (35)	Chinese astrologer (47)
Venus (35)	The Great Deluge (47)
India (36, 66)	
America (38)	
Russia (64)	

Against this hybrid context, a good number of topical references to the more immediate concerns of nineteenth-century China are interpolated in the text. Such references, for which the Aesopic fables are justly famous, are targeted at specific groups. These include the pedantic Confucian scholars in some cases, and corrupt government officials and ineffectual ministers in others. These happen to be repeatedly singled out and pilloried in Chinese fiction of the time, collectively designated "condemnation novels," such as Wu Jianren's (1866–1910) *Strange Events Witnessed in the Past Twenty Years* and Li Boyuan's (1867–1906) *The Bureaucracy Exposed*.[8] Examples of castigations of educational and legal personnel include the stories about the fly spitting ink (Z1), the scholar who lectures to the child about to be drowned (Z43), and the adjudicator who seeks to resolve the conflict between two men who catch a clam on the beach (Z49). The first two of these provide the occasion for a diatribe against the bookish Confucian scholar who engages in nothing but empty talk, and the last is a veiled attack on judges in the Qing system.

While such adaptations in *Haiguo miaoyu* are limited, the generic assimilation, or the recasting, of the stories in Chinese literary "form," is quite thoroughgoing. The paratextual material mentioned earlier, as well as the use of the fables as satiric stories targeted at specific groups, as noted in the last paragraph, are already indicative of a different orientation. Defined simply, assimilation is the process whereby a source text is given properties that make it similar to counterparts in the target language, or rendered so familiar to target readers that they would treat it as if it was written by an indigenous author. The opposite phenomenon is differentiation, where a translated text remains foreign, unfamiliar, and incongruous with native expectations. Of course, assimilation in translation takes many forms: it can

---

[8] The former has been translated in part by Liu Shih-shun as *Vignettes from the Late Ch'ing: Bizarre Happenings Eyewitnessed over Two Decades* (Liu 1975).

be linguistic, cultural, thematic, and so on, while terms like "acculturation," "domestication," and "naturalization" are loosely linked to it. But in Zhang Chishan's tales it is generic assimilation that explains the way his texts have been reconfigured. The process involves more than just the transformation of some fables into satiric stories in the Chinese literary tradition. The preface by Zhang gives the clearest hint as to the kind of assimilation in question: in *Haiguo miaoyu* Aesop's fables are evidently modeled on an entire tradition of classical literary tales in China.[9]

In the assimilation mode, *Haiguo miaoyu* should be read against the textual norms and conventions from the target literature. Formally, many of the translated stories read more like Chinese literary tales than they do Greek fables, especially where there is better acculturation (or Sinicization). To begin with, one notices that these "fables" contain more details than the Aesopic originals even though they were translated in classical Chinese, which is a condensed literary language. Among the longer ones are "The Two Virtuous Men" (Z21), with about 525 words; and "A Case of Emergency" (Z38) and "The Dead Donkey," with about 400 words each. On the average, the stories in this collection are longer than Handford's or Daly's renditions in English. Yan Ruifang has also highlighted the length of some of the tales, noting that some are so wordy that one critic has complained of their "tastelessness" (Yan 2011: 9). "The Web" (Z28), with 910 words, is unmistakably the longest of all of Aesop's fables translated into Chinese, reading more like a classical Chinese short story than an Aesopic fable. Interestingly, the plotline is not much altered in the translated versions; only the texture is denser and the plot elaborated at greater length.

In addition, a large proportion of Zhang's translated stories involves human characters. Though the beast fables in Aesop are better known and more often translated, there are many Aesopic fables with human protagonists, and Zhang shows a strong preference for these. Examples are those of the thief who talks his way out of the scheduled execution (Z8), the overly worried woman (Z25), and the child who drowns in the water (Z43). In effect, though human fables do not dominate in Zhang's version, the balance between the two types of fables in the original is skewed. Zhang's selection of fables is also in marked contrast to later, twentieth-century collections where the beast fables figure more prominently. While it is questionable whether Aesop translations introduced the animal fable to China (as some

---

[9] One can also say that the tradition of classical tales provides more than one model into which non-Chinese fable-lore can be assimilated, since this tradition is made up of diverse genres: jokes, accounts of strange phenomena, humorous tales, stories of marvels, fables, and so on.

early twentieth-century critics averred), it is true that Chinese fables had traditionally been dominated by those with human characters, supernatural beings, and mythological beasts like the unicorn and the dragon (see Ning 1992; Wu 1994) rather than animals. The extent to which Zhang's version has somehow been influenced by generic considerations in the target literature is evident.

"The Web" is worthy of closer examination in this connection. It presents a conversation between a fly and a spider, in which the latter persuades the former of its friendly intentions. When the fly finally surrenders to the charm of the spider, it gets trapped in its web and then eaten up. Stylistically, the story betrays many similarities to the classical Chinese literary tale, including the adoption of its "register."[10] For purposes of comparison, we can cite a classical tale by Shen Qifeng (b. 1741), "The Conversation of the Chickens," which revolves around a verbal contest between a cock and a hen (see Chan 1995: 32–3). Among the features that make "The Web" look similar to "The Conversation of the Chickens" and different from its Aesopic original are the allusive language and the classical references. The two main characters in "The Web" are given literary names—"Young Master in Green" (the fly) and "Weaver of the Net" (the spider). There is, then, the use of a fictitious commentator "Master Awakening the World" who inserts the moral of the fable at the end. This is in contrast to the Aesopic fable, where the moral lesson does not come from any particular individual. The equivalent convention in Chinese short story literature is the appended commentary, by some mysterious figure like the "Fantastorian" in Pu Songling's (1640–1715) *Strange Stories from the Leisure Studio*. Another non-Aesopic element in "The Web" is the comparison, near the end, of the spider to the vixen. The vixen, it must be noted, has long been used as a trope in Chinese tales for seductresses and licentious women, and it opens up avenues of meaning not inherent in the original fable. Finally, the moral didacticism typical of traditional classical tales in China also appears: "I hope men of this world will not emulate the fly's arrogance and court destruction, nor model themselves after the spider and use trickery to deceive others." In sum, the tale has virtually been rewritten in the form of a classical literary tale, though without radical changes to the core plot elements. The norms of the target literature

---

[10] The superimposition of a new register borrowed from the target culture on a text to be translated has been superbly illustrated by John M. Foley's study of the Old English poem "Andreas" as an "indexed translation" of the Greek "Praxeis" (Foley 1995: 181–207). "Indexed translation" can equally well be used to describe the story "The Web": it becomes indexed when a new set of codes derived from the traditional Chinese repertoire with their distinctive signifying capabilities is used, serving to reorient the translation by placing it in its target context.

have been forcibly superimposed and the tale undergoes a process of generic assimilation.[11]

But how did Chinese fabulists at the time respond to the influx of translated fables from the West? There is no mistaking the fact that indigenous literary productions were stimulated by the translations. The sheer number of fables that appeared in Chinese newspapers and magazines in the late nineteenth century bears testimony to the fledging interest in writing fables, especially ones involving animals. How the cross-fertilization of indigenous fables and translated fables occurred is textually exemplified by a tale like "The Web."[12] From the mid-nineteenth century on, foreign elements thus infiltrated the Chinese tradition, and the process is chiefly observable in the translations of Aesop. Theoretically, a fable translator could come up with more "indigenous" tales than the Chinese fabulist of the same period if the strategies of acculturation and assimilation go far enough, and it is not inconceivable that the former would try to discard the exogenous elements as far as possible. This is at least one possible view of Chinese translation history of the period.

Of course, Indian fables had been translated into Chinese, an earlier example being "The Wolf of Zhongshan," which was derived from the Pancatantra (see Mowry 1984). But never before had the writing of fables coincided with such intense translation activity as was witnessed in the latter half of the nineteenth century. The direct social critique that we have noted in *Haiguo miaoyu* was carried out more pointedly, for instance, in Wu Jianren's fables in his *Witty Stories* (1906). The most important collection of autochthonous fables in the late Qing, it exemplifies the nineteenth-century Chinese fabulist at his best, writing in the face of an influx of translated imports. Without any doubt, as its title suggests, this compilation carries on the tradition of social criticism in Chinese joke literature.[13] As in *Haiguo miaoyu*, bureaucrats are the target of derision: they are compared to mice (in "The Resignation of the Cat" and in "A World of Beasts"), dogs (in "Promoted by Three Ranks"), wild roosters (in "Wild Roosters"), and turtles

---

[11] For generic assimilation in translation, see Armin Paul Frank (1992), Dirk de Geest (1992) and Itamar Even-Zohar (1978), among others.

[12] The native tradition is believed, by general consent, to have begun with Zhuangzi. He was the first person to use the word "fable" (*yuyan*), in Chapter 23 of the book by his name. There are, however, slight differences between this word as it was originally used and the English word "fable," so the latter can only be a makeshift translation (cf. Hartmann 1986: 946–8).

[13] In terms of what has just been said about the process of generic assimilation occurring to translations, it can also be argued that the translations of Aesop's fables were also assimilated to Chinese joke literature.

(in "The Literary Name of the Turtle"). But Wu became dangerously specific in some of his stories. In the opening story in the collection, "Other Names for Beasts," he inveighed against the anti-reformist group in the government, likening them to pigs. Then, in "The World of Insects," he foretold sarcastically the demise of the dynasty. In this way, Wu gave back to the Chinese fable the age-old function for which it was originally conceived—to make an indirect political statement to the emperor—but added to it the animal characters found in non-Chinese fables circulated widely at the time. The impact of translated Aesop fables is thus seen in the work of indigenous fabulists, with genealogical roots that extended beyond China.

Yisuo yuyan and Ideological Appropriation

Lin Shu's (1852-1924) *Yisuo yuyan* was the most complete translation of Aesop's fables at the time it was published, with a total of 295 stories.[14] It was in fact a collaborative effort with Yan Peinan and Yan Ju, the two sons of the renowned late Qing translator Yan Fu (1854–1921), though for obvious reasons (see below) it should simply be attributed to Lin. In his preface Lin describes the rather casual conditions under which the translation was initiated. He was introduced to a few Western books by the Yan brothers while sojourning in Peking, and decided to translate the fables of Aesop. Lin also referred to a tradition of fable-writing in China in the preface, mentioning, among the more reputable fabulists, Su Shi (1037–1101) and his book of anecdotes, *Master Ai's Miscellaneous Sayings*. He considers the Aesopic fables, however, to be far superior as an instrument for educating youngsters. Yet Lin's translation is certainly not meant as children's entertainment. Nowhere in the preface, however, did Lin make explicit his motivation or the readership he envisaged for the translation.

Lin Shu's translation clearly differs from its predecessors, as can be seen from a brief comparison of different versions of "The Cat and the Mice." Zhang's version (Z4) is nothing more than a copy of Thom's (T49), with only minor changes to the wording. The greatest difference is found in

---

[14] The issue of how many fables by Aesop exist has been debated for centuries without any definite answer. The difficulty lies not only in the fact that there might not have been a historical person called Aesop, but also in that efforts were only made to preserve the tales long after they began to be circulated—in fact only in the fourth century BCE by Demetrius of Phalerum. This complicates the issue of the translation of the fables. There are later retellings, like those by Babrius and Phaedrus, and by La Fontaine later. Li Shershiueh has ventured the suggestion that La Fontaine's version might have served as the source text for Trigault's translation (Li 1990: 131–57).

the commentary, for Zhang added one more sentence at the end, "That is detestable and pitiable." But the moral lesson is essentially the same as that of Thom's translation, namely that "certain things are easier said than done." In Lin's rendition (L103), the fable proper is shorter than the commentary, which is also less of an exhortatory nature, and more concerned about using the right strategies or making the proper decisions. Here is the commentary translated into English in its entirety:

> Comments by Weilu (i.e., Lin Shu): It is already a mistake to let the shallow-minded decide. It is even worse to gather together a bunch of dim-wits and allow each one to put forth his ideas. How can we decide wisely? Often I have come across impossible suggestions from those who never give a thought to their implementation, although they do expect others to carry them out. Such cleverness is the cleverness of rats. Alas! How can we decide on anything of moment with people no cleverer than rats?

One can simply conclude that, if anything, Lin's rendition belongs to a different stratum of Aesop translations in China than the others.

The most prominent feature in Lin Shu's *Yisuo yuyan* is the extended commentary, whose dual origins are: (i) the parallel convention in Chinese histories and short story collections, and (ii) the epimythium in the Western fable, a conventional formula placed at the end of a story to explain its moral application. In some Aesopic fables, however, the epimythium is absent, replaced by the promythium, the message placed at the very beginning. Yet the promythium never shows up in the Chinese versions under consideration, showing how the epimythium was favored as the convenient meeting point between two textual traditions, Chinese and Western. But whereas earlier translators simply supplied a moral epigram, in the form usually of one sentence, Lin chose to appropriate and functionalize this formal feature. His use of the commentary can be related to the *maxim* (gnome), which refers to "general statements [truisms] about human affairs [that] become complete enthymemes if a reason or conclusion is added" (Hill 2003: 101)—a part of the Greek rhetorical tradition as exemplified by Aristotle. This shows Lin's effort at appropriating the stories to make a point relevant to his own world. As in many of Zhang's Aesopic fables, Lin's commentaries also are very specific in reference; they were a vehicle for the expression of his views on the political scene (see Hill 2013: 83–8). Yet Lin's prime targets were not corrupt government officials in general; like Wu Jianren, he aimed directly at the incompetence of the Qing administration in handling China's political crisis at the turn of the century.

Once again it was the intended purpose of the target text that determined the choice of a translation strategy. Fidelity to the source text was not Lin's concern, nor was it Thom's or Zhang's. Lin Shu departed drastically from the original not because he was unable to read the source language and had to rely on oral intermediaries, nor because he had scant regard for faithfulness in translating Aesop. In rendering his fables freely, Lin was intentionally manipulating the text for his own purposes, and this aspect of Lin's free translation method can be seen clearly in his translated novels. The alterations in the text were not meant to make the reading easier for target readers, as was the case with the assimilation strategies in Zhang's version. Put simply, the translation served a different function than the original. Its ties to the original text were snapped and refastened to a specific target situation—China's political predicament at the time.

That the acculturation strategies in Thom and Zhang do not figure so prominently in Lin's version is seen in the fact that the Chinese proverbs and folk sayings have almost entirely disappeared. For example, the well-known Chinese proverb about the snipe and the clam (meaning: "two parties fight for a bone, but a third party runs away with it"), which concludes the story of the lion and the boar fighting over the lamb in the two earlier versions (T2, Z63), is not found in Lin's (L148). Instead, there is a preference for exoticization as seen, for instance, in the renderings of the names of the Greek gods Hermes, Jupiter, and Mercury. The decision not to replace them with the names of Chinese deities signals different priorities on Lin's part. Only bits of Western exotica are left here and there in the Chinese text, like the reference to the Arabs as lovers of camels (L139). The moral didacticism, too, is much less conspicuous.

As for the commentaries, it is obvious that Lin Shu was most keenly interested in the power relations of the animal world. This in fact furnishes a clue as to why Lin translated Aesop's fables. As we know, the late nineteenth-century Chinese intellectual scene was swamped by Darwinian theories of social evolution, introduced to the Chinese public through Yan Fu's translation of T. H. Huxley's *Evolution and Ethics* in 1898. An entire generation was affected by it: the reformists used it to justify their program of political changes; key cultural figures like Wang Guowei (1877–1927) and Lu Xun (1881–1936) subscribed to the theory of natural selection and the newly discovered rationale for social progress and change and eagerly promoted it. That Lin was unaware of the connection between the Aesopic fables and Darwinism is thus highly unlikely. It is even more unlikely that the Yan brothers' suggestion that the Aesopic fables be translated was just a coincidence. It was, after all, a time when the traumatic effects of the Boxer Uprising and the defeat of China by an alliance of Western powers were painfully felt. It may not be too far-fetched to suggest that one motive behind the translation of the fables was to popularize the ideas of Darwin among the general public and to urge them to take action before the country got devoured, like the lamb· by the wolf.

From the perspective of Darwinism, Aesop's fables depict a hierarchized animal world where the fittest survive. That much is evident through the recurrent stories of the lion bullying the other animals in his kingdom, in addition to those about the wolf killing the lamb, the horse teasing the donkey, and so on, as well as those narrating the disputes about which animal is most powerful. These fables allowed Lin Shu to issue his clarion call to· the Chinese of his time. He cautioned them against imminent national disaster by drawing attention to the rule of the jungle, namely, that the weak are eaten up by the strong. Commenting on the story of "The Wolf Devouring the Lamb" (L2), Lin said that weaker countries are like the lamb, and stronger countries, the wolf. He added one sentence to this fable that is not found in the earlier renditions. When the wolf fails to come up with a plausible excuse for killing the lamb, after trying out several, it says, "I might not have made a sound case for myself, but there is no reason why I should let you go because I am at a loss for words," and eats the lamb all the same. The lesson is that it is futile to reason with those wielding more power, as the lamb does. In concluding the story of the wolf's making a meal of the heron that just saved it by removing a bone stuck in his throat (L4), Lin Shu does not offer a moral remark on human ingratitude (cf. H29), but sourly notes that there is nothing surprising about stronger nations wishing to "devour" weaker ones.

Through the translated fables, Lin Shu freely offered his views on the international situation and suggested possible courses of action for the weaker countries. He spoke against international treaties that favored the stronger nations through the story of the hound catching the rabbit (L176). In commenting on the tale of the father who advises his sons to stick together after his death, Lin Shu argued for closer cooperation among the weaker nations. For him "the European nations are strong because they act in unison" (L5). If weaker nations do not band together, according to Lin, they will be annihilated. It is the lesson taught by the story of the donkey letting the mule carry the whole burden, till the latter dies and then it is his turn to shoulder the entire load (L50). This case shows the extent to which Aesop's fables fitted Lin's purpose quite well, and what Lin did was simply Aesopic, for hidden meanings were attached to an animal story. This strategy has been widely seen as an invention by Aesop: Andrew Ford has noted how, as a slave, Aesop learned how to "talk around a point when addressing a superior" (Ford 2002: 97). To understand the true meaning of Lin's freely translated narratives, they will have to be decoded.

Above all, in *Yisuo yuyan* Lin Shu is advocating a philosophy of action, privileging Machiavellian adaptability in the face of difficult circumstances. While many of Aesop's fables show the elimination of the weaker ones in the game of natural selection, others tell how the weak can overpower their enemies and gain an unexpected victory. The tables are thus being turned against those more powerful, and there exists a rule for survival of the "not so fit." Aesop's stories reflect a world where cunning, cleverness, craft, wisdom, and "metic intelligence" (Raphals 1992) allow the weaker party to gain the upper hand when bullied. An excellent example is the fable, known the world over, of the fly proving that it is "stronger" than the lion by going inside the latter's nose and ears, the message being that ingenuity is more effective than brute force. Then there is the narrative of the (malleable) fox which wins the verbal combat with the lion intent on eating it and escapes unharmed, showing the triumph of practical wisdom. Even the story of the tortoise winning the race with the hare, which shows the need for perseverance, was presented by Lin as an example of the tactful defeat of an opponent. In outwitting the hare, the tortoise proves that the race is not always to the swift, nor the battle to the strong. In Lin's freely added commentaries, the oft-repeated keyword is *zhi* (cleverness), and his message to the reader of Aesop's fables is that it pays to be clever (see comments in L30, L57, L178). Even the cunning of the fox, the trickster figure in fable-lore, was not always condemned, while the donkey's stupidity was again and again singled out for ridicule (see L98, L113, L107, L122).

For H. J. Blackham, Aesop's fables do not teach a Sunday-school morality, but an "open-eyed Baconian morality" (Blackham 1985: 9). There are stories in Aesop's collection about how one's rightful claims are denied simply because one has not got the power to enforce them; how kindnesses are never repaid; and how one can attain by cunning what one cannot acquire by pleading. Yet there are tales denouncing vainglory, dishonesty, ingratitude, and so on, in the collection as well. There are diverse, perhaps even contradictory, strands of moral thinking embodied in the fables, but in his translations Lin Shu highlighted those aspects of Aesopian morality that did not find a comfortable niche in the Chinese moral system of his time. (By contrast, Zhang Chishan strives to present a traditional Chinese ethical outlook.) His commentaries contain few exhortations to moral behavior; instead, his emphasis was on action attuned to changing circumstances, on flexible response to crises. Traditional Chinese morality, strengthened by the retributive system of virtue rewarded and vice punished (which showed up most prominently in the commentary portions of classical tales) is *not* the fundamental operational principle in Lin's translated fables; practical cleverness is. In this manner, Aesop's fables were transplanted by Lin along with a more practical-oriented approach to real-life contingencies.

Free Translation in Historical Context

The functionalist approach proves to be fruitful not only in understanding the freely translated fables of the late Qing, but also in differentiating between the various uses to which the free method can be put. As Christiane Nord has said, a text has no fixed function; the function is only assigned by the initiator, or by the recipient through the initiator (Nord 1991: 16). In Thom's translation, it is the translator's perception of the language learners' needs that determines his acculturation moves. In Zhang's version, it is the desire to facilitate acceptance of the text by the Chinese readership that leads to the assimilation of many stories to indigenous narrative models. In Lin's translation, the Aesopic fables take on a kind of timely relevance and allow Lin to alert his readers to the national crisis through the incorporation of extraneous remarks in the commentaries. Ironically, none of the translations were meant only for consumption as children's literature; the adaptive mode unveils the intended targeted audience.

However, although the alterations to the original text can be functionally interpreted, one cannot underestimate the extent to which the fable, by its very nature, encourages adaptation, retelling and "re-version" (see Inggs 2019: 149–50)—in short, liberalism in translation. In the late Qing period when China was only beginning to be opened to the West, this necessity to make adjustments to suit the target culture and readership was compounded with the use of intermediary texts or interlingual assistance by a third party, ending up with outrageously liberal versions. Earlier we noted that Shi Zhecun considered Thom's translation as a "literal" one. This appeared to be so for him because a succession of Aesop translations was based on it and their translators manipulated them even further to produce Sinicized versions, so that each subsequent translation turns out to be freer than its predecessor. This trend continued until it was reversed in the early twentieth century, when the preference for literalism took over. On the other hand, collaborative translation was also a cause for the serious departures from the source text: Thom translated the fables with Chinese help and Lin relied on collaborators when he himself could not understand the source language. There are, in short, innumerable factors at work that, either singly or in combination, account for the liberties taken by Chinese translators in translating not just Aesop, but also other works in other genres, in the period immediately before China entered her modern era.

3

A Higher Loyalty? The (Ab)uses of Aesthetic Theories of Translation

One of the most controversial topics in modern Chinese translation theory is the precise meaning of *ya* (literally: elegance).[1] First presented as a cardinal principle and then transformed into a dominant concept of the Aesthetic School of Translation, it commanded the attention of a succession of mainstream theorists from Yan Fu (1854–1921) to Xu Yuanchong (1921–), both doyens of twentieth-century Chinese translation theory. Yan foregrounded *ya* along with two other principles of translation—faithfulness (*xin*) and comprehensibility (*da*)—in the preface to his translation of T. H. Huxley's essay on social Darwinism, *Evolution and Ethics*, in 1898. According to him:

> *The Book of Changes* says: "Fidelity is the basis of writing." Confucius said: "Writing should be comprehensible." He also said, "Where language has no refinement, its effects will not extend far." These three dicta set the right course for literature and are the guidelines for translation. In addition to faithfulness and comprehensibility, we should strive for elegance in translation. This is not just for extending the effects far. (trans. C. Y. Hsu; Chan 2004: 69–70)

While all three principles have dominated the discourse on translation in China throughout the long twentieth century, *ya* has been subjected to an inordinate amount of interpretation and reinterpretation, and praise and blame, after it entered the theoretical battleground with the prestige bestowed upon it by Yan Fu (see Wang 2007). Quite unlike faithfulness and comprehensibility, which have gone virtually unchallenged as essential criteria for evaluating any translation, *ya* has been treated with great skepticism by those who call attention to its nebulous nature. Some sought to make it

---

[1] In addition to "elegance," *ya* has had a number of variant translations, for example "embellishment" and "refinement." To cover the range of meanings in the present discussion, however, it could mean something like "aesthetically pleasing."

relevant and serviceable by emphasizing certain connotations that they said Yan Fu intended, saying, for instance, that *ya* is the equivalent of "beauty."[2] Others, however, tried to justify it with reference to the special historical moment at which it emerged; it was said that the archaic style he deployed is a standard valorized by his well-educated peers. At the disapproving end, however, *ya* is sometimes viewed as a misguided and misleading principle. According to detractors, it does not deserve our attention because Yan Fu only included it in his tripartite model due to his personal preference for the ornate, archaic style that he used himself in translating Huxley into Chinese. Yet times have changed so much in the intervening century that such a style is now seen as anachronistic at best, and genuinely obfuscating at worst, especially as the plain, colloquial style is now the order of the day.

Over the years *ya* has evolved into the Aesthetic School of translation in China, as it was made to connect with concepts of "spiritual resonance" and "realm of transformation." Together these ideas form an integrated body of theory about "translating with style." At the same time, by reaching back to the past, theorists have drawn upon traditional Chinese aesthetic philosophy to create a rubric under which "elegance" can be seen as an essential element in the search for artistic merit.[3] Ma Hongjun has traced the genealogy of twentieth-century theorists who have contributed to the construction of this "school" of thinking (2006: 43–52). In particular, he pointed out how aesthetic translation theories are made to appear coherent through some ingenious pyrotechnics on the part of those involved. Their success is seen in the way an artistic principle (*ya*) is raised to a level on par with the ethical (*xin*) and communicative (*da*) principles in Yan's tripartite formulation. By referencing the ancients, including Confucius and Zhuangzi, the Aesthetic School attains the status of "a translation theory with Chinese characteristics." Thus the meaning of *ya* becomes broadened, as Luo Xinzhang said in his *Collected Essays on Translation*: "*Ya* does not imply sophistication or adornment; instead it suggests higher literary or aesthetic value" (1984: 500). Xu Yuanchong, the last in line, went one step further: he believes that the aesthetic approach to translation has effected a shift from the realm of "what must be done" to that of "what one can freely do." In such a context, *ya* is beauty attained in "the realm of freedom" (Ma 2006: 44). Departures from the original text are not only permissible but also actively encouraged.

---

[2] Among those who sought to redefine *ya*, and extrapolate from this term possible implications is Lin Yutang (1895–1976), who said it actually means *mei* (beauty). This is an improvement on "elegance," while allowing Lin to retain the two other principles.

[3] Chinese philosophizing on the "beauty" that resides in a literary work dates back to antiquity (see Wu 2009: 93–4).

Translating the Spirit: From Beautification to Transcreation

As the brief account of the development of the concept of *ya* into an aesthetic school above shows, it is both elusive and enigmatic. Its elusiveness can be seen in the shifting interpretations given to it, as well as the growing number of loosely related notions that get attached to it. Its enigmatic nature is evident in the fact that it actually contradicts Yan Fu's first principle of fidelity. Theories of "elegance" and "beauty" legitimize stylistic intervention as the translator is given a free hand in handling the source text, working under the premise that adherence to the sense is of lesser significance than recapturing the essence of the work as revealed in its style. Because *ya* runs counter to faithfulness (*xin*), justification for it is presented in one way or another. One prevalent line of defense is to emphasize it as an alternative kind of fidelity, "equivalence on a higher plane," or "fidelity to the spirit" (not the content) of the source text. The argument is that translators should be allowed to aestheticize the foreign text as they engage in the pursuit of "re-creation" or "transcreation." How the concept of *ya* is deployed in Chinese translation theory is an illustration of the fluidity as well as malleability of concepts when applied to practical circumstances. In the case of *ya*, we see some mid-century theorists who propounded the need for stylistic embellishment with reference to a theory of the "spirit" of the original. This was then given a further twist in the 1990s when the notion of transcreation was introduced as the ultimate goal of *ya*.

We begin with the 1920s. In his article on "On Translation" (1929), Chen Xiying (1896–1970), an outspoken cultural critic of the 1930s, drew a link between translation and Chinese painting, making reference to the native tradition of imitating notable masters.[4] He distinguished between three kinds of "resonance" in translation that serve as criteria in judging translation quality: formal, semantic, and spiritual. Viewing the first of these as inferior, he castigated literal translation, used by those who "translate word for word and line by line but also abstain from adding or omitting one single character, and changing the order of words" (trans. Chapman Chen; Chan 2004: 95). It is unsatisfactory because it is "no more than rendition of the shape or form [and it] emphasizes content at the expense of style" (trans. Chapman Chen; Chan 2004.: 95). The subject was then taken up by Zeng Xubai (1894–1994), who used instead an analogy with musical performance, quoting what Anatole France said in *Le jardin d'Épicure* about the difficulty of pinning down the spirit

---

[4] Luo Xinzhang (Luo 1984; see also Ma 2006: 44–7) also links the impulse for embellishment (or beautification) to traditional Chinese thinking about artistic creation as seen in the critical discourse on poetry and painting that spanned the premodern era.

of a literary work: "every word in the book is a finger of the Devil plucking our mental strings as with a harp, allowing the music of our souls to be played out" (trans. Chapman Chen; Chan 2004: 99–100). For Zeng, each reader's subjective response to the source text being different, what the "spirit" turns out to be will depend on the nature of each translator's "mental strings." The two theorists thus helped pave the way for succeeding generations to enlarge on the possibilities of conveying the more ineffable elements of style—and disregarding formal or surface resemblance to the original.

In the 1950s, the Aesthetic School found a new spokesman in Fu Lei (1908–66). Today, Fu's reputation rests primarily on his fourteen Chinese translations of Honoré de Balzac's novels, including *Le Père Goriot*, *Eugènie Grandet*, *Le Cousin Pons*, and *La Cousine Bette*, in addition to renditions of Mérimée's *Colomba* and Voltaire's *Candide*. He advanced his manifesto on "spiritual resonance" in "Preface to the Retranslation of *Le Père Goriot*" (1951). Lamenting the difficulty of replicating Stendhal's style owing to the vast disparity between French and Chinese, he quoted Bo Le, a horse connoisseur in ancient China with special talent in judging other people's abilities: "Value its essence and forget its crudity; treasure its intrinsic qualities and leave behind its external form" (trans. May Wong; Chan 2004: 102). For him, the translator should do likewise, which makes faithfulness a stylistic rather a content issue. Like Chen Xiying, Fu was full of praise for the "imitation" method in Chinese painting, which seeks to capture the essence of the original artwork rather than its shape or form. In this way, he made "conveying the spirit" and "seeking the sublime" the ultimate goals, while speaking against the practice of "holding fast to the dictionaries and following the syntactic structures of the source text" (trans. May Wong; Chan 2004: 102). In giving artistic considerations utmost importance, he epitomizes a new phase in the reinterpretation of Yan Fu's *ya*. Although he did not discard fidelity altogether, he nevertheless clearly distinguished translating the meaning from rendering the style, and then prioritized the latter.

In this way, the post-Yan Fu generation made possible the morphing of "beauty" or "elegance" into "adherence to the spirit." The next (and most recent) phase in the reinvention of *ya* in the 1990s is crystallized in Xu Yuanchong's view that a re-creative translation can displace the original. According to Xu, deviations are acceptable if they are ingenious and bring pleasure to the reader. In striking contrast to Yan Fu, for whom *ya* is the least important of his three principles, Xu puts it before faithfulness and comprehensibility. On that basis, he puts forward his proposal for re-creative translation, illustrating it with his own rendition of the last sentence in *Le rouge et le noir*—*Elle mourut* (she died)—as *hungui lihen tian* (a literary expression meaning "the soul returns to the painless realm"). This translation, challenged by many as hyperbolic and grossly exaggerated but touted by Xu himself as a superb example of beautification (*meihua*) and emulation (*jingsai*), has landed him in a heated controversy (see Xu 1996). His response to the criticisms was to query how fifteen other translations of the same sentence can outperform him "in conveying the message and communicating the emotions" of the original (trans. Orlando Ho; Chan 2004: 262).

Xu believes that he outshines not only Fu Lei but also the author of the original work (Stendhal). In his critical assessment of Xu, Ma Hongjun (2006: 105–11) concedes that, under specific conditions (such as the translation of literary texts), the goal of surpassing the original may be condoned. However, the underlying rationale for Xu's project—that of showcasing the superiority of the target language (Chinese) and winning the contest with non-Chinese cultures to be translated—is a controversial one. Ma points out that Xu's theory of emulation takes us nowhere, since the style of one language cannot be equivalent to that of another (2006: 109). Nevertheless, Xu's theory is of interest because it stands as the pinnacle of a century's ruminations on how to convey the aesthetic essence or spirit of the source text, although he stretches the accepted standards of faithfulness to the utmost. Unfazed, Xu supports his theories with his own translations, known for their unrestrained character. Besides Stendhal's *Le rouge et le noir*, Xu's other translations, both into and out of Chinese, are used to prove the applicability of his theories of "beautification" and "transcreation."[5] Xu avers that, because of the "elegant" style, translations are no longer secondhand copies, but take their pride of place alongside their sources.

The many theories on the translation of style spawned by Yan Fu's *ya* show how far Chinese theorists have traveled in building on the concept of beautifying the original. Despite all the disagreements with Xu Yuanchong's "New Age" translation theory, the fact is that a continuous tradition of thinking has developed that links up contemporary with traditional Chinese aesthetics. Most significant is the alignment of *ya* with "spirit" to begin with, and then the forging of a connection between these and the concept of style. In her survey of the history of the Western understanding of style before the advent of modern stylistics, Jean Boase-Beier (2006) notes that the notion of "style as ornament" actually goes back to antiquity, although the linkage might have been due to a mistranslation (2006: 12). The conflation of "spirit" with "style" from the Renaissance on, by contrast, can be illustrated with reference to the ideas of key figures like Peletier du Mans ("spirit and intention are often bound up with [the author's] style"),

---

[5] In this regard, one may recall what the famed Brazilian translator Haroldo de Campos has said on the same subject. For de Campos, transcreation occurs when "in translating, the poet (cannibalistically) creates an original work in his or her own right, one no longer beholden to the source" (Bernstein 2010: n.p.).

Alexander Pope (the "spirit" and "fire" of a text), and Friedrich Schleiermacher ("the spirit not only of the language but also of the original author") (2006: Chap. 1). While the concept is no longer current, the Chinese theorists' views are not so different from those of some stylisticians today. They were all aware of the need for the translator to capture "what goes beyond content, and especially with the manner in which it is expressed" (Boase-Beier 2006: 11) when they have put behind them surface meanings and features.

As these same theorists have noted, attention to the aesthetic values of a literary text is essential to a successful rendition. But because style is not fixed in a text, and different translators can read the same source text differently, there is room for creativity, and it is this line of thinking that informs Xu Yuanchong's conception of translation as "transcreation." Xu is evidently an active (rather than a passive) translator who strongly believes in the worth of a translation, while his hope that his translations can surpass rival ones shows what Boase-Beier says: "a literary translation, especially if it is informed by stylistic awareness, will be a more literary text than an untranslated text" (2006: 148). His position also tallies with that of Roman Jakobson, for whom translation in the ideal sense is not possible, and there is only creative transposition. Such a view of translation creates favorable conditions for manipulation in order to achieve certain literary effects. Indeed, Xu's ideas furnish us with a perspective from which to understand certain translation practices in contemporary China. Below we will examine one striking instance of the transcreation method used by Lin Shaohua, who stands at the center of the so-called Murakami Haruki Fever that has taken China by storm in the last two decades. How successfully does the translator re-create the "spirit" of the original author through stylistic means? Given that each language has its own characteristic properties, can Japanese style be rendered in Chinese? What kind of aesthetic equivalence can one speak of?

"Aesthetic Fidelity": Lin Shaohua Translating Murakami

The Murakami Haruki Fever is one of the most spectacular events in modern Sino-Japanese translation history.[6] The vagaries of translation

---

[6] Fujii Shōzō dates the beginning of the Murakami "boom" in Taiwan to 1989, and in Mainland China to 1998—the delay attributable to what he calls the "principle of the pace of economic growth" (2007: 165), which is one of four that undergird the popular reception of translated Murakami novels in East Asia. The other principles are those of "clockwise dissemination," "post-democracy movements," and "preference for *Norwegian Wood* over *A Wild Sheep Chase*" (2007: 76–7). It is obvious that these have less to do with the stylistic elements affecting reception. For an exhaustive bibliographical account of the translation history of Murakami in China, see Wang (2012).

reception are exemplified perhaps nowhere more blatantly than in the changing volumes of translation traffic between the two countries in the course of the twentieth century, as statistically documented by Tam Yue Him (1981). The directionality of translation, whether into Chinese or Japanese, is symptomatic of shifts of power. At the beginning of the century, consequent to Japan's rise as an East Asian power after China's defeat at the Sino-Japanese War of 1894, translations from Japanese into Chinese saw an immediate boom, increasing till it was almost sixty times those in the opposite direction. This completely reversed the situation of centuries of interaction before that fateful year. In premodern times translations from Chinese into Japanese completely dominated the transtextual interchange (even if the huge number of *kundoku* texts is to be regarded as a variant form of translation from Chinese). However, almost exactly a century later, a second reversal occurred with the rise of China to become a world superpower. Since the 1990s translations from Chinese into Japanese have once more outnumbered those in the other direction, so that the balance is again tilted in China's favor. Given such a background, the tremendous success of the translated novels of Murakami Haruki in China is most exceptional, particularly in light of the turbulent political relationship between the two countries in the 1990s.

Lin Shaohua was the first to translate a Murakami novel on the Mainland: his translation of *Norwegian Wood* appeared in 1989, but its reception was lukewarm at the time. It was in the 1990s that Chinese readers were drawn to the Japanese novelist, such that "Murakami" became a household name in China. According to Lin himself, only when the book cover was redesigned and much better quality paper was used did his reprinted translation become a blockbuster (Ya 2006). In two years it sold over 200,000 copies, and by 2006 the total number of sales was 1,400,000, making it the best-sold Chinese translated novel of all time and inaugurating the Murakami Fever. In fact, this was a belated response, since almost a decade before another translation had already taken the book markets of Taiwan and Hong Kong by storm. The extent of the Fever in Mainland China is seen in the fact that Lin's translation of *Norwegian Wood* was reprinted nineteen times by 2004. Lin boasts translations of works by other modern Japanese writers, including Yukio Mishima, Yoshimoto Banana, and Akutagawa Ryūnosuke, but he is now renowned as *the* Chinese translator of Murakami. In 2003–04, riding the wave of success, the Shanghai Translation Publishing House brought out as many as 240,000 copies of *Kafka on the Shore* in translation. As far as overall estimates go, an impressive 2.5 million copies of Murakami's works in Chinese were sold in the fifteen years up to 2004, roughly equivalent to the sales of all translated Japanese literature since 1976 (Lin 2005: 60).

The special characteristics of Lin Shaohua's translations are highlighted by a fierce debate concerning his corpus vis-à-vis that of the Taiwanese translator Lai Mingzhu. As soon as *Norwegian Wood* was published in Japan in 1987, it was overwhelmingly received, immediately taking its place as the Japanese mega-bestseller of the century. Soon afterward, the craze swept through Taiwan. Although this novel was first rendered into Chinese by Liu Huizhen et al. in 1989, Lai's version is now credited with having started the Murakami Fever on the island. Not only was Lai the first person to translate Murakami in 1986 (*Pinball, 1973*), but she also single-handedly translated all of Murakami's novels into Chinese as they appeared—including a translation of *Norwegian Wood* in 1997. Now Lai is considered the authoritative Taiwanese translator of Murakami, just as Lin Shaohua is on the Chinese Mainland. However, with almost every one of Murakami's works being translated twice into Chinese, a debate arose as to whose version was better.

The debate was sparked off by readers of the translations and took place online through the website "Murakami and the Beatles" (www.goosky.com). Launched at the height of the Murakami Fever, the website held a contest in December 2006 on "Who's the Better Translator—Lin Shaohua or Lai Mingzhu?," asking readers which of the two translations of *Norwegian Wood* they preferred. For months readers flooded the website with their evaluations of the two versions. In the end Lin Shaohua got 87.5 percent of the votes cast, while Lai Mingzhu secured only 12.5 percent. Most comments zeroed in on the stylistic differences between the two translations. The majority favored Lin's translation because it is more "embellished" (*ya*), and they felt more "comfortable" reading the Sinicized text. By contrast, it seemed generally agreed that Lai's translation is more literal and source-oriented, as it often reminded readers of the language of the Japanese original. It is clear that few commentators lost sight of Lin's conscious attempt to "beautify" Murakami's text. Of some interest, too, is the fact that the debate sometimes spilled over into discussions of the linguistic properties of Chinese versus Japanese. According to one commentator with the pseudonym "Born Witch": "Mainlanders are gruff and tough when they speak, not so much given to the deployment of end-of-sentence particles, so Lin Shaohua's translation is not as 'effeminate' as Lai Mingzhu's" (see http://majo.dominatus.net/?p=85).

The debate is thus multifaceted, focusing on not just readers' personal preferences and the different translation strategies used in the two versions, but also differences between what may be called "regional registers," the expressive potential of Chinese versus Japanese, and the ideological factors impacting the stylistic choices made by the two translators. It has continued unabated, and recently Fujii Shōzō, a Japanese professor of modern Chinese literature, entered the fray to lend support to Lai Mingzhu's renditions. He pointed out how Lin's translations were colored by a "nationalistic" agenda, which the style he deployed was meant to promote (Fujii 2009). In response to this, scholars from the Mainland defended Lin's approach and refuted the charge of Sinocentrism, or an ulterior purpose, imputed to his translations. Lin also wrote essays and gave interviews in which he explained the translation method he adopted, justifying it by recourse to a theory of "aesthetic fidelity." In what follows, through a close look at the "embellishing" translation method he used with *Norwegian Wood*, we will analyze the nature of Lin's "aesthetic improvements" on the original text, with special reference to the Chinese tradition of thinking about *ya* in translation.

It can easily be seen that Lin's alterations to the content of the original Murakami novel are minimal, though many mistakes were made due to oversight or miscomprehension of the source text. Fujii Shōzō notes a number of these in Lin's *Norwegian Wood*, showing his failure to understand certain terms and expressions. To the list of forty-six errors already spotted by another commentator, Fujii adds a few more himself, like the rendition of "(Eugene) Ionesco" as "Ibsen." Yet clearly his dissatisfaction with Lin's translation pivots on the stylistic. He understands the particularities of Lin's style in this way: by including a range of embellishing strategies like allusions and parallelisms which can elicit a stronger emotional response from readers, Lin is not faithful to the original. His argument is two-pronged: not only does Lin's domesticating style do Murakami an injustice, but Lin's Sinicization strategy also prevents Japanese culture from impacting—and transforming—China. Somewhat unlike other critics who have faulted Lin's translations for failing to present the "real Japan" to a Chinese readership, Fujii mainly criticizes Lin for not helping to bring about the benefits of cultural interaction, shown (as he said) in the long history of Sino-Japanese translational interchange through the centuries. He explicitly declares his support for Lai's more faithful or foreignizing translation, which for him is "overwhelmingly superior" (2009: 114).

In turn, Lin Shaohua expounded in several publications his philosophy of translation, particularly his choice of a hybrid Chinese prose, with the classical language embedded in the modern idiom. To some critics, this is the prime factor contributing to the overwhelming popularity of his translations in the Mainland. There his renditions are simply dubbed *Linyi* (see Ya 2006), a coinage meant to apotheosize Lin's signature style and distinguish his works from those of rival translators.[7] At the height of the online readers' debate, Lin and Lai had a chance of confronting each other in cyberspace. Both the differences between the source and target languages, and the extent to which Murakami's style can be reproduced in translation, were issues that the two addressed. In a posting on March 24, 2004 (see "Murakami and the Beatles"), Lai Mingzhu noted how translators must not ignore fundamental differences between Japanese and Chinese: the former is "gentle and elegant" and the latter is "laconic and forceful." As for capturing the style of the original work, she said she had translated Murakami with an eye for his more Westernized flavor, calling it "Western dress for a Japanese soul." For her, Murakami's style contrasts with Tanizaki Jun'ichiro's (1886–1965) "ornateness and fluidity" and Natsume Sōseki's (1867–1916) "simplicity and directness"; these two older novelists wrote more like the Chinese than does Murakami.[8] Lai responded, too, to readers' preference for Lin as revealed in the above-mentioned poll by saying that Mainland readers made up a greater percentage of the voters and they had reason to feel more comfortable with Lin's style. By implication she was suggesting that her faithfulness to Murakami's style was not appreciated.

In a rejoinder to Lai's defensive arguments, Lin Shaohua had an interview with the German international broadcaster Deutsche Welle in December 2006 (http://www.dw-world.de/dw). Concerning the stylistic gap between the two renditions, Lin said he had chosen to translate Murakami's prose with a more refined style, freely interpolating elements of the Chinese literary language to enhance the aesthetic effect. For him, this aestheticizing move is justified because "Japanese literature is plain and unseasoned, like Japanese cuisine." In fact, beautification of the original text is widely applauded as Lin the translator's stylistic trademark, and he is also well known to have a special fondness for classical Chinese verse, which he writes and publishes. His translation of *Norwegian Wood* is characterized by the following:

(a) word choice: suggestive, ornate, and emotionally charged terms greatly outnumber straightforward, direct, and conventional ones;

---

[7] This is a typical strategy applied in many translations of Japanese literature into Chinese; Lin Wenyue's delicately crafted, densely allusive translation of *The Tale of Genji* (Lin 1973–1979) is a notable example. The long history of linguistic contact between Chinese and Japanese—in particular the incorporation of Chinese characters into Japanese—creates conditions for Chinese renditions of Japanese literature to be "Sinicized" to an extent not possible with translations from non-Asian languages.

[8] Tanizaki Jun'ichirō, who sometimes deployed a classical Japanese style with frequent use of Chinese characters (*kanji*), can easily be rendered in a more Sinicized idiom. An example is his "Portrait of Shunkin" (*Shunkin shō*), of which there are translations in a semiclassical Chinese prose. Natsume Sōseki wrote and published Chinese classical poetry throughout his lifetime, and his knowledge of the language is reflected in his writings.

(b) four-character set expressions: examples are abundant, the translation critics' favorite example being the passage describing Reiko's playing of the guitar before Toru in Chapter 6 in which four such expressions are compressed into one sentence (see Sun 2004);
(c) literary style: preference for an archaic style—Sun Junyue calls it an "ornamented Six Dynasties prose style" (Sun 2004)—which contrasts strikingly with Murakami's Westernized, modern "oral" idiom; and
(d) rhetorical devices: among the most frequently encountered are metaphors, parallelisms, reduplicatives, alliterations, and classical allusions—all absent from the Japanese original.

Much as they are part of his aestheticizing strategy, these features also reveal an effort at intensive domestication. One critic has said that Lin's "high" style caters to the expectations of an expanding literate bourgeoisie in China (Wang 2009: 121). To those who malign him for his misrepresentation of Murakami's style (Sun 2004), Lin Shaohua countered by explaining at some length his own approach. He claims, first, that he aims to eradicate any trace of *washū* (Japanese odor). This is a term that, paradoxically, was used in traditional Japanese literary criticism to castigate the Japanese elements (seen, for instance, in deviations from the Chinese lexicon, expressions, and rhyme schemes) appearing in Sinitic poetry penned by Japanese men of letters.[9] For Lin, as a medium of artistic expression, Japanese differs substantially from Chinese. Believing that the latter is arguably "the most beautiful language in the world," he highlights his effort to rid his translations of the "Japanese odor" that is intrusive and unpleasant (Lin 2006: 138–9). His aim is to transfer wholesomely the "spirit" of the work being translated through thoroughly domesticating its style:

> Literary translation is an art, which in the last analysis is a feeling—one's own feeling artistically conveyed. On the basis of this definition I would like to summarize my concept of translation in one word: "taste." . . . It can either be "smelled" or "swallowed." The former refers to the use

---

[9] The Edo scholar Ogyū Sorai said there are three aspects to *washū*: using Chinese characters in their wrong meanings, making grammatical mistakes in writing Chinese sentences, and inserting Japanese expressions in Chinese essay compositions. He was quite fond of Chinese classics and he considered *washū* a deficiency. His comments on *washū* became a yardstick for generations of Japanese scholarship on the subject. In considering *washū* as a negative element, Lin was following the same line of argument, although the situation is reversed in the case of Chinese translations from Japanese. For further discussion of Sinitic poetry written in Japan and the problems of *washū*, see Chapter 8.

of translationese or "Japanese odor" (some call it *washū*, which I have sought to dispel as best I could, rightly or not). The latter is the "spirit" or inner "flavor" that I strive to capture assiduously. (Lin 2005: 179)

Incidentally, this is in line with present-day cognitive linguists' understanding of the aesthetic as that which is underscored by "the evidence of the senses and the appeal to emotions" (Boase-Beier 2006: 73).

Second, Lin Shaohua emphasizes translation as an act of re-creation, or of "second-order creation." This reverberates with Xu Yuanchong's view of translation as creative rewriting, as a result of which the translation can lead an autonomous existence of its own. As proof of his success, Lin refers to the overwhelming reception of his translations in the Murakami Fever; they have eclipsed all the other translations—by Zhong Hongjie/Ma Shuzhen, Yi Meng, Zhang Bin, Li Huan, Li Ji, Ye Hui, among others. He praises assertive interference by the "strong" translator who is a master stylist. Support for this stance has come from Yang Bingjing, for whom Lin has made an interpretive difference through giving a new identity to Murakami's works. Yang opines that "translated literature" must ultimately not be viewed as a subcategory of foreign literature, but gain autonomous status as home literature. Lin's translations are in a class of their own, and the coinage of *Linyi* is meant to distinguish Lin's oeuvre from Murakami's (Yang 2009: 126).

Third, there is the issue of Lin's "use of excessive makeup," an epithet used by Fujii Shōzō when comparing the two translators. By now, it should be clear that Lai's more "faithful" approach as well as her adoption of Murakami's "oral" and "foreignizing" (in the sense of "Americanizing") idiom contrasts strongly with Lin's disparagement of close stylistic correspondence. At an extreme, Lin would even render dialogues quite flatly, dropping Japanese end-of-sentence modal particles that reflect characters' emotional affective states. Rather than considering these as infelicities, many Mainland Chinese critics have endorsed Lin's translations as more "elegant." On this basis, they explain the incomparable charm of the translations and, accordingly, their success with readers. For his own part, to counter criticism of his "unfaithfulness," Lin offers his theory of "aesthetic fidelity," which brings him into line with the entire tradition of Chinese theories that engage with (and expand on) *ya*, even arguing that it is compatible with Yan Fu's first principle of "faithfulness."

> My own view, similarly, is that translations should accurately render their originals, although there are different interpretations of this "faithfulness." I am mainly concerned with being faithful to the original style, artistic conception and implicit charm, not with word-to-word semantic correspondence. . . . As Weng Xiliang has put it: translation

seeks to break through the surface structures of the original, and achieve faithfulness at a deeper level. (Lin 2005: 139)

Nevertheless, Lin Shaohua is perhaps not incognizant of the difficulty he would run up against when talking about fidelity while the stylistic deviations in his translations are so easily discernible. One might ask: Can the original style be altered to achieve a "higher loyalty"? Lin's answer is that while equivalence is not attainable, at least "aesthetic fidelity" can serve to narrow the gap between the source and target texts. In another essay in his anthology *The Beauty of Falling Flowers* (Lin 2006), he defends his position with some gastronomic metaphors:

> Japanese literature is like Japanese cuisine: light food is best; it is beautiful. The problem is that if the lightness is preserved in translation, the Chinese will not appreciate the beauty. . . . In order to shorten the aesthetic distance between the Chinese and the Japanese, I have made some adjustments, when circumstances allow, by adding a pinch of salt. In this sense, it is not just beautification but a kind of faithfulness— or simply "aesthetic fidelity." In literary translation this is not only permitted, but also necessary. (Lin 2006: 234)

Like Xu Yuanchong, Lin does not see his stylistic departures from the original as unwarranted. In his essays and interviews (see Zhang 2013: 27–9), he makes reference to nearly all the key theorists of the Aesthetic School described in our last section, but most specifically Qian Zhongshu, "the pre-eminent Chinese scholar of the century." Though more of a literary and cultural critic than a translation theorist, Qian is famous for his preference for extreme liberalism (see Chapter 5). His essay "The Translations of Lin Shu" (1963), apparently an appreciation of Lin Shu's work, actually presents the strongest theorization yet in China of translation as transmigration (trans. George Kao; Chan 2004: 104–14). A question may be asked as to why Qian is also classified as belonging to the Aesthetic School. One notes that, in this essay, he said that translational transmigration means discarding "the external shell" and focusing on "the spirit and style" (trans. George Kao; Chan 2004: 104). Lin Shaohua would have seen that as justification for what he did to Murakami.

The Problematics of Aestheticization

While Lin Shaohua's project for making Murakami "stylistically acceptable" to Chinese readers is quite singular in that he has carried it out more consistently than any other translator, it must be noted that, as a general approach, the aestheticization of the source text by translators can be problematic. There are texts for which an elevated style is simply not desirable. The use of an "elegant" style has often been conflated with the Chinese conception of "literariness," but such an equation may not be universally applicable. Inheriting a centuries-old tradition in which students acquired writing skills by imitating master prose-stylists of the past, some Chinese writers still labor under the premise that an ornamented language not only is aesthetically pleasing but also demarcates the literary from the nonliterary. The Chinese term for literary talent, *wencai*, which literally means "colorful writing," shows the inseparability of stylistic elegance from literary quality; they are, after all, etymologically linked. The two definitions given for the word *wencai* in *A Chinese-English Dictionary* are "stylistic elegance" and "literary talent" (*Hanying cidian* Group 1981: 721); this once again underlines the connection between the two. This partly explains the priority accorded to *ya* by translation theorists in the Aesthetic School, just as it had served as a tool for measuring original literary composition in China over the millennia. To follow this golden rule in literary translations into Chinese, however, creates certain difficulties. For one thing, stylistic refinement may be out of place in certain kinds of narrative fiction.

As Bakhtin puts it in "Discourse in the Novel," narrative genres showcase "a diversity of social speech types" (Bakhtin 1986), and the use of idiolects and registers can play havoc with the principle of *ya*.[10] There is, naturally, no stigma against translating vulgarisms as vulgarisms, as shown in drama translation. They are exempted from the requirement of elegance or decency because drama translators, out of necessity, aim for the accurate reproduction of daily speech, however idiosyncratic or nonstandard. In the translation of novels, registers are usually confined to dialogues, and coming from the mouths of characters, they are conveniently exempt from the criterion of *ya*. However, problems occur with novels narrated by characters who consistently deploy slangy speech and abusive language, and the situation is exacerbated when the narrator's speech idiosyncrasies are thematically significant, or when they are used to construct the impression of a distinctive subjectivity. For example, in J. D. Salinger's *The Catcher in the Rye*, a first-person narrative, a linguistic medium is used that powerfully conveys the novel's message, but almost all of the existing Chinese translations are far too

---

[10] Olga Brodovich has written on the ways of tackling nonstandard speech in fiction, especially the linguistic resources available in Russian for rendering it from English (Brodovich 1997).

"polite," and none can reproduce adequately the narrator Holden Caulfield's horrendous teenage idiom.

Almost all the Chinese translators of the novel have chosen a higher (i.e., more decent) register that is not in character. To avoid vulgarisms in the novel, Wu Youshi and Liu Shoushi (1968) consistently omit words like "crap" and phrases like "what the hell," which Holden is particularly fond of using, presumably to make their rendition meet standards of acceptability. In another translation, Zhang Zhihu shies away from Clegg's swear words by constantly deleting words like "bastard" from the text; for instance, the word "bastard" in "It wasn't allowed for students to borrow faculty guy's cars, but all the athletic bastards stuck together" is neutralized in translation with *ren* (humans) (Zhang 1985: 64). Similarly, stylistic improvements are found in Jia Chang'an's translation where obscene expressions are bowdlerized (Jia 1972). Yang Yuniang, in her preface to a fourth translation (1991), makes the observation that a contrast is created by Salinger between those parts where obscenities are abundant and other parts where Holden reverts to a more decent idiom when he thinks (or talks) about his much-loved sister Phoebe. So she is not unaware of the intended effects to be achieved through Holden's use of abusive language. That the contrast is not even factored into her own translation reveals the restraining force of the unspoken decree of *ya* in the Chinese tradition and the preference for the high style.

It may be argued that the cases of stylistic alteration in the translations of *Norwegian Wood* and *The Catcher in the Rye* are differently motivated: there is a degree of conscious intentionality in the case of Lin Shaohua and a lack thereof in the Salinger translators—a contrast between strong and weak translators. Whereas Lin can describe his re-styling of Murakami as a transcreative move, the stylistic alterations in the translations of *The Catcher in the Rye* mentioned above can be seen as the result of self-censorship. Since Lin propounded his ideas of re-creating the original novels for readers well after his body of translations had been hailed as classics, and he tried to capitalize on the theories of eminent predecessors like Xu Yuanchong, it is clear that the preference for a high style in literary writings in the Chinese tradition still retains some of its influence well into the twenty-first century. The use of an elevated register is, of course, deemed appropriate in the translation of works in some genres as well as certain texts from earlier periods. For instance, there is the comparable case of the tradition of "academism" in the French language, which requires a certain style to be adopted in the translation of the classics (Vanderschelden 2000: 286). But such a practice as seen in the translation of texts as different as Murakami's and Salinger's shows that the Aesthetic School has been influencing practicing Chinese translators at a much deeper and subconscious level.

Whether theories of "spiritual affinity" and "transcreation" are adequate as explanations for Lin's departures from Murakami's texts, and whether the conceptual slippages from *ya* to style/spirit, then to transcreation, are just a theoretical sleight-of-hand—these are matters that cannot be resolved easily, especially in a context where translation issues are inscribed within national language (Chinese vs. Japanese) debates.[11] Perhaps most questionable is Lin's assertion that his renditions are faithful to the spirit rather than the letter of the source text: who decides what the true spirit is? In light of all this, it may seem that, while translation theory can inform practice,[12] it can also be used to rationalize practice.

---

[11] In fact, the scholarship on premodern Japanese literature often considers the Chinese and Japanese language as binary opposites. For a discussion of this issue, see LaMarre (2000).

[12] Note the dialogue on the relationship between theory and practice in Chesterman and Wagner (2002). For the present case, theory does aid practice, though not in the terms that these two theorists are addressing.

Part II

4

Adaptation Studies through a Translation Lens

Both forms of transtextual rewriting, translation and adaptation, have co-existed as half-identical twins, similar yet separable. Literal translations are meant to be close reproductions of source texts which enable readers to overcome linguistic barriers, whereas adaptations that involve transfer into a foreign language depart from their sources to greater or lesser degrees. The academic study of these two forms has led to the creation of autonomous academic disciplines for each. Their developmental trajectories show the two fields as moving, apparently, further and further apart even as both have flourished. As it seeks to establish an identity, translation studies has been enlarged—and revolutionized—by "borrowing" from a wide range of disciplines, including linguistics, literary studies, cultural studies, sociology, and so on. Meanwhile, adaptation studies, at first dominated by research on screen adaptations, has also more recently broadened its outlook to include a growing range of verbal and visual genres. However, despite the vast common ground they share, attempts to bring them together have had only limited success. This is unfortunate since, from the translation side, some scholars have asserted that completely faithful translations are an imagined ideal and that adaptation as a method is widely used in translating, while a handful have felt the need to stress the link by proposing the use of an amalgam like "tradaptation" or "transadaptation."

In contrast to the scant interest on the part of adaptation scholars in reconnecting the two fields, translation theorists have engaged intensively with this issue since the 1990s. In fact, as early as 1959, even before translation studies became an object of academic study all its own, the Prague structuralist Roman Jakobson had shown the connection when he distinguished between three categories of intralingual, interlingual, and intersemiotic translation. According to him:

1. Intralingual translation or rewording is an interpretation of verbal signs by means of other signs of the same language.

2. Interlingual translation or translation proper is an interpretation of verbal signs by means of some other language.
3. Intersemiotic translation or transmutation is an interpretation of verbal signs by means of signs of nonverbal sign systems (Jakobson 2000: 113).

Since Jakobson is not, strictly speaking, a translation scholar and his main interests lie elsewhere, the last category ("intersemiotic translation") is of special significance. As it is used to denote the substitution of semiotic signs of one system by those of another, it can be said that all intermedial (or transmedia) adaptations—novel into film, comics into TV drama, and so on—can be placed within this category. According to the logic behind Jakobson's taxonomy, adaptations are a type of translation, not the other way around. In the search for a distinct disciplinary identity for "translation studies" in the past few decades, researchers have been keen to explore the possibility of including adaptation within their fold in spite of indifference from the adaptation side. The distance that both groups have traveled, the attainments (and failures) so far, and the hurdles yet to overcome are the focus of the present chapter.

Three Kinds of Adaptation Studies

It seems best to begin with the emergence of adaptation studies as an independent discipline (or subdiscipline) in the last few decades. Of course it is virtually impossible to present even a rudimentary history of its birth and growth, or portray the magnitude of its scope. The streams of thinking that fed into it defy any attempt to give a brief account. If one were to describe only the poststructuralist contribution, even a condensed list will have to include Roland Barthes ("death of the author"), Mikhail Bakhtin ("dialogism"), Homi Bhabha ("in-betweenness"), Maurice Blanchot ("complementary unity"), Julia Kristeva ("intertextuality"), Jacques Derrida ("transformation"), Gérard Genette ("literature in the second degree"), and so on. One can do better by noting that, for long, literary scholars and historians have seen a tendency in all human societies to rewrite texts, and one kind of textual product consists of versions that are closely or loosely connected to their sources. Adaptations, as works derived (and bent and twisted) from a stated source, have thus been with us since ancient times.

Included for study in Boldt, Federici, and Virgulti's recent volume of articles (2010) on adaptation are Samuel Johnson's "The Vanity of Human Wishes," an eighteenth-century adaptation of a Latin poem; Shakespeare's "rewriting" of *King Leir* as *King Lear*; Jonathan D. Syss's *The Swiss Family*

Robinson (1812), remodeled on Daniel Defoe's *Robinson Crusoe* (1719); Charlotte Bronte's *Jane Eyre* (1847), a reworking of *Pamela* (1740); and Titian's painting *Diana and Actaeon* (1559), which is a transformed version of Ovid's myth in *Metamorphoses*. These Western adaptations find their counterparts in the East, where texts from China were avidly adapted for consumption by Japanese, Korean, and Vietnamese readers. The long history of derivative literature in China itself has been discussed by Karl Kao (1985). Prominent in that history are stories of how poetry of ancient times was rewritten by Chinese poets of later generations, while storytellers' use of narrative techniques adapted from Indian Buddhist tales reached a high point in medieval times. It is only in our digital age that attention has shifted, and most adaptations now serve to carry cultural subjects across not just verbal (literary) and visual (filmic) media, but East-West geographical boundaries as well.

To illustrate the subjects of interest for adaptation studies scholars recently, we can think of work done, first on adaptations in the same medium, like Matthew Bourne's *Swan Lake* (dance), Bob Rafelson's *The Postman Always Rings Twice* (film remake), Barbara Walker's *Feminist Fairytale*s (rewritten folktales) and Picasso's cubist version of Velásquez's works (painting), as well as those in a different medium, like Graham Greene's *The Third Man* (film into novel), Sergei Prokofiev's *Romeo and Juliet* (drama into ballet), Peter Jackson's *The Lord of the Rings* (novel into film), BBC adaptations of the Victorian novels (novels into TV drama), Oliver Stone's *JFK* (biography into biopic), Benjamin Britten's *Death in Venice* (novella into opera), and *The Matrix* (film into video game). Adaptations appear omnipresent.

The diversity of concerns and the range of textual materials covered clue us in to the fact that adaptation scholars are not a closely knit group with a well-defined disciplinary identity. In the past few decades, the study of adaptation as a mode whereby cultures cross national and linguistic boundaries has flourished on the back of research carried out by three groups.[1] To begin with, as briefly described in Chapter 1, since the 1950s, there has been an accumulation of research on adaptation into the various media, which has led to calls for institutional recognition. Often simply designated as "adaptation studies" (though "film adaptation studies" is more appropriate), this discipline began with the analysis of films based on novels as pioneered by a spate of publications on theory and book-length studies of screen adaptations of novels by British and American authors (Naremore

---

[1] There are, of course, other innovative approaches to adaptation studies, such as travel theory (see Clifford 1997), but for the purposes of the present discussion only the text-oriented ones are highlighted.

2000; Stam 2005; Leitch 2009). The conferment of academic recognition is, then, seen in the launching of two journals that spell out the special direction to be taken by the fledging discipline. *Adaptation: The Journal of Literature on Screen Studies*, inaugurated in 2008, devotes primary attention to filmic adaptations of novels, although the editorial statement states that the journal publishes articles on other media, like theater, television, and animation, as well. The other one is *The Journal of Adaptation in Film and Performance*, whose first issue appeared in 2007.[2] That they both, at least initially, sought to build some kind of disciplinary identity has resulted in a narrowing of focus, since they drew heavily on the expertise of subject specialists in literature and film departments (see Raw 2009: 72–4). While instances of literature-into-film are innumerable and inexhaustible, the approach must be seen as somewhat inward-looking, seriously limiting the full-range exploration of the nature of adaptations. Besides Raw, another vocal critic of this brand of adaptation studies is Costas Constandinides (2010), who points out the limitations of Robert Stam, who fails, among other things, to consider cases of adaptation into new digital media like video games.

Although one can easily point to early film adaptation scholars' neglect of adaptations based on sources other than the novel, like comic books, graphic novels, and reportage literature, there is also no doubt that their input has stimulated thinking on approaches to film and literature. As the discipline develops, fresh approaches have been adopted and breakthroughs attained by research on intermediality (Elleström 2014; Rippl 2015; Bruhn 2016). Research interest has shifted away from textual transformations within one medium to the many interlocking relationships between the verbal and the visual. While film-to-film remakes and novel-to-film adaptations are still studied, they are balanced against a growing interest in media characteristics as they affect intermedial transformations. Another change can be observed in the shift from "between media" to "between cultures." This intercultural orientation is seen most conspicuously in the analysis of the cross-cultural element in adaptations (Stam and Shohat 2009), which actually aligns adaptation with translation studies. Where, previously, examples involving the film adaptations within one culture or country have engaged critical attention, those involving two are now no longer in the periphery. What is more, interest in trans-Atlantic adaptations have been partly displaced by burgeoning concerns with trans-Pacific ones. Prominent examples are Hollywood adaptations of movies from Japan, Korea, and Hong Kong (see

---

[2] One should also mention the founding of the Association of Adaptation Studies, based at De Montfort University, Leicester.

Lim 1999). Adaptation is thus turned into a quintessentially intercultural project.

Outside of film-related adaptation studies, two other groups of scholars working on adaptations find their disciplinary homes elsewhere. There are those studying contemporary postmodernist drama who deal with "adapted" plays that successfully enter, and become integrated into, new (target) cultural environments. Sparked off by the spectacular success of Peter Brook's 1985 adaptation of the Indian epic *Mahabharata*, intercultural theater has garnered great attention, and attempts have been made to replicate his success in which Asian staging and acting practices, as in the Noh and regional Chinese operas, are borrowed for experimentation with global theater presentations for worldwide audiences. In response to this euphoria, intercultural drama scholars like Patrice Pavis and Rustom Bharucha, most of them based in theater and performance studies departments at universities, have moved to engage with related research issues. Their studies often center on verbal play texts, but their contribution lies in their foregrounding of innovative features inserted into a text when it is performed in cultures other than that of the original. Building on the work of Pavis (1996), the Taiwan-based scholar Iris H. Tuan analyzes performances of adapted drama in the past two decades like Wu Xin-chu's *Slut Antigone,* Richard Schechner's *Oresteia*, and Wu Xin-kuo's *The Kingdom of Desire* (based on *Macbeth*) to show the artistic strategies whereby Greek and Shakespearean plays are recast in Chinese form—one version utilizes the Beijing opera style, and another uses the Fukienese dialect and Hakka costumes. In Tuan's view, adaptation is a measure of how, with the advent of globalization, the Other can be in(ter)corporated into the Self, the West into the East, and vice versa. She looks optimistically into the future and projects that "on the basis of equal cultural interaction, more plays can be adapted in an appropriate way" (Tuan 2007: 153).

Already mentioned in Chapter 1, Catherine Diamond (1993) classifies four types of adaptations, with examples for each one: the generic (e.g., fiction into film), the diachronic (e.g., the contemporary Puerto Rican context for *West Side Story*), the ideological (e.g., Brecht rewriting an old Chinese play as *The Chalk Circle*), and the cross-cultural. In the last category she places the "Little Theatre" Movement. Focusing on this category and placing a strong overall emphasis on interculturality, Diamond examines in detail the mediating role that adapted dramas can play between cultures. She applauds the potentialities opened up for transcultural research by drama adaptations because they can cross borders and be transformed into the familiar. But as noted earlier, she is skeptical about translation, an activity pejoratively viewed as existing only at the border of adaptation. The stigma attached to it is revealed in its being seen as "an attempt at faithfulness toward the original text" (Diamond 1993: 131). Such a restrictive view of translation is, of course, at variance with current theories of translation that accept deviation from the source text, as well as hybridization, as very much part of the nature of translated texts.

The third group consists of literary scholars working on the cross-cultural adaptation of children's literature—a subfield in literary studies that also holds out promises for creating a meeting point between translation and adaptation studies. Children's literature has been explored with rigor by critics working on the ways in which literary works, produced initially for children in specific locales, are "culturally altered" to suit different readerships in the countries to which they travel. Adjusting the content (by additions, substitutions, etc.) is a key strategy used to cater to the tastes of readerships in target cultures, and this has been standard fare for adaptors from time immemorial. Two extensive surveys of this approach, one closely linked to translation studies although it has its own roots elsewhere, have been given by Reinhert Tabbert (2002) and, more recently, Cecilia Alvstad (2019). The latter, in particular, gives a panoramic view of the way children's literature has been adapted to smoothen reception by a range of target readers. Of special interest to us are the works of Cay Dollerup, who charts the routes of transmission of Brothers Grimm's fairytales across Europe as they assume new forms in a host of languages (Dollerup 1999), as well as Riitta Oittinen, who examines adaptation as a form of translation using a corpus of West European translations of classical fairytales (Oittinen 2000). Oittinen moves beyond written versions, however, and draws attention to modern movie adaptations, showing the full manifestations of rewriting across space, time, and media. In her view, adaptation, as a strategy that permits great liberty, gives new life to canonical works. Both Dollerup and Oittinen exemplify the route that can be taken both in adaptation scholars' "translational turn" and translation scholars' "adaptational turn."

Understandably, reception by the reader is the "ecological" factor that determines the nature of adaptive changes made to children's literature transmitted abroad. As with film and drama adaptations, the range of cultural adaptations studied has been expanded in recent times. For instance, Lan Dong discusses how the Chinese fairytale of Mulan can travel to the Western world and induce a full range of adaptations, including a Disney version (Dong 2011). Olga Papusha analyzes the two versions of A. A. Milne's *Winnie the Pooh* by a Russian (Boris Zakhoder) and a Ukrainian (Leonid Solon'ko) adaptor. She concludes that both works must be understood in terms of the much enlarged, new readership that belongs to a new post-Soviet, post-totalitarian space (Papusha n.d.: para.14). With regard to three Brazilian Portuguese versions of Lewis Carroll's *Alice in Wonderland*,

Lauro Maia Amorim highlights how the adaptation in Brazil by Nicholau Sevcenko is affected by its target readership, eleven- and twelve-year-olds (2009: sec. 3). This impacts the adaptor's choice of vocabulary and use of colloquialisms, among other things. Readers' expectations need to be taken into consideration, and they determine directly how the adaptors alter the original text. Often radical moves are undertaken in response to an anticipated readership, resulting in "adaptive reinterpretations" of the original. Amorim cites examples where the adaptor even intervenes into the story by assuming the persona of a storyteller (see Amorim 2009). In sum, reception, translation, and adaptation studies conjoin to offer a multidisciplinary perspective on children's literature crossing linguistic, national, literary, and (even) age boundaries.

Grounds of Compatibility

Significantly, despite the remarkable insights they contain on the nature of adaptation, two widely read monographs on the subject of adaptations by literary comparatists Julie Sanders (2006) and Linda Hutcheon (2006) barely touch on the relevance of translation to adaptation studies.[3] An increasing number of translation scholars have sought to highlight such relevance, however. John Milton issues a call to investigate how translation studies can play a central role in the strengthening of adaptation studies (2007: 56) and raises the possibility of joining the two fields of enquiry through the concept of transculturation (2009: 19). Citing adaptive techniques used in the translation of genres like advertisements, theater texts, and fictional classics, he points to the interface between the two disciplines. The applicability of translation concepts to adaptation, however, is underscored by an article by Lawrence Venuti (2007), who is of the belief that the critical methodologies of translation can be usefully transferred. His test-case is the Italian film director Franco Zeffirelli's 1968 adaptation of Shakespeare's *Romeo and Juliet*. Embedded in Zeffirelli's version is an elitist homoerotic subtext that is latent rather than explicit in the original. Zeffirelli can be said to have actualized (or "translated") the deeper meanings inherent in Shakespeare's play, or he was simply making a personal commentary on the classic. In his analysis, Venuti capitalizes on a number of translation concepts like "abusive fidelity,"

---

[3] Designations used for individual scholars in this chapter (comparatists, translation scholars, etc.) are not intended to strictly compartmentalize them. They just point to the different, but changing, disciplinary factors that inform the development of the two disciplinary fields under discussion.

"intertextuality," "recontextualization," "norms," and "isomorphism" when applied to film adaptation. For him:

> [T]ranslation theory can advance thinking about film adaptations by contributing to the formulation of a more rigorous methodology for studying them. If we abandon the communicative model of translation and instead consider its relation to a source text as hermeneutic, the interpretant can assume crucial importance in analyzing both translations and adaptations. . . .The hermeneutic relation can be seen . . . as interrogative, exposing the cultural and social conditions of those materials and of the translation or adaptation that has processed them. (Venuti 2007: 41)

More boldly than some of his predecessors, Venuti erases the unneeded distinctions between adaptation and translation: one of the sections in his article has the subheading "adaptation as translation." This signifies the shift away from the exclusionary view of adaptations on the part of translation theorists, who stigmatize adaptations because they are unfaithful to their sources. From his more inclusionary vantage point, Venuti understands the departures from the original as hermeneutically motivated, and this aligns him with someone like George Steiner.

In fact, a decade earlier, Venuti had touched on the close link between translation and adaptation in *The Translator's Invisibility* (1995). There, looking at the history of English-language translation in Anglo-America, Venuti notes translators' strong preference for ethnocentric domestication, whereby the strange is made familiar, and the Other is turned into the Self. This strategy stands in contrast to "foreignization," which allows differences to be inscribed. Partly owing to his covert proposals, in recent years the foreignizing mode has been increasingly upheld as the preferred alternative. Yet ironically it is the "invisibility" approach that undergirds the many cases of adaptation over the centuries that are the subject of his monograph. Adaptations are nothing less than domesticated translations, where target values, conventions, and norms are superimposed on the source text, cultural differences are erased, and the foreign becomes the familiar for the local audience. Recognition of the applicability of translation theory to adaptation studies—due to the former's capability to unravel what happens to texts undergoing cultural reconfiguration—may have been a recent trend, but the skills and terminology used by translation scholars in tackling crosslingual textual issues give their approach special utility. Perhaps this is the much-needed response to Laurence Raw's dissatisfaction with adaptation studies, especially his wish to "learn about the process of textual evolution rather than reading endless commentaries on completed texts" provided by an abundance of publications in the field (Raw 2009: 73).

Another staunch defender of the need to reinterpret the relationship between translation and adaptation, seen both as strategies and as overall orientations, is Georges Bastin, who has published extensively on issues related to the nature of adaptation. His article on "Adaptation and Appropriation: Is There a Limit?," coauthored with Hugo Vandal-Sirios, and published in Laurence Raw's collective volume (Raw 2012), begins by surveying the work of several scholars who wrestle with the distinction between translation and adaptation. Notwithstanding the difficulties involved, the article asserts the possibility of drawing a dividing line between the two, and on that basis to analyze the "freedoms" enjoyed by adaptations. The interface between the two forms is a complicated one, with some overlap despite evident differences. In underscoring this ambiguity, the two authors quote from an earlier piece by Bastin, who points out that adaptation may be seen "as a set of translative operations which results in a text that is not accepted as translation but is nevertheless recognized as representing a source text of about the same length" (2012: 25). In striking contrast to Venuti, Bastin and Vandal-Sirios stress the communicative or receptive (and not the hermeneutic) purpose of adaptations, using as examples the translations of educational and marketing material to highlight the laudatory uses of adaptation—to convey a point, convince the reader, facilitate reception (2012: 30–3), and so on. On the strength of these translated vocative texts, which make up a substantial portion of the translation work being done today, the authors draw the conclusion that the differences between translation and adaptation should be seen as largely a matter of degree.

While a few other authors in Raw's anthology also highlight the connectivity between translation and adaptation—one calling them "two sides of an ideological coin" (Krebs 2012: 42), for instance—it is Bastin who has consistently worked on the problematic issue of their compatibility despite their ontological differences.[4] In a later article (2014), he further elaborates on the linkage between the two, although he also points out several differences, noting, for instance, that the act of adapting is a performative one (with the adaptor at play). In addition, for him, *telos* (deep down gut feelings) rather than *skopos* (a key term in functionalist theories of translation) should be the term for what governs the adaptors' decisions to alter the source text. Significantly, he notes an important point of connection: both translation and

---

[4] For another survey that seeks to disentangle the complexities of the case, see Minier (2014). For Minier, the contrast is stated in terms of "a fully new work" and "a mutation of the original matter" (2014: 21).

adaptation involve "interventions," either compulsory or deliberate, which are undertaken for reasons that are ideological, cultural, and historical. In reiterating the fact that there are only different emphases between translation and adaptation, Bastin exemplifies a strong trend among those scholars of translation who wish to capitalize on the similarities to build a bridge between the two disciplines.

In Henrik Gottlieb's semiotically based taxonomy for the plethora of translation types (2005), adaptation is seen from an even broader perspective than those of Venuti and Bastin. Gottlieb moves beyond theorization on the basis of conventional concepts of translation (such as interlingual transfer) to ponder what he calls multidimensional translation, an attempt no doubt necessitated by the increasing prominence of new media, and the reduced interest in traditional forms of translation activity. The abundance of publications in intermedial forms (for example, audiovisual translation, audio description, sign interpreting), which recent film adaptation studies has come to acknowledge as well, has called for yet another turn in translation research. In presenting his comprehensive map of "translation in its totality" (2005: 2), Gottlieb starts off by schematizing on the basis of distinctions between: (a) mono-semiotic and poly-semiotic texts, (b) verbal and nonverbal materials in human communication, and, particularly significant in the present context, (c) conventional and "inspirational translation" (i.e., production of "inspired" texts only loosely connected to the original, like adaptations and imitations). The first two of these sets of distinctions are typified by novel-to-film translations, the almost exclusive focus of early film adaptation studies, but Gottlieb also gives a long list that includes translations from poetry into song, the decryption of messages in Morse, and so on.

After a preliminary discussion of the various forms of "translation" under his emphatically semiotic design, which is also a simplified version of Jakobson's threefold division that combines the interlingual and intralingual categories (2005: 3), Gottlieb inserts two diagrams. The first shows intersemiotic translation, which involves a shift from one channel to another (like a novel reworked into a film); the second shows intra-semiotic translation that may or may not involve a language shift (as in a foreign language remake versus a local remake). He then adds to the first diagram a verbalization dimension: texts may be verbalized or de-verbalized in translation. With these considerations in mind, and by eliminating a number of subcategories used by Gottlieb, I have worked out a version in Table 4.1 with a focus on the range of possible adaptations, highlighting the degree of liberty taken by the adaptor in the left-hand cloumn, in contrast to the faithful translator on the right. ("Intra-semiotic translation" is now the equivalent of Jakobson's "translation proper.")

Table 4.1 Translation and Adaptation from a Semiotic Perspective (Adapted from Gottlieb 2005)

I. INTERSEMIOTIC TRANSLATION

Adaptation (More Free)			More Faithful (translation proper)
	De-verbalization*	Verbalization	
Different channel	Story → pictures, for example, *Little Prince* (mono-semiotic → mono-semiotic)	Ball game on radio	*Morse Code interpreted*
More channels	Story/novel → film, for example, *Rouge*; Disney (mono-semiotic → poly-semiotic)	Ball game on TV	*Stage script acted out*
Fewer channels	Film → novel, novelization or movie tie-in (poly-semiotic → mono-semiotic)	Description of film for article	*Ballet notations on paper*

II. INTRA-SEMIOTIC TRANSLATION

Adaptation (More Free)			More Faithful (translation proper)
	Interlingual	Intralingual	
Same channel	Foreign film remakes, for example, *The Departed* (from a Hong Kong movie) (poly-semiotic → poly-semiotic)	Local film remakes, for example, Gus van Gant's version of *Psycho* (poly-semiotic → poly-semiotic)	*Written and oral translation*

*De-verbalization refers to both the reduction of the role played by verbal elements *and* their total elimination.

Gottlieb himself notes the relevance of notions of freedom to the enlarged definition of translation, one comparable to that which is proposed in the present study. Immediately after defining translation as "any process, or product thereof, in which a combination of sensory signs carrying communicative intention is replaced by another combination reflecting, or inspired, by the original entity," he notes a profusion of possible changes that can be made to the source text and varying degrees of freedom for the translator (2005: 3). He alerts us to the room for laxity or unpredictability in the translated product through his creation of an "inspirational" category. Undoubtedly, in his advocacy of a broader notion of translation he finds it necessary to query the need for strictly separating adaptation from translation (2005: 5), even juxtaposing one against the other. Faithfulness, seen in the effort made to attain maximal correspondence and equivalence, becomes irrelevant in "inspired" translations, a term that can be applied not just to adaptation but also to "imitation" (as we shall see later). Most significantly, Gottlieb's study alerts us to one fact, namely that the perspective of intersemiotic transfer opens up the theorization of adaptation, so that alterations to the original must be seen as unavoidable because of a change in the medium used, and not just caused by a different interpretation, or an attempt to translate what is untranslatable, or a result of carelessness or misunderstanding.

Adaptation and Transculturality

Where does adaptation studies stand in relation to translation studies? There is little possibility of answering this question without clarifying the relationship between the two forms of transtextual rewriting. In the endless debate on the similarities and divergences, the linkages and disconnections, and the overlap and discontinuations between the two, perhaps we can better conceptualize the two related forms metaphorically. Other than as "half-identical twins," which I mentioned in Chapter 1, Patrick Cattrysse has, in his recent article on research and disciplinary boundaries between the two, called them siblings sharing close family resemblance (2018). As twins they are umbilically linked, look remarkably similar, and yet have independent existences. As siblings they are genetically connected, have inherited different traits from their parents, and share less physical resemblance than twins. Having described the evident likenesses between the two forms of rewriting, then, we can more profitably move on to consider differences. To my mind, adaptations that do not effectively allow foreign cultures, lifestyles, and modes of thinking to be transferred are not irrelevant to the present discussion of the interface between translation and adaptation. As is clear by now, in giving priority to changes of content consciously introduced by the author rather than to shifts necessitated by a change in medium, we are excluding from our discussion adaptations that are more properly the subject of media-specificity studies. Three "trans" dimensions—the transnational, the transcultural, and the translinguistic—lie behind our study of how adaptations work in introducing the "alien" to target recipients in a way comparable to translation.

In particular, there has been recent interest in exploring how adaptations can be explained in transcultural terms. In the introductory essay to one issue of *Journal of Intercultural Studies*, Suzi Adams and Michael Janover note two contrasting approaches to the study of the contemporary "clash of civilizations." For them, "[either] the cultural 'other' is reduced to the identity of the 'self' or 'the same,'" or "'cultural otherness' is envisaged as alterity, as unbridgeable and ultimately untranslatable" (2009: 227). The dichotomy can be expressed in a number of paired terms, each of which encapsulates one aspect of the dialectical relationship between two perspectives on intercultural processes: acculturation versus alienation, domestication versus foreignization, translatability versus untranslatability, and so on. If we take either of these alternative paths to understanding the two modes of rewriting in question, then we can see obvious differences in emphasis. Adaptation better enables the Other to be transformed into the Self, while translation displays more clearly the alterity of the Other. Adaptation leans toward the theoretical positions of acculturation, domestication, and translatability; and translation, toward those of alienation, foreignization, and untranslatability. While this systematization of differences may not be applicable to all the forms that adaptation and translation can take—for instance, translations can be domesticating—it is one fruitful way of characterizing the ontological distinctions between the two.

We will have occasion to further elaborate on these contrasts, although it should be clarified that no claim is made as to which form is superior or better suits specific historical and social circumstances. In the world we inhabit, there is no place for a "multiple-worlds" approach where cultures are seen as separate and unbridgeable; in contrast, the idea of a "shared universe" is actively promoted in work done in the fields of globalization studies and multicultural studies, among others. As disciplinary newcomers, translation studies and adaptation studies can both help increase our knowledge of the myriad ways in which cultural texts cross national and linguistic boundaries as they are rewritten for different audiences. The difference between the two forms, then, is a matter of degree. That being the case, any attempt to make either translation or adaptation a subcategory of the other is contestable.

With this as a basis for establishing the significance of translation and adaptation in transcultural terms, we can explore the meaning of adaptation in translational terms. Among the diverse views on adaptation as outlined above, it is clear that it is somehow unified around certain core concepts, most notably that it has an active role in giving texts new incarnations in target cultural contexts. Intercultural studies has emerged as a discipline because differences between cultures are considered to be a constant cause of conflict and misunderstanding, arising from people's different perceptions and thought patterns.[5] Perhaps it is time that transcultural studies be introduced as a parallel discipline that deals with how texts from one culture *enter* another, through interventions in one form or another. The interventions used in adaptive rewritings show that they can be a strategy for the assimilation of differences (or for acculturation) as the text mediator strives to either incorporate the elements from another culture, or make possible ready reception by the target audience. The need for adapting material across cultures is particularly strong in our time because of increased globalization processes and intensified cultural exchange. As a method for facilitating intercultural flows, adaptation easily meets the two crucial criteria for successful reception: effectiveness (because the receptor feels secure) and comfort (because any cultural shock is removed) (Barnett and Kincaid 1983: 172).[6] It succeeds through the adjustments made as a text is transferred from one culture to another. And by departing from the original text through strategies more drastic than those found in prototypical translations, an adaptation enhances the infiltration of what is foreign.[7]

Judging from the fascinating work done in adaptation studies, it is evident that the status of adapted works has risen. There is clearly no justification for regarding adaptations as of a lower order than translations. After all, efforts to manipulate the foreign have as much right to exist as attempts to present the foreign work as it is—if that is at all possible. Although some earlier scholars of film adaptation, laboring under the fidelity principle, saw departures from the original as undesirable, in subsequent years the group

---

[5] One must add that the relevance of translation to intercultural studies has been underscored by the title of one of the largest organizations of translation scholars—International Association for Translation and Intercultural Studies (IATIS), founded in 2004. According to its official website description, it is a "worldwide forum designed to enable scholars from different regional and disciplinary backgrounds to debate issues relating to translation and other forms of intercultural communication" (https://www.iatis.org/index.php).

[6] Since the discussion here is concerned primarily with the cultural contexts for the reception of adaptations, we will not mention the personal reasons that prompt adaptors to alter the source texts.

[7] For instance, there are the Japanized versions of Shakespeare in the cinematic adaptations (Hoenselaars 2004).

has advocated dual-perspectival "readings" leading to re-assessments of adaptations that put them effectively on a par with their originals. Theater adaptation scholars, who conceive of adapted foreign drama as providing new impetus for innovations in postmodern theater, praise it for how it achieves deep significance "through releasing the intercultural signs and the multiple meanings in performances" (Tuan 2007: 153). In the case of adapted children's literature, given that it is a genre requiring constant textual adjustments across national and linguistic borders, scholars have not lost sight of how adaptations give stories, fairytales and myths their "afterlives" as they travel around the world in new guises.

Of course, certain negative evaluations of adaptation persist, including doubts about their worth. Some argue that they hinder, rather than promote, genuine exchange, ostensibly because of the "partiality" on the part of the adaptors. Manipulation, a method generally deployed by adaptors strong or weak, has also not been looked upon favorably. In this connection, adaptations have been critiqued with reference to notions of "interference" and "lack of originality," as might be expected. Non-Western scholars have pointed out the hidden agendas of adaptors who serve as accomplices to Western hegemony (Lim 1999), while reception critics have wondered if comfort and ease of reception is a desirable goal, since "textual fissures and disjunctions" can jolt receptors' sensitivity to cultural incongruities and incompatibilities. Attacks have also zeroed in on adaptations as acts of conquest, on how adaptors "borrow" or "steal" from their precursors, at times without an understanding of what they have done (Diamond 1993: 161). In the translation studies field, too, despite a surging interest in adaptation as noted above, the centuries-old belief that faithfulness to the original is a supreme virtue dies hard, and adaptive modes are still faulted by many. As we shall see, many of these criticisms apply with even greater force to imitations, a strongly appropriative form of rewriting that is the subject of Part III of the present book.

It makes little sense to denigrate adaptation in any way, much less compare it unfairly with translation. Instead, the transcultural operations of adaptations can throw into high relief the different concerns of the two forms of transtextual rewriting under consideration here. To begin with, they present different degrees of responses to the alien and unfamiliar. In making an effort to use concepts already available in the target culture to assimilate elements of foreignness, adaptations naturally stand at the far end of a spectrum of degrees of freedom as exercised by text rewriters.[8] The

---

[8] There is no denying that many adaptations present novel, even idiosyncratic, readings of preexistent texts. The emphasis on the assimilative aspects of adaptation in the present study is, of course, based on a restricted definition of the term that allows us to position it vis-à-vis translation as modes of cultural transfer.

choice to turn the alien into the familiar can be viewed positively: it reflects the adaptors' desire to transmit what may not be ferried across cultures easily. They do not take seriously the requirement to be faithful to the source text that ensnares every translator. By contrast, when they refuse to pander to the wishes of receptors, translators allow us to see more of the outside world through retaining the foreign and refusing to localize and erase differences. Even though it is virtually impossible for translations to be completely faithful, theoretically speaking adaptations are a lot more free, resulting in a "fidelity gap." Obviously, the more the adaptors alter their source materials, the less they transmit to their receptors, so that one can say that adaptations are not "acceptable" translations. Yet it is equally true that, by departing from their sources (especially in situations where they are dislodged to another medium), the adaptors can more than compensate for the "loss" they have caused to their receptors by giving them more than the original authors did. All in all, adaptation studies shows the diversity of means whereby textual materials from one culture can be migrated to another, much as translation studies does, albeit in its own way.

5

Accommodation and Adaptation

The Case of East Asia

The problem of demarcating translation from adaptation has preoccupied translation theorists to a greater extent than those outside the field. Although it has been said that adaptation is not translation (e.g., Nogami 1938, qtd. Wakabayashi 1998: 60), emphasizing only the distinctiveness of translations, rather than the areas of overlap between the two forms, is less than helpful. While some may think that the thorny problem should be better left untouched, the connection between the two makes it difficult to relegate adaptations to a realm outside of translation. It is particularly difficult to disengage one from the other, especially when free translation is tantamount to adaptation of a less liberal kind. We saw in the last chapter the troubled relationship between the disciplines of translation and adaptation studies. Some works, most notably dramatic productions based on a foreign source and children's literature being circulated in non-native versions, simply straddle the two realms, while adaptive strategies are indispensable in certain spheres of translation, like advertising. With translation being consistently enlarged as a research field, it becomes incumbent upon us to consider the question: What is the ontological status of adaptation when it is seen from a translation viewpoint? In what ways can its intrinsic characteristics be seen to overlap with those of translation?[1]

The relegation of adaptations to a minor position because they are not "faithful" to their originals is still very much in evidence in some quarters of translation study. It may be said that, with better mastery of the foreign languages to be translated than previously, faithful renditions can now successfully supersede adaptations where they have not previously done so, and literal translation can play a more important role. Historically, freer methods of translation were often adopted because of the lack of translators

---

[1] Excluded from our discussion will be adaptations that do not involve interlingual transfer. Adaptation studies have proliferated dramatically in recent years, as a cursory look at the tables of contents of the journal *Adaptation* reveals, but a significant portion of articles published there does not involve more than one natural language (e.g., August 2018 issue).

with sufficient competence in lesser known languages, and so make-do translations had to be tolerated. Examples are the early European translations of the classical Chinese works, such as Joseph Henri Marie de Prémare's adaptive version of *The Orphan of Zhao* and the nineteenth-century Chinese adaptations of Dickens's novels by Lin Shu. After at least a century's linguistic interaction, not even minor languages are a hassle, as shown by the spate of Chinese translations of works in those languages without the use of an interim rendition in either English or French, the major intermediary languages (Branchadell 2005). It is perhaps worth noting that the respect for the original text has not diminished in our age, one that has seen not only the ascendancy of deconstructionist thought, but also its impact on translation theory (see Venuti 1992; Davis 2001). Nevertheless, in practice, the adaptive method continues to be favored by many translators who take their role as mediators seriously, ready to intervene and make alterations where they think necessary.

The present chapter takes a look at the nature of adaptations with reference to theories in East Asia, with the aim of answering the question of ontology from an alternative to the dominant Eurocentric position. While Western materials have been addressed in the previous chapter, attention will be paid here to theories and supporting evidence in the last few centuries from China, Korea, and Japan before the "arrival" of the West. Preference for adaptive translation is seen in isolated periods of Western literary history like seventeenth- and eighteenth-century France, when it was dominated by the "unfaithful beauties" (*les belles infidèles*) tradition. Less often scrutinized from a translation perspective is the remarkable history of adaptations in East Asia, where free renditions of source texts have contributed enormously to the translation field in the Sinosphere. The Western, post-Romantic disparagement of adaptation was never a part of East Asian translation history if the evidence from the past is closely inspected. Bearing in mind our primary objective—namely, to give an ontological description of adaptation—we shall look below at three categories of works: first, the novel adaptations spawned in Korea and Japan by Chinese classical novels since the eighteenth century, in particular the deluge of popular Japanized and Koreanized re-versions that formed the staple for the reading public up to the end of the nineteenth century; second, the fad for adapted, domesticated, or localized adaptations of Western literature in Meiji Japan (1868–1912), which prepared the country for the massive importation of Western texts via translation later; and third, free translations in China of Western literature from the nineteenth century on. Covering broad yet different historical periods in the countries in question, this chapter deploys an ecological framework, which, hopefully, will mitigate much of the theoretical obfuscation in much discourse on translation versus adaptation.

One caveat must be repeated before proceeding further. One major contemporary form of adaptation is that which takes place on an intersemiotic level. Our age bears witness to the growth of interest in adaptations that cross media and, in the process, are transformed. Traversing different semiotic systems is, of course, an adaptive move: the adaptor needs to adhere to the conventions and modalities of the target medium, regardless of whether interlanguaging is involved. This is the core meaning of "adaptation" for film theorists working mostly on same-language remakes of film classics. But in our present discussion, the central focus is on interlingual adaptation, where linguistic elements interact with the ideological and political factors that come into play when cultural borders are crossed, rather than on adaptations of all kinds. It is to be expected that, with rapid transformations in the textual-visual landscape, adaptation will elicit more and more attention because of its strong presence in intermedial forms, understood in terms of the crossing of sign systems. Of greater interest in the present study, however, are the shifts in content rather than form.[2]

Ecological Adjustment: The Terms Explained

The meaning of the term "adaptation" has been so broadened that it now covers any text that has been altered in the process of being transwritten across languages and media. (The situation would be worse if we include for consideration non-textual phenomena such as those in the physiological and behavioral sciences.) In fact, a dictionary definition of "adapt" gives simply: "1. To make fit or suitable by changing or *adjusting* 2. To *adjust* (oneself) to new or changed circumstances" (Thomsett and Nickerson 1993: 111; italics added), yet it is a meaning seldom attributed to adaptation either as a genre or as a technique. We can, therefore, define it not as any "changed" text, but one "adjusted" to suit a different environment, with all the ecological implications that this may entail. A cornerstone of modern biology, "adaptation" has a special status in Darwin's theory of natural selection as presented in *On the Origin of Species* (1859). Darwin understood it to be a key process in evolution

---

[2] Even in the example analyzed in Chapter 5, the emphasis is on how the adaptors make the TV drama versions accessible and palatable to the local audience on the cultural level, and not on the medium-related adjustments.

whereby organisms undergo mutations in order that they be better fitted to survive in the environment. In transtextual terms, adaptation is therefore nothing less than a form of "textual evolution." The success of an adaptation is to be measured genetically, that is, when desirable traits are preserved in reproduction. In the past decade or so, such a theory has been borrowed to interpret the functioning of translation by some China-based scholars. An Adaptation School of translation studies came into existence through the launching of the International Association of Eco-Translation Research under the headship of Hu Gengshen, who introduced the concept of "eco-translatology" in several publications, held regular conferences, and founded a journal specifically devoted to research in the area. According to Hu, in response to the target linguistic, cultural, and social environment, the translator adapts his text so that it attains maximal success with authors, clients and readers (2003: 283–4). Along these lines other Chinese articles were published in the field, and the topics dealt with include the adjustments made to Thomas Hardy's *Tess of the d'Urbervilles* when the folk idiolects of major characters are translated into a Chinese dialect (Sun 2009); Yan Fu's adaptation of Thomas Huxley's *Evolution and Ethics*, which combines Huxley's version with his own interpolations (Huang 2009); and free translations (into English) of the play *The Peony Pavilion*, in which cultural elements are tampered with (Jiang 2009). Hu's focus, at least in the early stage of his work, is on the translator's use of effective strategies to deal with a range of ecological determinants.

Not all of Hu's suggestions are relevant to the present discussion, however. For example, the idea that the adaptation—and selection—processes in translation are ultimately determined by principles in the natural world (2003: 289) needs to be qualified, since the natural and cultural do not follow the same paths. But his notion of a translation's "survival" being dependent on its adjustment to the new socio-cultural environment in which it finds itself is particularly illuminating in that adaptations find new life through departing from, rather than faithfully replicating, the original. Proper adjustment to target conditions ensures renewal and an "afterlife" in a different context. In the final analysis, this process is operative at the core of all transtextual rewritings, even in translations (where ideal literalism is not achievable). The term "adaptation" has indeed lost much of its specificity and usefulness because it has been extended to refer to texts containing alterations of any kind regardless of the reason or motivation. As should by now be clear, core definitions like this one serve to better differentiate between translation, adaptation, and imitation given their many commonalities.

If adaptations are to be successful in textual transfer, the method for effective transplantation into new environments deserves a closer look. In this connection, it may be useful to look at three frameworks proposed to explain cross-cultural transmission. First, in the introductory essay to their edited volume on theatrical performances that cross cultural barriers, Bonnie Marranca and Gautam Dasgupta venture a workable definition of "recontextualization," a term also relevant to the study of adaptation as a form of translation. It is for them "the inscription of a preserved foreign code in a native structure, which implies that an ideology is inscribed with it" (Marranca and Dasgupta 1991: 35). The "inscription of a foreign code" occurs in adaptations too, when textual elements are transferred from the hypotext to the hypertext, finding a "home" in the native context. This is an acculturation process whereby imported items are lodged comfortably in an indigenous setting, although it is an operation that comes with an ideological baggage. "Localization" and "reframing" are two strategies that are frequently invoked in conjunction with acculturation, and both are subsumable under "recontextualization."[3]

Second, in cross-cultural transmission, because of the barriers separating one culture from another, adaptors not only situate their texts in a new context, but also interpret them for a different audience. In transtextual rewriting, meanings are added to literary texts as they are rewritten for wherever they are destined. After a plethora of modifications has been introduced to the text, their new significance has to be enunciated. In referring to the methods of handling culture-specific elements that resist literal translation, Patrice Pavis has coined the term "cultural reinterpretation" (1989: 38–9). This is the practice whereby adaptors assimilate the source culture to the target culture by ironing out differences between the two and then injecting new meaning into the combination of plot, structure, and characters. In other words, the adaptor is given a free hand to make more out of the text than the original author. Understandably, given that the universals transcending individual cultures are limited, these adjustments can at times be quite substantial. But although the extent to which the traces of the original are removed differs from one case to another, a certain degree of rereading is almost always present in adaptations, and more pronounced with aggressive, manipulative adaptors.

Since recontextualization and reinterpretation will inform the ensuing analysis, we need to note briefly the term "transculturation." It has been

---

[3] For a succinct discussion of localization as a category of translation, see Pym (2010: Chapter 7).

defined as "the destruction of a text/code and its wrenching displacement to a historically and socially different situation" (Marranca and Dasgupta 1991: 35).[4] The relevance of this concept in light of what was said in our last chapter about transculturality (as different from interculturality) probably needs little explanation. More concretely, it refers to adaptive alterations (i.e., departures from the source text) that enable the transfer of cultural content to a different milieu as a text is rewritten. This anthropological term, which originated in Latin America (with Fernando Ortiz) and then traveled to Anglo-American academia (via Bronislaw Malinowski among others), has become influential in cultural studies and literary circles (through the work of Mary Louise Pratt). It eventually found its way into translation studies through two seminal publications by Maria Tymoczko (2007) and Edwin Gentzler (2008). Jesús Sayols Lara, who brilliantly summarizes this history, stresses the bi-directionality of cultural influence in the translational process, in contrast to Tymoczko's concern with "the capacity of transculturation to transmit, uptake and disseminate elements from one cultural *environment* in a unilateral direction towards another cultural *environment*" (Sayols Lara 2015: 68; italics added). It is eminently suitable as an explanation of why adaptations are found acceptable in target contexts. When elements borrowed from the source text become integrated into the new ecological environment, we can speak of "effective transculturation."

In what follows, we will first introduce East Asian theories of adaptation in the premodern age. This will set the stage for the more detailed discussion of "ecological adaptation" with reference to two examples of translations in the East Asian context, namely a seventeenth-century Japanese adaptation of a Chinese story from Qu You's (1341–1427) *Trimming the Wick* (1378) and a late twentieth-century adaptation of Oscar Wilde's *The Picture of Dorian Gray* by the Taiwanese writer Wang Dahong. They showcase an array of strategies (accommodation, acculturation, relocation, reframing, etc.) deployed for purposes of recontextualization, reinterpretation, and (ultimately) transculturation, as adjustments are made by adaptors such that source texts can be integrated into the new ecology. Needless to say, a measure of these successes is the extent to which they have been favorably received by the target audience. We will then end with a brief look at the third

---

[4] Marranca and Dasgupta also express a preference for understanding cross-cultural adaptations on stage as "transcultural" rather than "cross-cultural." They wish to emphasize the transformation the textual elements are subjected to when moved from one culture to another.

example, which shows the strong reception accorded the adaptations of Western novels by Lin Shu.[5]

Adaptation Theories in the Premodern Sinosphere

Adaptations in East Asia are best illustrated by those of the classical Chinese novels, especially *Romance of the Three Kingdoms*, *Journey to the West* and *Water Margin*. The first specimens appeared as early as the seventeenth century in Korea and Japan, and then they proliferated, with variant versions appearing over several centuries before Chinese cultural dominance was undermined by the incursion of the West in the nineteenth century (Lee 1986; Pollack 1986b). Seldom studied in any depth and generally unknown to the West except in a branch of comparative literature studies, these adaptations constitute a treasure-trove of material giving us a glimpse of the unique nature of the cross-cultural traffic between China, Japan, and Korea (Salmon 1987). Especially noteworthy is the fact that most of the Chinese texts were fervently adapted and published alongside the much fewer literal translations, giving rise to arguments, like that by Cho (2016), that adaptation was the primary mode of transtextual rewriting in premodern East Asia.

A recurrent pattern of transmission pertains to the adaptations of classical Chinese novels in the Sinosphere. There is the well-known case of a Vietnamese adaptation of the novel *The Story of Jin Yunqiao* into *The Tale of Kiều* (1820) by Nguyễn Du (1765–1821), a poem that is often seen as representing the pinnacle of the Vietnamese literary tradition. With reference to this example, Ha Kim-lan explains the particular nature of transtextual rewriting in the region, noting in particular the element of transmittability (2001: 24–6). To her transmittability is a factor as important as "readability" and "scriptability" in determining the circulation of textual products in the Asian context. We should add that "transmittability" is nothing less than ecological adjustability. Chinese cultural artifacts were easily transmittable, traveling with great speed through the countries concerned. The regional proliferation of adaptations, rewritten from a canon of Chinese source texts, is a premodern cultural phenomenon determined by the specific geopolitical configuration of

---

[5] Since an attempt is often made in adaptations to minimize the cultural shock and make the resultant text conform to the expectations of readers, adaptations also often turn out to be "domesticating translations." By contrast, literal translations are "foreignizing" in nature.

East Asia, with China occupying the center and flanked by tributary or vassal states. The sharing of Chinese culture and literary sensibilities by the nations in the periphery enabled easy movement of the original texts, while their adaptations show signs of these texts acclimatized to local conditions. In this way, the adaptations participate in a unique Sinocentric Model of Textual Transmission.

Among the earliest and best-known adaptations following an itinerary of this kind is the fifteenth-century Korean story collection, *New Tales from Mount Kŭmo*, by Kim Sisŭp (1435–93), adapted from *Trimming the Wick*, the aforementioned popular Chinese collection of short tales about romantic encounters and supernatural occurrences. Unlike *The Tale of Kiều*, which was written in the ancient Vietnamese script (*Chữ-nôm*), *New Tales from Mount Kŭmo* was written in *wenyan*, classical Chinese. Both adaptations, however, stood at the apex of their respective literary traditions. Careful comparison of the Korean adaptation to the Chinese source shows the resemblances in theme and plot, but the locale was completely nativized (i.e., Koreanized). For example, "Park of Assembled Scenery" becomes "Manbok Temple," and "Mirror Lake" turns into "Pubyŏk Pavilion." Nevertheless, the story of the journey taken by *Trimming the Wick* does not end here. When it landed, with an added Korean commentary, in Japan in 1646, it spawned a handful of Japanese adaptations and imitations, and is generally viewed by scholars as having inaugurated the genre of fantastic tales in Japan. In Vietnam, too, there was Nguyễn Tu's (ca. sixteenth-century) adaptation, *Casual Notes of Short Stories* (1520–30), composed in classical Chinese (see Riftin 2007; You 2017).[6] This completed the cycle of East Asian transtextual adaptations.

The traditional Korean and Japanese conceptualizations of adaptation can be read against these practices. On the theoretical front, the Korean understanding of adaptation is contained in their word for "adaptation" or "rewriting." *Bun-an*—literally "reversing the verdict" or "overturning an established theory" (Kim 2000: 24)—has legal connotations and meanings. Many Korean adaptations of *Romance of the Three Kingdoms*, Korea's most adapted Chinese novel, are to be differentiated from literal translations because they have been given local color through the interpolation of elements of Korean life (customs, place names, and proper names) into the

---

[6] Similar to the Korean and Japanese versions, the Chinese characters in the original were also replaced by Vietnamese ones. For a close analysis of the Vietnamese adaptation as compared to the Chinese original, see Nguyen (2005: 352–443).

text.[7] The tampering with the original is tantamount to an attempt to reverse the original judgment. The Japanese term for "adaptation"—*hon'an*—also connotes "reversing the verdict" (Nakamura 1968).[8] Just like the Koreans, over the centuries the Japanese eagerly adapted classical Chinese fiction, relocating it to the indigenous context. This reached a peak in the latter half of the eighteenth century. Adaptations were made not just of *Romance of the Three Kingdoms*, but also of *Water Margin*, a novel about bandits-as-heroes that we shall look at later in Chapter 8.

The contrast between adaptations and literal translations is reflected in Japan, both past and present, through terms in daily use. As J. Scott Miller has pointed out (2001: 9–21), the antithesis is expressed in the terms *hon'an* and *hon'yaku*—counterparts of which can be easily found in different cultural traditions like the Chinese, the English, and the French, to name just a few. On the one hand, *hon'an* is akin to "adaptation"; on the other hand, *hon'yaku*, denoting a method used mostly with scientific and medical texts, is a term similar to "(literal) translation." The former connotes transmutation whereas the latter suggests correspondence—and both are distinguished from the Japanese word for imitation, *mosaku*. Rebekah Clements (2015: 10–11) disagrees with this distinction between translation (*hon'yaku*) and adaptation (*hon'an*), pointing out that the contrast was not supported by usages from the nineteenth century, the period that Miller discusses in his book. The possibility is that the division is a modern, Western construct. The imposition of Western categories on non-Western contexts certainly has the effect of detracting from a more accurate understanding of an East Asian past.

Recontextualizations of "The Peony Lantern"

Against this backdrop, we can review an example of a Sino-Japanese adaptation: Asai Ryōi's "The Peony Lantern" (1666), a tale of the fantastic adapted from "The Chronicle of the Peony Lantern" (1378) in *Trimming*

---

[7] Concerning this novel, apart from translations that sprang up after the introduction of the Korean alphabet in 1446, there were many adaptations, carried on over a long historical span, and not ceasing until the twentieth century. In explaining the appeal of the adaptations, Kim Dong-uk says that the novel could have shown "the imaginary victory looked for in the Koreans' consciousness of life . . . a consolation for their own philosophy of dedication to a great cause" (Kim 1987: 69).

[8] In the terms used in the revisionist approach adopted in the present study, *bun-an* and *hon'an* can also be translated as "imitation," the more extreme form of adaptation.

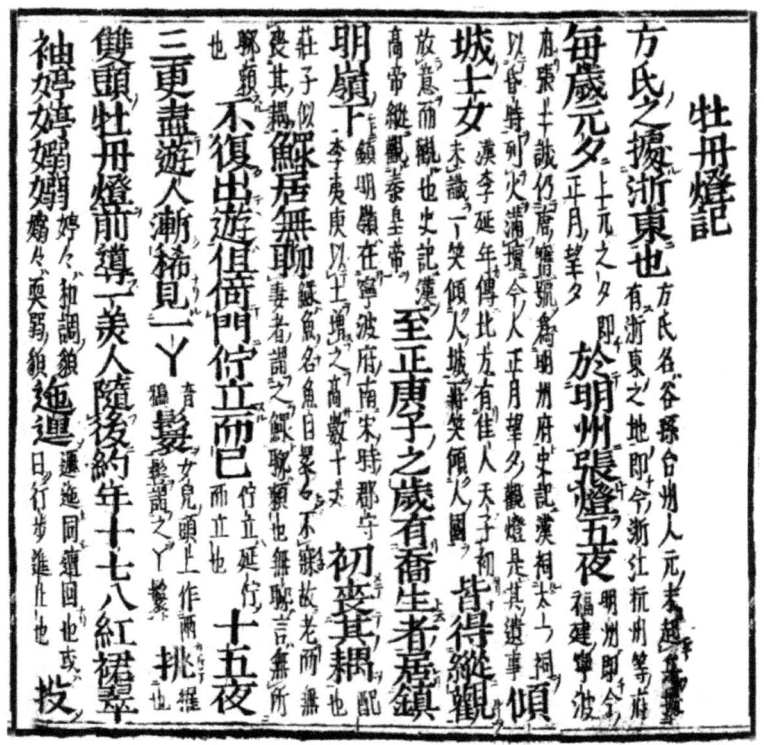

Figure 5.1 "The Peony Lantern" with *Kundoku* Notations.

the Wick (see Figure 5.1).[9] The original Chinese narrative by Qu—about a licentious scholar (Qiao) carrying on a sexual affair with a woman of unknown background (Fu Liqing) whose true spectral form is revealed to the elderly neighbor peeping at the two through a hole in the wall, and the disastrous consequences that ensue—is closely replicated in the Japanese adaptation, for there are minimal alterations. All the major characters from the source story (including the maid, Golden Lotus, who carries the peony lantern) reappear in the adaptation. All the basic plot details—the chance meeting, the sexual liaison, the female seen by her neighbor as a skeleton, the intervention of the exorcist, the separation of the couple, the tragic death of the scholar, the marriage in the underworld, and the final subjugation of the

---

[9] For a translation of "The Peony Lantern," see Shirane (2002: 33–8); for that of "The Chronicle of the Peony Lantern," see Harmon (1985: 193–203).

ghosts of the three major protagonists—are retained. But it is in the following details that divergences can be detected:

1. the Chinese scholar is turned into a samurai named Ogihara Shinnosuke;
2. the location is removed from Mingzhou (in China) to Kyoto;
3. the events of the Chinese tale occur in 1360, those of its adaptation in 1548;
4. Scholar Qiao first meets Fu Liqing at the Lantern Festival in the first lunar month of the year, while Ogihara encounters Iyako at the Japanese Festival of the Dead in mid-summer; and
5. the amulets used by the Daoist priest in Qu You's story are replaced in Ryōi's by a Shingon Buddhist priest's talismans.

Further signaling the recontextualization strategy is the fact that all the Chinese "cultural bumps" are removed in Ryōi's version. Literary allusions to Chinese classics like *The Book of Poetry* and *The Commentary of Zuo* are erased; instead, there are allusions to Japanese poetry. Whereas the Chinese text begins by mentioning various sacrificial rituals, its Japanese counterpart gives a description of the use of paper lanterns as decorations during the Festival of the Dead. Some significant traces left over from the Chinese original are the metaphors used to describe beautiful Iyako: the "lotus blossoms" and the "willow" (trans. Maryellen T. Mori; Shirane 2002: 34), whose provenance, according to Shi Zhiwu, cannot be traced to earlier Japanese literature (2010: 119). But the most conspicuous element of recontextualization comes at the end of the story, in the removal of a lengthy section about the netherworld officials' subjugation of the three ghosts (Qiao, Fu, and Golden Lotus) that haunt the town. The Chinese story records at length their written confessions and the Daoist priest's remonstrations, which bring out obliquely the moral message of the tale. The cumulative effect of all these modifications is to encourage a different reading—like the one given by Noriko Reider: "when Ryōi purposely chose to omit the underworld section from his version of 'Peony Lantern,' any overt ethical lessons were all but eliminated as well" (2002: 14). Thus the adaptation is more secular and clearly meant for entertainment, while the Chinese original, more didactic and moralizing, is a diatribe against sexual license. Encouraged by the textual alterations is an interpretation purged of the moralizing and thus altogether different from that intended by the source text.

The history of the Japanese adaptation of "The Chronicle of the Peony Lantern" does not end here, however. For many literary critics, Ueda Akinari's (1734–1809) "The Cauldron of Kibitsu" (*Kibitsu no kama*), in the collection *Tales of Moonlight and Rain* (1776), is also a rewritten version of the same story. But the deviations from the Chinese tale are so numerous that Tachikawa Kiyoshi (1999), after a close textual comparison of the two texts, concludes that Akinari's work cannot be said to be directly adapted from Qu's.[10] This view is contested by Shi Zhiwu, for whom the many divergences between the two texts are balanced by a web of correspondences, with the Japanese story alluding to some Chinese literary classics (2010: 115–18). A third critic, Shen Fei, also lists linguistic similarities between the Chinese and Japanese versions (1985: 48). When, as proposed in the present study, an adaptation becomes extremely "deviant," and departs radically from its purported source text, it can be said to have crossed the blurry lines between the adaptive and imitative modes,[11] between borrowing substantially from an antecedent and being simply "inspired," lending itself to being classified as an imitation.

Not all of the East Asian adaptors relocate their source texts to new settings—geographical, religious, social, or otherwise—although in the majority of cases, cultural adjustment is a key characteristic of adaptive translations. *Trimming the Wick* in fact spawned a cornucopia of adaptations, and examples are found beyond Japan. Su Heyun (2013) has unearthed a rare instance where the original Chinese cultural references were retained as they were, in a nineteenth-century Korean adaptation of the story "Drunk Teng Mu Visits the Jujing Garden." This is an exception to the popular Korean practice at the time of "spicing up" Korean adaptations of Chinese fiction with local settings and characters. In this case, in the face of the Japanese invasion near the end of that century, a sense of pessimism fueled the Korean nostalgia for the golden Song dynasty era in China (960–1279) (2013: 95), so the Chinese setting was transplanted rather than eradicated. A shared poetics, together with the factor of East Asian cultural proximity, renders it easy for Japanese and Korean readers to empathize with the characters in the Chinese originals and appreciate the themes and emotions expressed therein, with the result that textual modifications can be applied in a piecemeal manner, rather than holistically.[12]

---

[10] By contrast, a play by the late Edo playwright Sanyūtei Enchō that bears the words "peony lantern" in its title can more properly be regarded as an adaptation of the Chinese tale.

[11] Ōki Yasushi and Ōtsuka Hidetaka have compiled an exhaustive list of adaptations during the Edo period from the seventeenth right up to the nineteenth century (Ōki and Ōtsuka 1987: 135–8). In it, adaptations are placed against translations, showing a clear awareness of the two different categories that are separate but closely related.

[12] One might ask whether partial translations are adaptations. For instance, the 100-chapter *Romance of the Three Kingdoms* gave rise to many partial, though literal, renditions in Korea and Japan. My view is that incomplete versions are not "adaptive." They should be seen as constituting a separate category.

Reinterpretation of Oscar Wilde's *Dorian Gray*

It may appear to be a big leap from an intra-Asian example to an "international" example like that of Wang Dahong's rewriting of *The Picture of Dorian Gray* (1891) as *Du Liankui* (1977), but the two cases are perhaps not so dissimilar. An instance of manipulative rendering in which "surgical" alterations to the source text are made, Wang's adaptation shows the extent to which the English original can be boldly acculturated and optimally naturalized. What distinguishes this adaptation is that the intentions of the adapter can be clearly determined, and the resultant text builds up to a rereading of the original novel. As noted above, all adaptations bear distinctly the marks of a new context. Wilde's late Victorian novel is relocated to Taiwan, its textual elements adjusted accordingly. More broadly viewed, all translations are recontextualizations since the source text is removed to new cultural, linguistic, and hermeneutic contexts, but adaptive translations recast textual elements in a more daring manner. Even though they never shed completely the traces of the original text, they do not work on the principle of semantic equivalence, which also marks them off from nonadaptive translations.

Considered the foremost of Taiwan's "First-Generation architects," Wang Dahong left behind him a wealth of biographical information and personal commentary that help us judge how Oscar Wilde's "intentions" may have been displaced by his own in the adapted novel. Concerning *Du Liankui*, which took him ten years to complete, Wang said at a recent interview that he hoped it would exhort the younger generation "not to seek wealth and prosperity, for they are like passing clouds," but "to practice abstinence and restraint in all matters" (Shyu 2007: 19). He Sinicizes the names of major characters from *The Picture of Dorian Gray*, converts places in England into well-known locales in Taipei, and invents rough Taiwanese equivalents for items of material and cultural life in Wilde's tale of nineteenth-century British upper-class affluence. The changes are meant to give readers an impression of the life of the *nouveaux riches* in 1970s Taiwan; it is a world replete with fashionable conveniences and enticing commodities. The substitution of one way of life (English) by another (Taiwanese) is a strategy for recontextualizing the source novel.

Perhaps of greater significance are some apparently minor changes to the plot. Wang turns Sibyl, with whom Dorian is infatuated because she is "a pretty boy" in the original novel, into a female singer at a dance-hall, thereby making the relationship a heterosexual one. He also deletes the reference to the "yellow book" (Joris Karl Huysmans's *À Rebours*, "the Bible of Decadence" given to Dorian by Lord Henry) as well as a lengthy passage in Chapter 11, which is replete with allusions to key figures in Roman homosexual history and Greek personages of ill repute because of their promiscuity. Wang substitutes for this passage Du Liankui's (Dorian's counterpart) travels to London, Paris, Cannes, and so on—cities that he delights in comparing to Taipei. Whereas the reader of the original will interpret Dorian as the latest in a long line of exemplary decadents and homosexuals in the West, in the adaptation the gay implications of the story are done away with. At the same time, Wang introduces Chinese culture and history into his adaptation, including allusions to real or fictitious figures like Jia Baoyu (hero of *Dream of the Red Chamber*), Pan An (medieval paragon of male beauty), Li Bai and Li Yu (both Chinese poets), and Empress Dowager Cixi (1835–1908).[13] Clearly Wang intends to impose his own reinterpretation on Wilde's novel, as his friend Gao Xinjiang points out in the preface to the book:

> People may not easily recognize the materialistic world accurately depicted in the translation . . . one cannot ask them to ponder the corruption and decline of civilizations, or the evil of human nature. These are things occurring to Taiwan as it becomes increasingly materialist and sophisticated. (qtd. Wang 1977: 2)

Thus *Du Liankui* becomes an indictment of materialistic trends in Taiwan, uncovering the capitalistic greed that accompanies rapid economic progress. The infiltration of Western lifestyles into Taiwan, when it enjoyed the boon of the Asian Economic Miracle, was believed by Wang to be the cause of moral degeneration on the island.

More recently, Richard Rong-bin Chen has delved further into the "local" meanings of *Du Liankui* against the background of 1970s Taiwan. Using Mikhail Bakhtin's concept of the chronotope, which is "the intrinsic connectedness of temporal and spatial relationships that are artistically expressed in literature" (qtd. Chen 2012: 165), Chen elaborates on the subtle shift that Wang Dahong has effected by transforming London's East End–West End contrast in the original text into the juxtaposition of East Taipei against West Taipei, which symbolizes the confrontation between affluence and degeneration. In reframing the story in this way, according to Chen, Wang also deletes Wilde's references to English fin-de-siècle decadence, the unrefined manners of the middle-class in England, and so on. What Wang has achieved is the creation of a premonitory "Taipei fable" in which the "Soul engages in a full-scale transaction with unrestrained Desire . . . ready

---

[13] For a more detailed analysis of all of Wang Dahong's textual modifications, see Chan (2010: 61–83).

to sell itself in exchange for the beautiful and fashionable, for wealth and knowledge, so long as it stands in the forefront. Faustus from the West has arrived in Taipei" (Luo 2006: 36). Whether Wang has intended this reading is perhaps irrelevant, for beyond doubt the adaptation engenders a new interpretation of Wilde's story, now transposed to a Taiwanese setting.

The Appeal of Lin Shu's Translations

It should be obvious by now that receptivity is a key to the use of adaptive strategies. It not only clues us to the motivation for the alterations; it is also a measure of the success of the adjustments made. A revealing case in the Sino-foreign context is that of Lin Shu (1852–1924), who, with his collaborators, churned out over a hundred adaptations, mostly of Western literary classics, in the early years of the twentieth century. In Chapter 2, we saw his departures from Aesop's fables, but even more blatant are those in his translated novels, which exhibit the following features (cf. Compton 1971: 206–14):

(1) words and phrases are not given equivalents in the adapted text;
(2) images replace commonplace expressions found in the original;
(3) extra words and phrases are freely added to enhance the flow of the text;
(4) many details are omitted, including proper names and background information (transliterations are also kept to a minimum); and
(5) paraphrase is used where the literal meaning is not rendered.

These changes to the original have been variously explained. One explanation, advanced by his biographers, is that Lin translated at great speed most of the time, in order to meet deadlines. He is said to have been in desperate need of the money derived from the sale of his translations. Another is that because Lin did not have a mastery of the foreign languages he was translating from, which ranged from English, French, Spanish, and Japanese to Russian, he relied on the oral, vernacular translations of his collaborators—working in the "tandem translation" mode (Hill 2013: 32–6)—so a literal rendition was difficult to achieve. Both of these explanations contain some truth, but more to the point is that Lin's textual adjustments were meant to create a readable version for readers accustomed to Chinese fictional genres but unfamiliar with Western ones. After all, the appeal of adaptations often cannot be dissociated from the accommodations made to pander to the target readership, which, in the final analysis, is the primary "ecological" factor. This can best be illustrated by the evaluation of an admirer of Lin Shu's adaptations. Quoted at some length here is how the polymath Qian Zhongshu described his response as a reader in "The Translations of Lin Shu":

> Recently, I happened to be flipping the pages of one of the novels translated by Lin, and to my surprise it had not lost its attraction. Not only did I read the book through, I went on to read another, and still another, until I had re-read a major portion of the Lin translations. I found most of them to be worth re-reading, notwithstanding the omissions and errors encountered at every turn. When I tried reading a later—and doubtless more accurate—translation of the same book, it gave me the feeling that I would rather read the original. This is most intriguing. Of course, for one who is capable of reading the original, to check through a deficient translation might be an amusing pastime. Some say that the more outrageous the translation the more fascinating it reads: when we check it against the original, we see how the translator lets his imagination run wild and how he uses guesswork to fill out the blanks in his comprehension, freely inventing and distorting, almost in the manner of a surrealist poet. But my interest in the Lin translations emphatically does not lie in any searching for boners to make fun of. Nor are the infidelities and "misrepresentations" in Lin's translations due entirely to linguistic deficiency on the part of his assistants. (trans. George Kao; Chan 2004: 107)

Worth noting here is not just Qian Zhongshu's decided preference for Lin's versions, which he prized above the translations in circulation. Interestingly, Qian also expressed his unmitigated fondness for precisely those parts where Lin departed from the original text. Even checking Lin's version against the source text does not lessen admiration for the adaptor; hence the paradoxical statement, "the more outrageous the translation the more fascinating it reads." Placed in context, Qian has inadvertently provided personal testimony to the allure of adaptations: they far exceed more "faithful" translations because they fit comfortably into, and are part of, their target environment.

Re-evaluating Adaptations

As should be obvious by now, the aforementioned adaptive translations in China, Japan, and Korea over the centuries have flourished alongside more source-text-bound ones, but there is no evidence that the former have been viewed as inadequate or undesirable. In Western literary theory, it is an accepted notion that the Romantic Movement led to the "retreat" from adaptive practices for a long time. If different kinds of transtextual rewriters are seen as differently motivated, then the appearance of both literal and liberal versions of even the same source text would not have been otherwise than natural. Apparently, the weight of proof shows that adaptive translations take more risks but are less restrained. The privileging of fidelity is the root cause of the phenomenon of "the rise of translation" in modern times. Such an attitude came to affect East Asia (as elsewhere) when the three countries there, hitherto existing in their own intertextual web, were opened up to the West in a process that began in the nineteenth century.

As a method, adaptation has had fluctuating fortunes, in both East and West. In his study referred to earlier, Miller compares the dichotomous stances of the Germans and the French—who historically leaned toward literalism and liberalism in translation, respectively—that underlie a fundamental theoretical opposition (Miller 2001). The preference for literalism was a product of the Romantic Movement in Germany, with its emphasis on inventiveness in artistic expression; in contrast, the liberal rendering of a text is looked upon as betrayal. In the twentieth century, again the literal method was eulogized by Walter Benjamin, whose advocacy of the extreme form of literalism (viz. interlinear translation) in "The Task of the Translator" (1923) has by now become almost a dogma in Western translation thought. On the other hand, the liberal, adaptive method also dominated in crucial periods in Western translation history. It was associated especially with the French, being the preferred approach during the French enlightenment. Miller has noted how the era of free translations in France only concluded with "the French turn towards literal translation following the example of the German Romanticists" (2002: 141). Unfortunately, then, the question as to why these shifts in taste occurred can only be answered with reference to Western intellectual or conceptual history. With regard to China, one can understand the rise to prominence of the literal method there around the second decade of the twentieth century along similar lines. The trend set in under the impact of no less a prominent translation theorist and practitioner than Lu Xun, for whom literal translations could inject foreign linguistic structures and expressions into the Chinese language, which desperately needed to be enriched at the time. From then on, the pendulum in the Chinese translation scene has swung toward the fidelity pole. Hardline literalists were in fact so emboldened that Lin Shu—the epitome of the adaptive method—was subject, in his later years, to some harsh criticisms and his translations disparaged for their scandalous deviations from the originals. In effect, the two modes—literalism (faithfulness) and liberalism (infidelity)—have taken turns as one advances and the other retreats in tandem with the tides of historical necessity.

An inclusive attitude to adaptive strategies makes possible an expanded concept of translation that incorporates scenarios where it performs other functions—those of accommodation and appropriation—than those conventionally attributed to it, like communication and information transfer. Enhanced acceptance of unfaithfulness is what is needed for future development of this research field. The existence of infidelities in adaptations compels us to confront and question the uncontested rule that the translated or rewritten text be a faithful replication or an exact mimetic copy. At the same time, pursuing this line of argument, one can see that the translator can play other roles than those traditionally ascribed to him—as an adaptor, an imitator, a manipulator, an intruder—and not the mechanical decoder, unerring mouthpiece, and faithful stand-in. Despite the special character of adaptations, in which the elements of domestication, acculturation, and reinterpretation are foregrounded, they still fall within the ambit of translation as broadly conceived. The adaptor is given free rein to modify, adjust, and interfere with, as well as tease out the meanings, apparent and latent, in the source text. By making space for adaptation as a component area of translation studies, we can enrich the latter and free it from the clutches of literal or faithful translation, which, while pedagogically justified, does not reflect actual practice, especially that of historical East Asia.

The conventional approach to translation, which puts a premium on equivalence in either value or meaning between source and target texts, is characterized by an inevitable bias against adaptations by its very nature. Inaccuracies in translation and departures from the original have customarily been singled out by translation commentators for censure. However, the increased prominence of concepts like "transposition," "transmutation," and "transcreation" today means that a subtle shift has occurred, as a result of which adaptations can be rethought and re-evaluated. Together with this, some older views about adaptation should be revisited. For example, it may be thought that, since adaptations are oriented toward the target culture and audience, they necessarily make for smooth and effortless reception, and are therefore less challenging. Yet, in view of the range of examples of adaptive translation cited above, it is perhaps time that we reviewed individual cases of adaptations to see ways in which they can be subversive and resistant, rather than tame and conformist. Since there are many instances where textual alterations give rise to reinterpretations, it should be said that adapters can also serve as active interventionists of the kind espoused in postmodern translation theory. Much work indeed remains to be done to unravel the amazingly complex "networking of languages and literary and cultural imaginaries" (Weiss 2004: 123) embodied in the amazing varieties of adaptive translations in the West and in the Far East. The next chapter presents one example of the latter.

6

Boys over Flowers

Localization in a Web of (Re)adaptations

A sizeable number of adaptation scholars have recently moved beyond literary products to focus on media materials, an example of the latter being those of East Asian popular culture, which have circulated with great momentum under the successive "waves" of Japanese and Korean TV dramas. Analyses of the phenomenon have concentrated on how Japanese, and then Korean, productions have impacted Greater China, especially Taiwan and Hong Kong, primarily the "trendy" love dramas. Two points are worth noting in this respect. First, the preponderant concern in these analyses is the reason for the spectacular successes achieved by these media products. With regard to this, views are divided between those who champion the "cultural proximity" thesis, stressing the close links between the three East Asian traditions, and those who uphold the "quest for modernity" thesis, viewing the upbeat, fashionable lifestyles depicted in the dramas as the root appeal for a middle-class Westernized audience.[1] Second, and more importantly, most Japanese and Korean dramas were adaptations of preexisting manga. They were so successful that they not only transformed TV drama production outside the countries of origin but also spawned further adaptations. Not surprisingly, therefore, in the scholarly literature one sees illuminating echoes of terms repeatedly deployed in adaptation studies, like manipulation, appropriation, and remediation. On top of this, localization, regionalization, and globalization serve as key elements of the transnational phenomenon in question.

Doubtlessly, one clue to the Japanization and Koreanization of Chinese-speaking communities effected through the two "waves" is to be found in theories of adaptation. Anthony Fung has attempted an analysis of the homologies between Hong Kong and Japanese TV soap operas (Fung 2007), whereas Wen Zhaoxia studies how Japanese and Korean "idol dramas" have

---

[1] On the Japanese Wave, see Nakano (2002), Cui (2010), and Lee (2004); on the Korean Wave, see Leung (2004) and Mori (2008).

led Mainland China to produce adaptations of her own (Wen 2006).[2] One problem is seen in some scholars' views of the reasons for the TV dramas' success with audiences from varying cultural backgrounds: they do not see the phenomenon in question as different from other kinds of intra-East Asian media traffic. Worse, while some attention has been devoted to the historical and social circumstances that inform these cultural productions, few researchers have focused squarely on the strategies deployed by the adaptors (like changes in plot, structure, and characterization) to enhance reception by audiences outside of the countries of origin. The present chapter reviews the many TV versions of *Boys over Flowers*—adapted from Kamio Yōko's immensely popular, thirty-six-volume manga series (Kamio 1992–2004)—to highlight the fact that some East Asianization processes need to be unraveled from an adaptive perspective, with the transtextual elements placed at the core.

One study of the Japanese and Korean waves can be singled out here for special mention. Lee Dong-Hoo has discussed how the inflow of Japanese TV trendy drama has given rise to Korean adaptations in the 1990s (Lee 2004: 251–74). Beginning with *Jealousy* (1992), she lists fifteen such examples, which are "suspected" of having copied Japanese versions (2004: 259). She focuses on the outrageous cases of *Chongchun*, condemned for its plagiarism of *Love Generation,* and of *Jealousy,* which is strikingly similar to *Tokyo Love Story* (Lee 2004: 267–71). Lee refers to the Korean versions as "adaptations": from time to time terms such as "transplant," "copies," and "plagiarism" are deployed, but basically she puts the examples she cites in the category of "transnational adaptations" (Lee 2004: 260, 266). However, other than the fact that only intramedial (rather than intermedial) modifications are involved, these cases evidently belong to a different category than *Boys over Flowers*, whose indebtedness to the source manga is acknowledged and for which copyright permission was obtained prior to production. Notably, most Korean producers of TV dramas at the time who borrowed from Japanese ones—like Lee Seung-Ryul (*Jealousy*), Auh Jong-Rok (*Happy Together*) and Zang Ki-Hong (*Tomato*)—denied any link between their works and the Japanese counterparts. While the adaptive nature of their work remains indisputable, their refusal to concede any linkage to predecessor TV productions means that they may appropriately be characterized as a different class of "adaptations"—or better still, as "imitations."

In any case, in most adapted TV dramas, there is much evidence of localized content and style. This is seen in all the transnational adaptations

---

[2] Of course these are adaptations in the same medium, one of two categories of adaptation addressed in this chapter—the other being intermedial ones.

and re-adaptations of *Boys over Flowers*. As the manga travels successfully to Taiwan, Mainland China, and South Korea in adapted forms,[3] it betrays a subtle privileging of the indigenous over the foreign. Anthony Pym opposes localization—making a product "linguistically and culturally appropriate to the target locale (country/region and language) where it will be used and sold" (Pym 2004: 29)—against "internationalization," which eradicates cultural differences instead of prizing them. This can be observed not only in adaptation, but also in written forms of translation with strong localizing tendencies, like dubbing. While often discussed in relation to translation for business, localization has assumed new importance in translation theory in general because of the advent of the international lingua franca, English, with its power to erase differences. Of course, adaptations can acknowledge the foreign by keeping certain elements of the originals unchanged, but it is in their active reshaping of their sources to suit local conditions that their strength is most keenly felt. Pym's view is that internationalization should be properly balanced by localization so that the two can work in a complementary manner. In the face of intense internationalization, localization can give the receptors what may be perceived as "the home product."[4] Such a binarism applies well to East Asian TV drama adaptations too, although (as we shall see) some slight qualification is in order: rather than the "localization of the global," localizing the *regional* is the order of the day.

Adaptations and Readaptations, Intermedial and Intramedial

The Original Japanese Manga (1992–)[5]

Boys over Flowers attained enormous success soon after it came out, becoming one of the bestselling *shōjo* manga (girls' comics) at the turn of the twenty-first century, along with such popular titles as *Nana* (2000) and *Fruits Basket* (*Furūtsu Basuketto*, 1999). It features Makino, a girl from a lowly family

---

[3] All textual references are made to Kamio Yōko's *Hana yori dango* (1992–).
[4] An alternative possibility is to think of "interlocalization" in the interaction between three major cultures of East Asia, all deploying "minoritized" languages: Chinese, Korean, and Japanese.
[5] The date given here is that of the publication of the first manga installment. Sequels to the story have appeared right up to the present. Similar continuations can be seen in the TV productions—for example, **Meteor Garden** was followed by **Meteor Garden II** (2002)—so that, taken together, we have a web of (literal) translations, adaptations, and (free) imitations.

who gets admitted to an elitist high school, but, because she stands up for a classmate, starts to be harassed by a group of four bullies who call themselves "Flower Four" (F4). However, Dōmyōji, the leader of the gang, gradually falls for her, though his love is unrequited at first because Makino has developed strong feelings for another gang member, the handsome but detached Hanazawa. On top of this love triangle, there are subplots that revolve around the other two members of the group, Nishikado, the playboy who is incredibly fond of traditional Japanese tea ceremonies, and Mimasaka, the peacemaker whose family has connections with the Japanese underground. In the main plot, matters come to a head when the hero declares his love for the heroine, although it takes a while for Makino to accept the relationship and change her mind about Dōmyōji, who is alienated from her in terms of class and social rank. As is common to these teenage romances, further obstacles are put in the way, in this case from a domineering mother, who tries in various ways to break up the couple. It is only when Makino enters the Dōmyōji household as a maid that the mother slowly comes to approve of her as her son's choice.

It can readily be seen, from the brief synopsis given above, that although the story features some universal themes in teenage romances, there is much that is not amenable to transference to non-Japanese contexts, even within East Asia. It is not surprising that adaptation methods are ubiquitously deployed when the story is transmitted to places outside of Japan. Apparently, the class issues can be appreciated by its two neighbors in the East Asian region, but culture-specific references, like those to family businesses of the well-to-do in Japan, pose barriers to direct transposition and therefore need to be altered. Above all, the abundant depictions of sex and violence in the original manga have to be drastically adjusted, or deleted, for transmission. For instance, near the beginning of *Boys over Flowers,* there is a scene that suggests gang rape, when male students at Eitoku High School, acting under the orders of Flower Four, chase after Makino, catch her and pin her to the floor, only to be stopped when Hanazawa shows up. The difficulties in moving these plot features, along with the Japanese characters and value systems, to other parts of East Asia are obvious.

Meteor Garden (Taiwan, 2001)

Fujii Shōzō's conception of the "clockwise expansion of a shared East Asian culture," introduced to explain how Murakami Haruki's *Norwegian Wood* traveled to Korea, Taiwan, Hong Kong, and the Chinese Mainland (Fujii 2007: 75–9), is applicable to the reception history of *Boys over Flowers*. Immediately after the manga's initial publication in 1992, a verbal (i.e., written) translation into Chinese was published in Taiwan, but in terms of impact it can hardly be compared to the many East Asian live-action TV adaptations in its wake. The first of these, the Taiwanese TV drama series *Meteor Garden*, aired in twenty-seven episodes, caused a sensation when it premiered in 2001 and gave instantaneous fame to the boys' band (F4, or "Flower Four") playing the four bullies. In this intermedial (manga into TV drama) adaptation, localization strategies are deployed at several levels. First, Eitoku High School, the setting for the romance between the story's heroine and her superrich boyfriend, is removed to a university campus in Taiwan; this makes more plausible the outrageous adult behavior of the unruly gang. The *kanji* (Chinese characters) in the Japanese names are mostly retained and pronounced as they should be in Chinese. For instance, "Dōmyōji Tsukasa" becomes "Dao Mingsi"; "Hanazawa Rui" is turned into "Hua Zelei," though "Hua" is not a common Chinese surname. The heroine is given a well-known Chinese surname (Dong), while her first name has a semantic link to the original Japanese word "Tsukushi," which means "weed."[6] A list of the characters' names as adapted into the three East Asian languages is given in Table 6.1. (The Chinese characters are shared by the Taiwanese and Japanese versions, but not used in the Korean one.)

Other than the name changes, the Taiwanese version freely interpolates "local" Taiwanese elements, including a profusion of popular colloquialisms used by the younger generation at the time. It also refers occasionally to

Table 6.1 Names of Characters in the Japanese, Taiwanese, and Korean Versions

Japanese	Taiwanese	Korean
牧野つくし Makino Tsukushi	董杉菜 Dong Sancai	甘艾草(금잔디) Geum Jan Di
道明寺司 Dōmyōji Tsukasa	道明寺 Dao Mingsi	瞿峻珀(구준표) Gu Jun Pyo
花沢類 Hanazawa Rui	花澤類 Hua Zelei	尹梓皓(윤지후) Yoon Ji Hoo
西門総二郎 Nishikado Sōjirō	西門 Ximen	蘇堯政(소이정) Soo Yi Jung
美作あきら Mimasaka Akira	美作 Meizuo	宋佑彬(송우빈) Song Yoo Bin

[6] There are actually two Korean names given to the female protagonist. "Jan Di" means "grass," while at one point in the drama Gu Jun Pyo confuses it with "Jap Cho," meaning "weed."

sensational current affairs (like the marriage of President Chen Shui-bian's daughter) and alters the venues in which some of the events take place. As far as the heroine's part-time job is concerned, whereas in the original Makino works in a shop selling Japanese delicacies, in the Taiwanese version Sancai is employed in a Western-style bakery, of the kind that sprang up and spread widely across Taiwan in the mid-1990s. Deleted from the original are the parts about the beauty pageant and a young woman undergoing cosmetic surgery. The use of coffee shops as a backdrop for much of the action in this adapted TV drama is another noticeable change. All these adaptations are meant to give color to the teenage love drama, relocated to a Taiwanese context that viewers can immediately relate to.

When the series was dubbed in Cantonese for Hong Kong viewers a year later, its success was repeated for a different audience, despite the fact that more fast-paced and action-packed narratives on TV are usually preferred there. In fact, owing to the divergence in taste, Taiwanese TV dramas rarely took up prime-time slots on Hong Kong's TV channels, and *Meteor Garden* was an exception. Thus, even before it entered Mainland China, the drama series had ignited great interest in its periphery. It finally took China by storm when aired on Hunan Satellite station in 2002. Its popularity was so overwhelming that, after only six episodes, the State Administration of Radio, Film, and Television (SARFT) ordered that the broadcast be halted on grounds that it "misleads our youths" just as the four great classical Chinese novels did: *Three Kingdoms* promoted factional rivalry; *Water Margin*, triad activity; *Journey to the West*, feudal superstition; and *Dream of the Red Chamber*, puppy love (Yamashita 2007: 140).[7] Similar successes were reported farther afield beyond the East Asian region, in the Philippines, Indonesia, and Thailand, where versions dubbed in the local Chinese dialects (like Cantonese) enjoyed spectacular receptions by the overseas Chinese community, as evidenced by record-breaking viewing ratings reported everywhere. In both the Philippines and Indonesia, *Meteor Garden* was the most popular TV drama ever, while in Thailand it was reported that a fad for learning Chinese was kindled after the series was broadcast on there in 2003.

Two TV Versions in Japan (1995; 2005)

Back in Japan, an intermedial (manga into TV drama) adaptation, starring teen idols Tanihara Shosuki and Uchida Yuki and produced by Toei Tokyo,

---

[7] For an account of the story of the censorship of *Meteor Garden* by the Chinese authorities, see Yamashita (2007: 129–41).

had appeared as early as 1995, though it was hardly the sensation that the later adaptations and readaptations in the other East Asian countries were.[8] It failed to cross national or cultural boundaries—not even in dubbed versions—and was virtually unknown outside Japan, quite the opposite of *Meteor Garden*. There is also no indication that the Taiwanese producer (Angie Chai) and director (Cai Yuexun) of *Meteor Garden* even made any use of it in their version. In 2005, perhaps as a response to the success of Chai/Cai's adaptation, the Japanese station TBS produced another TV drama series based on the manga. It met with great success locally—an example of outside success fueling audience interest back home—and also when it was "exported" overseas, in dubbed and subtitled versions, to non-Japanese communities in Asia. It was a much shorter version, consisting of only nine episodes and starring Matsumoto Jun, the lead singer from the pop group Arashi. But despite this, it still paled beside *Meteor Garden* as far as reception went. The dampened interest in Japanese TV drama at the turn of the twenty-first century, when the Japanese Wave was overtaken by the Korean Wave, must have been a contributing cause. While a case of transmedial adaptation involving a shift in medium, however, it bears few traces of cultural manipulation: it is, after all, a "local" production without the need for localization.

Let's Go Watch the Meteor Shower (PRC, 2009) and a Remake of *Meteor Garden* (PRC, 2018)

The next stage in the afterlife of Kamio's manga was marked by a Mainland Chinese TV version, *Let's Go Watch the Meteor Shower*. Produced by Hunan Satellite, the station that had run into difficulties with the censors in 2002, it was aired in 2009 in all the major cities of China, including Beijing, Guangzhou, Shanghai, Tianjin, and Chongqing, with over-the-top viewership ratings. This adaptation is probably the most localized version of them all.[9] It can be characterized as an intramedial adaptation, given its obvious indebtedness to the influential Taiwanese TV version. Besides the use of a rather different title, the characters are thoroughly Sinicized, being given Chinese surnames like Murong, Duanmu, and Shangguan (see Table 6.2, middle column). The Chinese background is accentuated, and the entire drama was shot on location in Xiamen University of Fujian

---

[8] There was also a TV anime adaptation of fifty-one episodes produced by Toei Animation Company, aired from 1996–7. Generally faithful to the original, it was subsequently dubbed in Cantonese (for ATV) and Mandarin (for TTV) for broadcasting in Hong Kong and Taiwan, respectively.

[9] At the time, despite its popular acceptance, there was strong Chinese reaction against the Japanese and Korean Waves at the time, expressed in newspaper articles like He (2005).

province. The sexually explicit material (like the kissing and caressing scenes), as well as the violent content in the adapted Taiwanese version, were deleted, ostensibly to satisfy the censors, since the official stance had remained unclear ever since the censorship of *Meteor Garden* barely seven years earlier. At interviews the Hunan producer Ren Yaojia insisted that *Let's Go Watch* was an original piece of work, although the parallels with its predecessor are blatant. With major roles played by winners in the well-known talent singing contest "Super Boy" hosted annually by Hunan Satellite, this "idol drama"—a new genre on the Mainland—captivated the teenage audience, despite the spate of criticisms that it also incurred. Paradoxically enough, one point of contention revolved around the failure to successfully accommodate the "foreign" work to a Chinese context. The adaptation, in other words, was seen by some as insufficiently localized. Comparing it with the Korean version, one commentator saw the latter as a more endearing adaptation, "aesthetically satisfying yet shot through with humor as well as a sense of real life experienced" (Dong 2012: 94). Albeit on a smaller scale, the same trajectory of success associated with *Meteor Garden* was repeated by *Let's Go Watch*. The key actors rose rapidly to stardom; audience rating records were broken, one after another; and associated products like soundtracks, CDs, and DVDs flooded the Chinese market.

Concerning this Mainland version, some "foreign" elements were obviously carried over from the Taiwanese adaptation, which was in turn based on the Japanese manga. The hero, Murong Yuhai, has curly hair, which is his "trademark" in the manga. Also he speaks Chinese awkwardly like Dōmyōji, but this is explained by noting that he is an Australian-born Chinese returning to the Mainland for schooling. Duanmu Lei, the heroine's initial love interest, has wavy, dyed golden hair. Both male leads, therefore, have a feminine, pretty-boy look, and in outward appearance they reflect a degree of non-Chineseness, departing from indigenous Chinese TV dramas in the same genre. On the whole, however, "local" elements dominate. The heroine's mother is the owner of a cafeteria, the Mainland Chinese equivalent to the small business run by her Taiwan counterpart. The bullying culture at school also figures in this adaptation, though no violence is presented. In the Japanese and Taiwanese "originals," references to virginity and abortion are conspicuous, while in the manga Nishikado is portrayed as a womanizer with many sexual escapades. All these are removed from the Chinese re-adaptation. In episode 23, Shangguan Duanqian, Nishikado's counterpart in the Chinese story, and his girlfriend book into a hotel room, but in no time at all the audience realizes that they are just playing a prank on the lead couple.

Plot-wise, one major difference between *Let's Go Watch* and its Japanese and Taiwanese pre-versions is seen in the account of how the heroine gets admitted to college in spite of her lower-class background. While both the earlier stories present the heroine's parents as snobbish money-diggers hopeful that their daughter will find a rich husband at the elite school, the Mainland adaptation shows Chu being motivated by a desire to improve her own prospects. The critique of money-minded seniors in the Japanese and Taiwanese versions does not inform either the Chinese or the Korean adaptations. Nevertheless, all three show the youths resisting their parents or guardians, symbolized to a greater or lesser degree by the figure of the scheming, domineering mother of Dōmyōji, though for different reasons. In *Let's Go Watch*, for instance, the gang H4 ("Handsome Four") is held together by the four rogues' shared reluctance to have their future careers carved out for them by their parents; they resort to all manner of mischievous behavior so they can be expelled from school. This is a little unexpected, since bullying would have been a taboo subject in China, but the generation gap problem must have figured as worthy of serious attention. On the whole, given the preponderance of plot elements it has taken over from the Japanese manga (like the love triangle, the conflicts between love and friendship, etc.), the disclaimer of the director simply cannot be trusted. Many of the deviations from the two source texts should be seen as an attempt to adapt to a new environment so that it can become palatable to the audience.

The story of the tangled web of adaptation and re-adaptation does not end here, however. In 2018, a second live-action Chinese adaptation of *Boys over Flowers*—also called *Meteor Garden*—was aired by Hunan Satellite station. Billed as a more faithful adaptation of the original Japanese manga, this version is more of a remake by Angie Chai of her previous, hugely successful work of the same name. Judging from the major protagonists' names, which keep nearly all the *kanji* from the source text (see Table 6.2, right column), it shows an effort to adhere more closely to the Japanese original. While the deviations are less pronounced, they are mostly introduced for the purpose of creating a "cleaner" version: the main lead is a high-flyer at Mingde University; F4's bullying of Dong Sancai is carried out on the Web, rather than physically; the attempted rape of Sancai in the original and the Taiwanese and Korean adaptations are deleted; there is no reference to the boys' clubbing and womanizing activities; the use of abusive language, which abounds in the Taiwanese version, is altogether absent. Sancai seeks admission to the elite university out of a desire to learn how to manage a business, as her mother has opened a restaurant for homemade cuisine. As the scriptwriter Fang Hui has said, many of these departures from earlier versions were carried out in accordance with the SARFT instructions on "no showing off on one's wealth; no references to money; no income gap; no bullying; no fighting" (https://www.zaobao.com/zentertainment/movies-and-tv/story20180712-874667).

Table 6.2 Names of Characters in *Let's Go Watch the Meteor Shower* (2009) and *Meteor Garden* (2018)

Japanese Names in the Original	Chinese Version 1 (Let's Go Watch)	Chinese Version 2 (Meteor Garden)
Makino Tsukushi	楚雨蕁 Chu Yuxun	董杉菜 Dong Sancai
Dōmyōji Tsukasa	慕容雲海 Murong Yunhai	道明寺 Dao Mingsi
Hanazawa Rui	端木磊 Duanmu Lei	花澤類 Hua Zelei
Nishikado Sōjirō	上官瑞謙 Shangguan Duanqian	彥西門 Yan Simen
Mimasaka Akira	葉爍 Ye Shuo	馮美作 Feng Meizuo

While this might be considered a tamer adaptation, the audience ratings were still high and those actors playing the lead roles were also propelled to stardom instantaneously.

Flower-like Boys (South Korea, 2009)[10]

In another bid to capitalize on the popularity of this manga, South Korea's KBS produced a fifty-two-episode TV adaptation in 2009, the same year that saw the first Mainland Chinese adaptation. The name of the heroine is Koreanized as Geum Jan Di; the leader of the Gang of Four and heir to the global corporation, Shin-Hwa Group, is renamed Gu Jun Pyo. In a similar move as the first *Meteor Garden* and *Let's Go Watch*, from episode 13 onwards the Korean adaptors of *Flower-like Boys* situate the story in a university, which furnishes a justifiable context for a story that is at times quite racy. Other evidence of localization abounds, but most significant are the changes made to the image of the family in the story. First, in the new adaptation Yoon Ji Hoo, the counterpart of Hanazawa, was orphaned when his parents died in a car accident; this piece of family history deviates from the original

---

[10] In the present chapter, *Flower-like Boys* is used as the title of the Korean adaptation, to distinguish it from the Japanese manga, officially translated as *Boys over Flowers*. For a synopsis of the story, see the Wikipedia article: http://en.wikipedia.org/wiki/Boys_Over_Flowers.

tale. Second, the heroine is offered a place in the elitist high school after she prevents a student from committing suicide; in the original Makino applies for admission to Eitoku High School because she wants to be near Tōdō, the rich heiress whom she adores. Incidentally, in sharp contrast to both is the unflattering portrayal of the family in the Taiwan version, in which the Cinderella-like heroine from a lowly background is forced by her parents to enroll in the elitist university because of the chance it gives for her (and her family) to move up the social ladder.

As much as the Taiwanese and the first Mainland Chinese adaptations foreground their respective cultures, *Flower-like Boys* showcases the lifestyle of the Koreans quite deliberately. It opens by introducing Shin-Hwa High School through a news report on its founder, the father of the hero Gu Jun Pyo. This is immediately followed by the sensational suicide of a bullied student as the audience watches a blood-smeared Lee Min Ha jumping off a building. The incident is witnessed by Guem Jan Di, who happens to be delivering laundry for the dry cleaner that her family owns. She works part-time at a congee shop, hardly a common establishment in Japan. Soo Yi Jung (the womanizer) belongs to a prestigious family engaged in the ceramics business, in contrast to his counterpart in the Japanese original, whose family organizes tea ceremonies. Besides showing people in their workaday roles, other elements of Korean culture, like religion, etiquette, and leisure activities (e.g., horse riding), are tactfully woven into the drama, where they are mixed with an array of Korean songs, high-end Korean fashion, and lavish settings, both interior and exterior.

The success of *Flower-like Boys* followed very much the path trodden by its predecessors. By the seventh week it had surpassed its fierce competitor, *East of Eden*, a drama series broadcast on another Korean channel in the same prime-time slot. It also got some unprecedentedly high viewers ratings (35.7 percent in Seoul and 35.5 percent in the country as a whole) in the course of two and a half months. The main actors, especially Lee Min Ho, the male lead, soon attained super-stardom and won a spate of acting awards. An avalanche of side-products, like original soundtracks and CDs featuring songs by the four male actors, was put into the teenager consumer market. The feverish adoration of the main male characters assumed unexpected proportions as young South Korean men started to pay greater attention to personal grooming and imitated the gestures and mannerisms of the characters. Males started to wear make-up, put on the flashy clothing of F4, and give excessive attention to accessories. Even the filming locations of the drama series have been turned into overseas tourist destinations for viewers from other parts of East Asia.

Seiko Yasumoto has carried out her empirically based research on the Taiwanese and Korean adaptations. Through a combination of textual analysis and qualitative survey methods (including the use of surveys and focus group discussions), she addresses the question of whether the TV adaptations in Japan, Taiwan, and Korea exemplify regional harmonization, whereby the discovered commonalities show shared views by the three communities, or the unavoidable existence of hybridism in East Asia, seen in the differences between the individual versions. While she notes that cultural harmonization is made possible by the adaptations—a position supported by the views she collected from her interviewees—her text-based analysis of the variant versions in fact tells a slightly different story. The fact that many culture-specific idiomatic expressions in the Japanese manga are totally eliminated from the Taiwanese and Korean adaptations (2015: 119–24) shows the importance of localization strategies used by the scriptwriters (Angie Chai in Taiwan and Yoon Ji-Ryun in Korea) and the difficulty of finding equivalences for cultural elements that are deeply ingrained in Japanese culture. Yasumoto further notes how the "Japanese odor" of the manga becomes diluted in the Taiwanese and Korean adaptations; in Japan's own adaptation it is as strong as ever.

According to Yasumoto, the thematic resemblances between the three versions can lend support to the harmonization thesis, which is in turn based on a perception of "cultural proximity" between the three East Asian countries. Nevertheless, her list of the different "textemes" gives us a glimpse into the range of localization strategies deployed by the Taiwanese and Korean adaptors. With regard to *Meteor Garden* in particular, she mentions two details: (a) the elitist lifestyle portrayed in the original manga is replaced by more mundane, or realistic, circumstances in the Taiwanese version; and (b) the high school setting in the source text is replaced by the campus of a recognizable Taiwanese university setting. In themselves these alterations may not mean much, but given the enormous popularity of *Meteor Garden*, the impact must be seen as crucial. Obviously, they must somehow have generated rapport with the Taiwanese audience. One could say that even minor localizing moves in *Meteor Garden* can contribute to its success. (By contrast, the later versions in Korean and Japanese could have enjoyed the "spill-over" effect of the earlier successes.) Hence, in evaluating the Taiwanese and Korean adaptations, one needs to carefully check the original against the adaptation, taking into special account the adjustments made with an eye to enhancing receptivity. The arguments for the attractiveness of "superior" Japanese culture alone, and for the allure of Western, global culture indirectly conveyed through the Japanese text, do not in themselves explain adequately the two successful adaptations from Taiwan and South Korea.

Features of Manga-Based TV Adaptations

The adaptation of manga like *Boys over Flowers* into Taiwanese and Korean TV drama is only one example of a recurrent formula adopted by East Asian media production companies. A recent publication by Tatsumi Publishing in Tokyo—*Kanryū and Karyū rimeiku dorama* (Inoue 2012)—surveys the current scene of TV drama adaptations of Japanese manga and novels in Taiwan and Korea. Inoue Yuhiko lists the differing degrees of affinity that the TV versions bear to the originals, although there is no mention of how the percentages were arrived at. While most likely these are impressionistic assessments, they are nevertheless helpful in revealing the viewers' perspective. Table 6.3 shows the Taiwanese adaptations assessed. Of these adaptations, only one is based on a novel—Yamazaki Toyoko's *The Great White Tower*; the rest, on Japanese manga. Taiwanese TV producers' efforts at adapting manga contrast sharply, too, with the much lesser interest in Mainland China and Hong Kong.

Comparable to the Taiwanese scene is that of South Korea (see Table 6.4). Three of the items listed were based on Japanese novels rather than manga: Morimura Seiichi's *Human Proof* (1977), Yamazaki Toyoko's *The Great White Tower* (1965), and Nozawa Hisashi's *Love Generation* (1996). Still, the strong

Table 6.3 Major Taiwanese TV Adaptations of Japanese Manga and Novels (Based on Inoue 2012)

Taiwanese Adaptation	Date	Japanese Original	Date	Affinity (%)
Absolute Boyfriend	2012	*Zettai kareshi*	2003	80
Skip Beat!	2011	*Sukippu bīto*	2002	90
Romantic Princess	2007	*Romansu godan katsuyō*	1989	90
Sweet Relationship	2007	*Oishī kankei*	1993	70
The Hospital	2006	*Shiroi kyotō**	1963	-----
For You in Full Bloom#	2006	*Hana zakari no kimitachi e*	1996	90
It Started with a Kiss	2005	*Itazura na Kiss*	1990	90
Mars	2004	*MARS*	1996	95
The Rose	2003	*Bara no tame ni*	1992	80
Tomorrow	2002	*Asunaro hakusho*	1992	70
Meteor Garden	2001	**Hana yori dango**	1992	90

* The original text is a novel.
# English translation given by the author.

Table 6.4 Major Korean TV Adaptations of Japanese Manga and Novels (Based on Inoue 2012)

Korean Adaptation	Date	Japanese Original	Date	Affinity (%)
Dr. Jin	2012	Jin	2000	60
To the Beautiful You	2012	Hana zakari no kimitachi e	1996	-----
City Hunter	2011	Shiteī hantā	1986	60
Royal Family	2011	Ningen no shōmei*	1976	60
Playful Kiss	2010	Itazura na Kiss	1990	80
Master of Study	2009	Doragon sakura	2003	80
Flower-like Boys	2009	**Hana yori dango**	1992	70
I Am Sam	2007	Kyōkasho ni nai-tsu	1995	60
White Tower	2007	Shiroi kyotō*	1963	90
Alone in Love	2006	Ren'ai jidai*	1996	80
101st Proposal	2004	101 kaime puropōzu	1991	90

* The original text is a novel.

preference for adapting manga, especially *shōjo* manga, is obvious. A special case is *Dr. Jin*, which is based on *Jin*, a Japanese manga by Murakami Motoka about the life of the much-loved historical figure Sakamoto Ryōma (1836–1867), a samurai renowned for his role in ousting the Tokugawa Shogunate and thus engineer of Japan's transition from the feudal to the modern age. In the completely Koreanized adaptation, the manga's setting is changed from the Edo period to the Joseon dynasty, and Sakamoto is replaced with the Korean political figure Lee Ha-eung, Regent of Joseon in the 1860s. For Inoue Yohiko, it is the one instance where the original is most radically altered; the affinity rating it received was 60 percent.

To sum up, a few traits can be deduced from a close inspection of TV adaptations modeled on Japanese manga that crossed national boundaries in East Asia at the turn of the present century. First, intermedial and intramedial modes of adaptation have gone hand in hand; some TV versions may have been based on the original manga, others on previous adaptations, and yet others probably on both. Second, the success of an adaptation in one place seems also to be linked to its counterpart's success in another, through some kind of snowballing effect. Several manga have been adapted in quite different ways and enthusiastically received in both Taiwan and South Korea—other than Kamio's *Boys over Flowers*, there are Nakajo Hisaya's *For You in Full Bloom* and Tada Kaoru's *It Started with a Kiss*, to name just the best-loved ones. The extent to which the appeal resides in the original manga as opposed to the adapted work is a question that can only be answered with reference to specific texts in specific contexts. Third, adaptations appear in most instances to "click" better with target audiences than subtitled or dubbed versions imported from the source country (Japan). A case in point is *For You in Full Bloom*, a story about a young girl disguised as a boy in order to attend the school of her athletic dream-lover. The Taiwanese version stars Wu Chun from the Mandopop boy band Fahrenheit, and Ella Chen, the tomboyish pop-singer of the girls' band S.H.E. In the Korean adaptation, Choi Min-ho from the South Korean boy group Shinee plays the male lead. Both adaptations scored spectacular successes with their respective audiences. There exist two Japanese TV versions of this manga series, one produced in 2007 and the other in 2011, but they were not "hits" when exported to the two target communities concerned.[11]

Local, Regional, and Global

Currently, in East Asian TV studies, adaptations appear to be a relatively neglected part of the bustling transnational textual traffic despite research by media and cultural studies scholars on the two "Waves."[12] In studies of the First Wave, it is sometimes said that the success of the Japanese TV "imports" is attributable to the attraction that the Western lifestyle as depicted therein has for the audiences. Globalization is in fact the common cord that many studies strike. This may be true of some "trendy" dramas from Japan and subsequent adaptations that used these as sources, but if viewed closely, the general tendency seems more of an adept use of an East Asianness, as the above discussion has delineated. While global Western values are often visible, more note should be taken of the transferred and transferrable cultural elements in the region. The reduction of intercultural processes to mere globalization, resulting in the disregard for local and regional features, can be redressed if adequate attention is paid to adaptive procedures. Prime mover behind the studies of the two East Asia Waves, Iwabuchi Koichi has emphasized the shortcomings of globalization studies and stresses the distinctiveness of the East Asian situation:

---

[11] Perhaps understandable in terms of contemporary Sino-Japanese relations, Mainland Chinese adaptations of Japanese manga are few and far between in the period under discussion. In Hong Kong, a different scenario exists: many of the adaptations discussed in this section are simply dubbed or subtitled.

[12] See bibliography in Wen (2006). "Translated," "adapted," and "imitated" TV drama in East Asia is a vast subject that awaits adequate research coverage.

"Global" is still apt to be associated with the West, and global–local interactions are mostly considered in terms of how the non-West responds to, resists, imitates, or appropriates the West.... [My book will] fill in the lacuna in the West-centered analysis of cultural globalization by ... attending to ways in which the intra-regional cultural flows forge transnational connections both dialogically and asymmetrically in terms of production, representation, distribution, and consumption. (Iwabuchi 2004: 43–4)

The ebbing of the Japanese Wave, as it was superseded by the Korean Wave since the 1990s, shows some of the weaknesses of the globalization/Westernization argument. Many of the conclusions drawn from the Japanese Wave could be turned on their head when one considers the appeal of the rather different Korean Wave, by which it was eclipsed. The popular Korean dramas are successful for rather different reasons. For instance, the value that the modern West attaches to youthfulness and urban living, said to be the root cause for the success of Japanese TV dramas, cannot explain the appeal of Korean historical dramas. The Korean period drama series *Jewel in the Palace*, in particular, shows the tremendous power of regionalism in the age of the global. It is interesting, too, that the claims concerning the allure of globalization are often based on the references to the material products as shown in Japanese TV dramas (e.g., Sony mobile phones, Mitsubishi washing machines, Sharp cookers, Nissan cars, etc.); what we have attempted to show are the localization processes in adapted TV drama by which the foreign is made familiar. If we look further back, the Japanization-as-globalization thesis is also undercut by the fact that Chinese TV drama, most notably the Taiwan series *Judge Bao*, was received enthusiastically elsewhere in East and Southeast Asia in the early 1990s, as were Hong Kong TV dramas like *Chu Liuxiang* and *The Good, the Bad and the Ugly* in the 1980s. The "waves" do not originate only from Japan, and reverse traffic is not altogether inconceivable, circumstances permitting.[13]

Of course, the local should not be conflated with the regional, which is also crucial to the present case study of adaptations. The issue of adaptability as it relates to the Japanese and Korean Waves must be understood in terms of the cultural proximity thesis, according to which East Asian cultures are closer to each other than to the West. Many "global" factors have been given for the phenomenal success of Japanese and Korean TV dramas, original or

---

[13] The vast differences between Japanese and Korean TV dramas, both of which find ready reception among East Asian audiences, also show that the argument for the attractiveness of Western modernity does not completely hold water.

adapted, including urban appeal, technical brilliance, skillful deployment of the romance and melodrama genres, glamorization of the teenage actors, and so on (see Leung 2004). But obviously some of these—especially the last two—are more regional than global. Whatever similarities exist among different East Asian peoples cannot all be consigned to the global realm. Unfortunately, non-global dimensions are generally ignored in much of the current discussion on the two Waves, as on many other fronts. To equate what is Japanese with "the global" is seen characteristically in a statement like the following: "The construction of South Korean popular culture is hybridization through the re-adaptation of Japanese popular culture *which is an adaptation of Western media culture or global consumer culture*" (Lee Dong-hoo 2005, qtd. Jung 2013: 111; italics added). To my mind, Younghan Cho presents a more nuanced understanding in his analysis of the spread of South Korean pop culture into all of East Asia:

> The asymmetric but synchronous spatialities expressed in the Korean Wave indicate that East Asian sensibilities are neither identifiable nor incommensurate with Euro-American modernity. Instead, East Asian sensibilities, already and always inscribed by global modernity, have been historically cultivated and generated by the national and by regional specifics. (Cho 2011: 395)

This throws some light on the adaptations of *Boys over Flowers* so far discussed, and allows us to say that Japanese cultural products, like manga, find easier acceptance among consumers in the region because of their much greater adaptability when compared with those from the West. Certain core values are shared by East Asian communities, especially Confucian ones like filial piety, respect for seniority, family centeredness, paternalism, and so on, which undergird a rather conservative outlook on life. It is the commensurability of lifestyles in the three countries concerned that enhances the adaptability of textual materials, many of which happened to have come from Japan during the last few decades of the twentieth century.

Between Adaptation and Accommodation

Though a major TV phenomenon of the past decade in East Asia, the adaptations of *Boys over Flowers* have received attention only in four English articles (Jung 2010; Deppman 2009; Choo 2008; Yasumoto 2015). Many critics have focused attention on the globalization processes at work in the region, and there is only selective treatment of certain kinds of popular cultural exports. The special nature of TV adaptations discussed in this chapter alerts us to a problem in adaptation studies, showing the need to be wary of the direct transference of Western models to the East Asian context. For Chua Beng Huat and Iwabuchi Koichi, "the multiple connectivities and socio-political implications of popular cultural flows and exchanges in East Asia . . . cannot be ascertained in existing US-centric analyses" (2008: 12). Might the same not be said of the transference of Eurocentric models of translation and adaptation to the East?

To continue our story, after *Meteor Garden*, an endless stream of adaptations has appeared in Taiwan, from *The Hospital* (2006) to *Sweet Relationship* (2007) and *Romantic Princess* (2007), all runaway successes. Besides *Flower-like Boys*, the long list of adaptations in South Korea of Japanese manga includes such rating triumphs as *Dr. Jin* (2012) and *City Hunter* (2011). Adaptations, in contrast to dubbed and subtitled TV dramas, exemplify the manipulations to which elements of cultural imports are subject when reconfigured for target audiences. It has been argued that intricate psychological mechanisms are at work when the receptors of a TV drama from abroad, whether Japanese or Korean, tackle elements of the foreign ("not us") and the familiar ("like us") (see Chua 2008: 73–89). Subtitling and dubbing, each in its own way (but especially the latter), help indigenize the media imports. The foreignness, Chua Beng Huat argues, is preserved most strongly in the visual elements, since the audience sees recognizably foreign locations and costumes on screen, no matter how the dialogues are subtitled and dubbed. Thus elements of both domestication and foreignization present themselves simultaneously to the viewer. By contrast, while adaptations contain traces of the foreign, they are highly "domesticated" products. In particular, they appeal to those viewers who are not cognizant of the Japanese "source" of the drama they are watching because the story is well Sinicized or Koreanized. In this way, localization may be said to have achieved its primary objective. It is like reading a translation that does not identify itself as such. Of course, the foreignness of TV adaptations remains rather explicit at times, but in any case adaptations are not geared to the display of the Other, and the Self dimension is usually strengthened, and that ensures that a text is accommodated to the target environment. One can even hypothesize that the eventual decrease in Japanese TV imports was attributable to the surge of adaptive productions. The increase in the number of adaptations in the period discussed here suggests that localized products appeal more to the audience than dubbed and subtitled versions—the more "faithful" imports.

The term "adaptation" can be used in two senses. Other than referring to modifications in content that have a localizing orientation and are introduced to "fit" the resulting product to audience expectations, it also denotes changes necessitated when a text crosses the borders between media. As noted above, our emphasis is on the former rather than the latter, so that the content shifts that occur when *Boys over Flowers* is transformed into TV versions receive more attention than the formal adjustments made for the purpose of accommodation to the target medium. Part III will address another peripheral form of translation—the imitation—through a consideration of its history, in parallel East-West traditions, and of a straightforward case (that of James Joyce's *Ulysses*) followed by the more complex scenario of over a dozen imitations revolving around a Chinese classic.

Part III

7

The Vicissitudes of *Imitatio*, Historically

Deployed to greater or lesser degrees in transtextual rewriting, free translation implies variance from the original. As a recurrent strategy, it is used in all genres (whether literary or nonliterary), as well as text-types (expressive, aesthetic, informative, or vocative). For texts in the vocative category, like advertisements, film titles, and promotional brochures, it is more the rule than the exception. For literary texts, it is most widely adopted in translated poetry, since the allowance made for poetic license is usually much greater than in prose writings. But in cases where transformative and creative elements are generously allowed in an extreme manner, the term "imitation" has been applied instead. As is well-known, imitation has a special history of its own, beginning with the concept of "mimesis," which for Aristotle underlines the relationship between art and life. Subsequent expositions of the term have furthered our understanding of the link between imitation and mimesis. Mihai Spariosu has made it clear that there are two kinds of mimesis: recognition mimesis (art imitating reality) and aesthetic mimesis (art imitating art) (Spariosu 1984: ix). While both are crucial to artistic creation, the latter is most apt as a characterization of derivative literature, the focus of the present study. A similar position was articulated by Edward Young in *Conjectures on Original Composition*: "Imitations are of two kinds; one of nature, one of authors," although he inherently posits an evaluation of the two by saying, "The first we call Originals, and confine the term Imitation to the second" (qtd. Sitter 2008: 387), obliquely privileging originals. In any case, the dichotomy thus constructed is the foundation for the Western discourse on imitation.[1]

The present chapter surveys how imitation has been understood as a form of translation in the West, referencing key thinkers and practitioners in the tradition from the Renaissance to the present, with a focus on why it has been sidelined in contemporary translation theory. The concept has fallen out of favor for some time, though some kind of revival is becoming

---

[1] There is a large cluster of terms that relate to imitation, as the following discussion will make direct or oblique reference to: transcreation, reactivation, reformulation, revival, resurrection, conversion, reconceptualization, and transposition.

increasingly apparent. Other than a handful of publications by translation scholars like Lawrence Venuti, Theo Hermans, and Willis Barnstone, as well as papers published in the journal *Translation and Literature*, the subject has received scant attention. Looking at the broader picture, it should be said that, since the eighteenth century, imitation has been slowly linked from translation. Now, with the fledging interest in imitation in areas like fan-fiction research, we might legitimately ask: Why, in contrast to the Augustan adulation of imitative practices and the concern at the time with imitation theory, was the subsequent attitude toward imitations so dismissive? Was the stigma attached to imitation related to developments in translation theory? What are the chances of its resuscitation in present-day contexts?

In England, the last Great Age of Imitation was the Augustan era, roughly the first half of the eighteenth century when reworking classical models was the order of the day, as exemplified best by Alexander Pope and Jonathan Swift. It was the Romantic Movement that pitted "originality" against "derivation," and elevated the former to be an ideal to be pursued, leading to the denigration of imitations. Augustan poetry translation, most notably of Virgil, Ovid, and Horace, was strongly imitative, and much valorized in literary production at the time. Paul Davis notes how there was "no watertight theoretical distinction between 'translation' and 'imitation'" (2008: 5), rightly emphasizing the kinship between the two, underlining the relevance of translational considerations to understanding Augustan imitations. Imitative poems deviated so much from their sources then that they could sometimes be read as "loose reminiscences of moods" (Davis 2008: 5) or as merely "allusive" (Brower [1959] talks of Pope's "poetry of allusion"), so why were they considered translations at all? Such extreme license warrants a close look, especially given the reversal of fortune that occurred when the curtains fell on the Augustan era.

Characteristics of Imitation: Early Views

We can begin by tracing, briefly, the history of *imitatio* back to its beginnings in Roman authors' imitations of Greek works—the earliest instances in which such a mode of transtextual rewriting is deployed in the West. Some of the basic elements making up the constellation of ideas on literary imitation later can be attributed to these early practitioners, backed as they were by a body of theory built on Aristotle's mimesis. In fact, the distinction made between imitation of nature (or reality) and that of art (or work originating from another poet)—as mentioned above—was crucial to Western thinking with regard to transtextual activity. Following Aristotle, further enunciation of the concept of imitation were provided by: Horace, who boldly asserted in *Art of Poetry* the use of imitation in breaking through the literal interpretation of a text; Quintilian, who advocated the use of eminent prior models in perfecting one's oratorial skills, and prioritized imitation of the "spirit" above that of the "letter" in *Education of an Orator*; and Longinus, who praised the aesthetic use of imitation in enhancing good writing in *On the Sublime*.[2] Together these constitute the essential ingredients of imitation theory as it relates to translation. Ever since then, the main concerns have been with how imitations can be used to improve one's writing or oratorical skills, emulate the achievements of one's forebears, reinvigorate antecedent models, and update past artworks (see Sowerby 2000). Early views informed later ones, especially with regard to: (a) the elements of the creative use of earlier textual material (as opposed to more literal reproduction), and (2) the wish to gain an edge on eminent precedents.

The next great period, one that witnessed the full flowering of the tradition, is the Renaissance, which saw more in-depth theorization of imitation as a mode of rewriting. In contrast to present-day approaches to translation that describe it with metaphors of gender and marital relationships (e.g., Arrojo 1994; Chamberlain 2000), the favorite Renaissance metaphors for imitations were, according to G. W. Pigman: apian (i.e., rearrangement), digestive (complete transformation), filial (genealogical linkage), simian (aping), concealing (disguise), and path-taking (following the master) (1980: 13–26). All of these, with the exception of the last, imply infidelity, or departure from the original work. In his landmark study of the Renaissance imitation scene, Thomas M. Greene (1982) added necromantic metaphors (communication with the dead). In his interpretation, imitators deal with a past enshrined in important cultural and artistic relics, and this entails a modernizing effort for fear that prestigious prior texts may otherwise be consigned to oblivion with the passage of time. Nevertheless, few of these metaphors find favor with the present generation of translation theorists. The greatest divergence, in fact, is the way the relationship between the source and target texts is theorized in terms of the husband and wife, in contradistinction to that between father and son, as reiterated in Renaissance views.

Three of Pigman's metaphors crystallize central themes in our analysis of imitative translations in the chapters that follow. First, the simian metaphor

---

[2] Quintilian's and Longinus's positions resonate with the Aesthetic School of translation in China that we discussed in Chapter 3.

can have serious or playful connotations. In the effort to surpass someone else's achievement, Renaissance imitators could choose not to follow their master or the existing model slavishly, and instead took great liberties with the precursor text, boldly rewriting it and even going so far as to subject it to parodic treatment. While serious Chinese imitations of James Joyce's *Ulysses* appeared in Hong Kong in the 1960s (see Chapter 9), the possibility of parody, one not available to the faithful translator, is exemplified by a good number of Japanese imitations of the classical Chinese novel *Journey to the West* (see Chapter 10). The two examples show that there is only a thin line between paying homage to an honored predecessor and deflating an acknowledged classic. Greene has underlined the difficulty of distinguishing between the two: "Every parody pays its own oblique homage" (1982: 46). In line with this, Greene proceeds to distinguish between four kinds of Renaissance imitation: (a) dialectical imitation, which works on the principle of competition, when two texts belonging to separate cultural, linguistic, and temporal systems are brought together via a web of transtextualities; (b) reproductive imitation, in which the original is regarded as inviolable, and hence not to be changed in rewriting; (c) exploitative imitation, where the source texts' topoi and allusions are re-used; and (d) heuristic imitation, which repositions the text in a modernized context. The *Ulysses* imitations fall mainly into the exploitative category, and those of *Journey to the West* are primarily heuristic. It may also be added that the former are in the transcreation mode; the latter, in the reconceptualization mode.

Second, the metaphor of disguise captures what Pigman calls the "dissimulative" (concealing) nature of imitation. That imitators did not identify their source texts or highlight their artistry is a feature worth noting in the Renaissance practice of imitation. Imitations were even sometimes disguised as originals, although this is often ignored in our time, when imitations are seen as equivalent to copying, and cover-up is viewed as an unethical act. The great extent to which these concepts were applied is seen in the fact that artistic productions may be textual or non-textual, imitation being virtually a way of life in the Renaissance and penetrating to spheres beyond the literary.

Third, the path-taking metaphor brings out the pedagogical aspect of imitative translations. To Christina Oberstebrink (2010), Renaissance imitation was poised between servility on the one hand and creativity on the other. Learning from the imitated work and transcending it are two sides of the same coin. In imitation theory, the positive aspects can be seen in a creative engagement with the past. In imitative Chinese painting, the artist reworks pictorial elements in order to reach the "ideal form," and predecessors are supposed to provide the materials for the later artists' extraction of the quintessential and ethereal. Apprenticeship to earlier artists was thus a "more heuristic comprehension of imitation" (Oberstebrink 2010: 52) for Renaissance imitators who made use of antecedent models inventively to embody a special kind of originality. Underlying this move, however, was the motive of emulation: "[the artist] should enter into a competition with his original, and endeavor to improve what he is appropriating to his own work" (2010: 57). In the final analysis, as the Renaissance people saw it, imitation was the springboard for original expression, a means whereby a disciple can—ironic though it may seem—outperform the master.

Above all, Renaissance imitations bore a special relationship to textual relics from the past, which they honored but also disobeyed. In imitating Greek and Latin works, writers looked past a temporal gap, although there was no desire to duplicate the classical literary models. Thus, researchers need to uncover the significance of intended and daring textual deviations from the original. It is by looking at the disjunctures between texts facing each other across several centuries that we can decipher the meaning behind the reworking of old texts from antiquity. In this way, Renaissance imitations can be appreciated from a transtextual perspective. In his landmark study (1982), Greene scrutinizes the way a body of Renaissance imitators—Petrarch, Poliziano, Ronsard, du Bellay, Wyatt, and Jonson—played fast and loose with their sources, and identifies the key terms which denote the range of freedoms that could be exercised (1982: 51): *translatio*, *paraphrasis*, *imitatio*, and *allusion* were all part of an arsenal of strategies at the rewriters' disposal.[3] Erasmus's view that "verbatim repetition is rated less highly than paraphrase; still more desirable is a conversion or transposition" shows how highly imitations were ranked, for they could "convert and transpose" (qtd. Greene 1982: 31). Put simply, license was imitation's most powerful weapon.

Dryden and the Augustan Imitators

There were imitators aplenty in the English Renaissance, but perhaps most representative of their position is Ben Jonson (1572–1637), an active practitioner whose conceptualizations of the imitative mode anticipated John Dryden's. In *Discoveries*, he famously stated that to imitate is "to be able to convert the substance, or riches of another poet, to his own use"

---

[3] Incidentally, Greene's book was also utilized by a generation of translation scholars from the Low Countries and Israel soon after its appearance.

(qtd. Sowerby 2000: 701), thus specifying a basic function of—as well as a justification for—the activity. Jonson also summed up the English conception of imitation at his time as a "middle composition" between translation and original writing. In saying this he was referencing the creativity debate, with imitation figuring as an in-between form that shares the features of both translated and original works yet not completely reducible to either. For Jonson, too, it was not just a technique but a genre with its own identity. He saw an imitation as vying for artistic excellence with the source text while retaining its spirit. He engaged actively in the imitative enterprise, which exemplifies the dialectic of preserving the "spirit" of the original versus intervening creatively. Reproduction-*cum*-recreation is the clue to the special character of imitations vis-à-vis translations, and the two were never kept far apart in the early history of textual rewriting in the West. Despite the fact that there were times when imitation did not take center stage, in Jonson it was clearly viewed as a preferred mode of composition.

As a leading theorist for the Augustan notion of imitation, John Dryden (1631–1700) also stands at the apex of that tradition. At the same time, probably since John Biguenet and Rainer Schulte's anthology entitled *Theories of Translation: An Anthology of Essays from Dryden to Derrida* (1992), Dryden has been extolled as the first major English translation theorist. He addressed issues relating to imitation in his oft-quoted "Preface to *Ovid's Epistles*" (1681), where he contrasted imitation with metaphrase (word-for-word translation) and paraphrase (line-for-line translation), though pointing out that the triad exists in a continuum. In effect, imitation was theorized by him as a kind of translation as well as a translation strategy—not as conceived by Jonson. This is how he described the differences between the three:[4]

a. Metaphrase: "turning an author word by word, and line by line, from one language to another"
b. Paraphrase: following the sense rather than the word; "translation with latitude"
c. Imitation: "to set [the earlier poet] as a pattern, and to write [as if he] lived in our age, and in our country"

---

[4] It is worth noting that, whereas for Jonson imitation enjoys an equal status with translation and original writing, for Dryden, whether as genre or technique, it has been "downplayed" to become one of three forms of translation. Could this be a reflection of Dryden's skeptical attitude toward it, a reaction to the copious instances of its failure?

It should be noted that, while Dryden preferred paraphrase as the "middle way" between the two extremes of metaphrase and imitation for rendering a source text, thus downplaying imitation, he did so only in reaction to the unsatisfactory imitations circulated in his time. Marie-Alice Belle (2011) has noted the popularity of imitations in the late seventeenth century; the existence of many poor specimens helps contextualize Dryden's criticism of the imitative methods used by Abraham Cowley (1618–67) and John Denham (1615–69) and the extreme laxity with which they handled their originals. Of course, there were also admirable ones: John Denham's "To Sir Richard Fanshaw upon His Translation of 'Pastor Fido'" (1648), Alexander Pope's *Imitations of Horace* (1730s), and Samuel Johnson's "London" (1738) and "The Vanity of Human Wishes" (1749).

Dryden's tripartite classification has deep historical roots, traceable to Quintilian and Pierre-Daniel, among others, and Dryden was simply reinvigorating it for his peers. With regard to the preface, Belle notes that "the dominating theme—and perhaps the most commonplace—is that of freedom" (2011: sec. 5), and if antipodal to metaphrase, imitation nevertheless shares with paraphrase the propensity for license. This threefold formulation, intrinsic to the premodern Western tradition of thinking on translation, entails at least an acceptance of imitation as a viable orientation (as is the case with the present study), despite the strong resistance to it by the advocates of fidelity. The Augustan period in England was followed by one which exalted originality as a fundamental virtue in artistic creation. In spite of the fact that the practice was not uncommon in earlier literature— one notes the appropriative use of textual predecessors by Chaucer and Shakespeare—imitation came to be frowned upon when Romanticism as a movement arose at the end of the eighteenth century. The emphasis on "individual attainment" thus bedeviled imitation until the pendulum began to swing back more recently. However, given the generally lukewarm interest in imitation in translation studies circles in our time, we might legitimately ask: What use can we make of the translator–theorists of an earlier period (cf. Steiner 1975; Gillespie 2011)? Are traditional Western views of imitation not relevant anymore?

The case of Dryden also shows that theory and practice do not always go hand in hand. Differentiating between "literal" and "libertine" methods, he had to confront issues involving the re-presentation of classical Greek and Latin authors to readers of his era. An abundance of modernizing imitations had flooded the literary scene of his time, with imitators freely shifting ancient locales in the source texts to Dryden's England—in an effort at "Englishing"—and deploying the parodic mode in order to mock-translate the Classics (2011: sec. 4). In such a trend, not only were domestic references substituted for foreign ones; ancient examples were replaced by contemporary "equivalents," and the living took over from the dead. This was the background to Dryden's denunciation of the use of parody and burlesque, and his calling imitation "an abusive form of rewriting" (sec. 4).[5] Nevertheless, while Dryden had praise for paraphrase in his "'Preface," his own approach (to Ovid, for instance) was in fact much freer, or more imitative, than he had recommended; this was evidenced by the abundance of omissions, additions, and distortions he used.[6] While proposing a limit to how much free rewriting was acceptable, he found himself in the realm of the lax and libertine. What is more, when he engaged in discussions of parody in his later essays like "Preface to Juvenal's *Satires*," he indirectly acknowledged the special role of imitations as a "creative" form of translation.

As an interlude, we should note a seminal figure in the twilight days of the pre-Romantic Imitation School, Sir William Jones (1746–94), who is another example of a translator not practicing what s/he preaches. He not only challenged the prevailing practice of imitation but also went so far as to suggest that Oriental poetry had no tradition of imitation. From early in his life Jones had acquired a knowledge of several Oriental languages, and he spent much time away from England—for the last decade of his life he lived in India. His imitative translations of Turkish, Arabic, and Persian poems were collected in his *Poems Consisting Chiefly of Translations from the Asiatick Languages* (1772). His renditions were presented as authentication of Oriental poetry for a Western readership. But given the license with which his sources were treated—seen by comparing his versions with their originals, some of which were printed as parallel texts—he was quite unrestrained in his approach. Many "source texts" were not named—which is not unusual since imitations can be composed with reference to a style or a genre, and not necessarily a specific poem. In fact, as Zak Sitter has pointed out, the 1770s was a period that saw intense discussions of imitation in England: in addition to Jones, cultural luminaries of the time like Samuel Johnson, Edmund Burke, and so on, also talked about it (2008: 387). Very soon, however, imitation came to be stigmatized and lost ground to original expression.

---

[5] Probably the best-known example of such imitation at the time is Alexander Pope's mock-epic "The Rape of the Lock" (1712), where the "high" style of classical texts was deployed in the rendering of a lowly subject.

[6] A comparable Chinese example that comes to mind is Yan Fu's famed translation of Thomas Huxley's *Evolution and Ethics* (as *Tianyan lun*) in 1900.

Imitation and Modernist Aesthetics

But the Romantic triumph only lasted until the next wave of fervent interest in imitation reared its head at the turn of the twentieth century, this time in Anglo-America, spearheaded by the modernists. Imitation in its full range—reproductive, exploitative, heuristic, and parodic, in terms used by Greene—returned with a vengeance. This time, too, the objects to be imitated were not just classical but also contemporary, as imitations once again became indistinguishable from, and even tied to, translation. In his monograph titled *Translation and the Languages of Modernism* (2002), Steven Yao surveys the imitative methods of modernist masters through the twentieth century, singling out for discussion the "translation" strategies applied to texts of foreign origin by writers like Ezra Pound, Robert Lowell, and Louis Zukofsky. As already pointed out by scholars on the derivative nature of modernist works (Cotter 2004; Piette 2008; Clej 1997), modernist writers saw "translation" as a mode of literary production, its creativity shown in their ingenious use of a source text, a foreign master, or an outside tradition. Not infrequently, an effort was made to appropriate novel styles and modes from the non-West, like China and Japan. The twin themes of creativity and appropriation clue us to the imitative nature of these modernist works, which makes it futile to expect even the semblance of correspondence between source and target texts. Only a genetic or generative model will allow us to see how foreign literary traditions were rejuvenated, or enriched, through modernist imitation. From a translational perspective, this model necessitates a more broadly defined, and less orthodox, understanding of "translation." Neither fidelity nor accuracy was a concern for modernist writers who dabbled with imitative translation in one form or another.

Pound's wildly experimental imitations of Chinese poems in *Cathay* (1915) on the one hand, and of Confucian canonical texts in *The Cantos* (c. 1915–70) on the other, exemplify the clever use of borrowed materials as a means of textual construction. Pound did not stop after his earlier achievement in *Cathay*: in his entire career, Pound continued to freely translate the Confucian classics in order to further his own political agenda. The original was invariably replaced by worlds of meaning created by Pound through his well-known "ideogrammic" method of translation. Although belonging to an altogether different generation than Pound, Robert Lowell and Louis Zukofsky were also imitative translators who deliberately broke the model of semantic and faithful translation. If poet-apprentices can learn their craft through modeling themselves on older poets, then Lowell and Zukofsky have done so remarkably with foreign models. More interestingly, there is also more than a slight hint that the two poets were playing with the expressive possibilities of their sources, so much so that the reader can perceive parodic elements in their works. This is a feat denied to the literalists: as Reuben Brower has pointed out in his book—now a classic of imitative translation—translators can be parodists (Brower 1974: 5).

When considered together, these not dissimilar cases make manifest certain characteristics of what can be termed a "modernist imitative aesthetics." First, most modernist translators who imitated foreign texts did not have sufficient knowledge of the source language that they were working with, though this was not necessarily an obstacle to imitating. Pound had hardly any knowledge of Chinese when he worked on *Cathay* (1915), though he became better at it when he came to the *Odes* and other Confucian texts, having studied the language through informants and dictionaries. Lowell did not have a mastery of many of the European languages he was translating from (see Wachtel 2017), nor did Zukofsky know any Latin.[7] Second, partly as a consequence of the lack of mastery of the source language on the part of these imitative translators, any degree of strict fidelity is out of the question. Lowell, for instance, was interested more in recapturing the style and "voice" of his originals than in being faithful to their meaning. Third, imitation was simply viewed as (a form of) translation, and the major modernists saw themselves as translators too. This view in fact relieves "translation" of some of the constraints advocated by those who insist on faithfulness to the original, and controverts translation theories that are based on prototypical translations. Fourth, the modernists prized a transcreative mode of translation rather than the "scholarly" mode (à la Matthew Arnold). On top of their practice of working on existing translations (for example, Pound's use of de Mailla and Legge), one can discern a desire on their part to impose their own interpretations on the originals—a method that translation theorists have designated as "manipulative."

A latecomer on the scene, Robert Lowell is representative of a mid-twentieth-century generation that found new uses for the imitative approach. In his *Imitations* (1961), he freely translated canonical poems by Homer, through Charles Baudelaire, Arthur Rimbaud, and Rainer Maria Rilke, to Boris Pasternak, recasting them in American language and poetic forms. In extreme cases, he made changes to theme, words, and even titles, adding and deleting freely to suit his own personal preferences and dispositions, yet he insisted on calling them "translations" from languages like Spanish and Russian, in which he had no competence at all (Wachtel 2017). Distinctly American but linked to the European tradition, Lowell's poems therefore

---

[7] It may be said, therefore, that translators can provide the channel whereby literary influence is exerted, and imitations are the result (and reflection) of such influence.

straddle the blurry borderline between translation and imitation, and the poet himself did not care for a clear distinction. While he emphasized in his preface that the collection was one of "translations," he had no qualms about calling them "imitations," as he had already done earlier with reference to "The Shako," a translation of a Rilke poem in his collection *Lord Weary Castle* that he said was amenable to being read as an original English poem (Heep 1996: 111). Lowell's case again exemplifies the inseparability of translation from imitation for Western poets.

The following are some of the characteristics of Lowell's imitations, as inferred from his rewriting of European sources:

1. Indigenization was a key imitative strategy, and used for the purpose of importing modes of European poetic expression (cf. the opposite attempt to remove foreign culture from the translated text). In this connection, it has been said that some kind of "colonization" of non-American poetry was being carried out.
2. While emulation of one's famous forebears might have motivated the imitations, the goal of "learning" from foreign models, was also a viable motive. The two are, after all, not incompatible.
3. By declaring his indebtedness to prior texts, Lowell was demonstrating an "alternative ethics." While (some) acknowledgement of the source is a central pre-requisite for translators, it is not always incumbent upon an imitator to identify the source of inspiration. This gives the imitator room to freely borrow, deconstruct, and even mutilate the source text.

By highlighting his sources, Lowell was driven by a wish to make transparent his compositional process.[8] Obviously, accomplished poet that he already was, Lowell should have no qualms about mentioning his literary debts. But because he left traces in his poems to signify his response to an "outside" canon, and the poets he imitated were well-known figures in the European poetic tradition, readers could see clearly the "remainder," as Lawrence Venuti calls it. In comparison with the translator, then, the imitator can show up textually as a strong and visible personality. If, as it is sometimes said, there is translation in all creative writings, and there is creativity in any translation, then imitations are translations of a most creative kind.[9]

---

[8] In this discussion of Lowell's "motives," I have benefited from personal communications with David Auerbach and Nat Paterson.
[9] The historical survey in this chapter, which covers major Western imitators and seminal research on them, is not meant to be comprehensive, much less exhaustive: my aim has been to uncover concepts and perspectives relevant to the analysis of individual examples of imitations in the chapters that follow.

Reconnecting Imitation with Translation

If imitation is a kind of translation, we can end with an overview of recent methods used to analyze imitations to see if fruitful and useful linking of the two is a possibility. To begin with, it should be said that the array of strategies in use in translations (as the term is conventionally understood) are fully deployable in imitations, except that an imitation may not bear a discernable link to one antecedent text to which it is linguistically related. On the contrary, it can display connections to a cluster of texts constitutive of a genre, texts that the imitation has drawn upon implicitly or explicitly. Furthermore, imitation can take place more conspicuously at the level of form than content, and an example relating to the borrowing of poetic forms is relevant here. While there was a consuming interest from the 1920s right up to the present in the potentials of using Western free verse and sonnet forms in composing "original" Chinese poetry, the incorporation of themes and subject matter of Western poetry was not widely seen in poems of the period.

As for imitative strategies, other than the ones mentioned above, mimicry, reduction, distortion, misrepresentation, recontextualization, localization, and so on, can readily be observed, all of them part of the transformational process undergone by the text being imitated. The important question is why these strategies (and not others) are used and the functions they serve. They may differ from the strategies used for prototypical or semantic translations, but many apply equally to both. There have been attempts, however, to introduce terms specific to the study of imitation strategies. For instance, Thomas McFarland presents his analytical toolkit for imitations, which focuses on five elements—*epanados* (repetition), *diadromos* (effect channeled into another country), *periodos* (effect returns to the original country), *hyetos* (theme dispersed in target culture), and *aphycton* (metaphorical usage transferred) (1985: 49–56). Hassan Melehy (2003) suggests looking at imitations on the basis of the following terms: reactivation, reformulation, revival, resurrection, conversion, reconceptualization, and transposition.

A slightly different perspective has been offered by Donna Hamilton. In her study of Shakespeare's strategies in his imitative use of Virgil's *Aeneid* in *The Tempest*, she notes that *imitatio* is a rhetorical move occurring not just at the microscopic (diction, sentences) level, but also at the macroscopic (structuring) level. Hamilton points out how the techniques of "disassembling, rearranging, redistributing" (1990: 4) were learned through classroom exercises by students who were taught at schools of earlier times to discover the artistry of famous literary works through detecting the textual echoes, analogies, citations, allusions, and repetitions that link an imitation to its precursor model. But of even greater interest perhaps is Hamilton's discussion of how attention was drawn by the teachers at these schools to the method for concealing the changes. It was thought that the links should only be detectable at a deep and not readily obvious level. This shows an understanding of imitation relevant to the present study. All that can be discerned in imitations may be just an "air" of resemblance, some suggestiveness. This contrasts sharply with adaptation, which makes explicit (rather than covering up) the textual connections. Of course, the analysis of imitative techniques in larger works like drama or the novel is more difficult than for poetry but, as an imitation, *The Tempest* shows the multifarious means (including even the insertion of stretches of text from the original and direct transfer of narrative segments) through which Shakespeare imitated Virgil.

Imitation is slowly emerging from the stigma placed on it for over a century to become a potent part of transtextual studies. The effort to return it to some degree of pre-eminence, through a reconnection to translation studies, is documented nowhere more clearly than in an article by Lawrence Venuti (2011). Although he uses the word "versionings," there is no mistaking its overlap with the imitative translation discussed in the present study.[10] To be sure, Venuti does not examine the possibility of using the term "imitation" in his study of several examples of modern "versionings"—cases of radical translation carried out by poets who have scant regard for fidelity but produce translations that are akin to originals through "mangling, shifts of emphasis, omission, deliberate mistranslation, the conflation of different poems, the insertion of new lines and on a few occasions the writing of entirely new poems" (Don Paterson, qtd. Venuti 2011: 232). Venuti's thesis, that all translations are hermeneutic acts whereby translators invariably impose an interpretation on the source text, is illustrated through a number of translations of works from antiquity, though he mentions the similarities that these bear to those by T. S. Eliot, Robert Lowell, and others.[11] A proliferation of interpretations is enhanced by these imitative efforts. While Venuti does note the difference between translation and adaptation (2011: 234), nevertheless

---

[10] Incidentally, the term had been used earlier by Karin Littau (1997: 70).
[11] Lawrence Venuti has voiced more than once his reservation about translation serving a purely communicative function. The use of the communicative model is, in my opinion, particularly problematic in the case of literary translations. In any case, it fails to explain how translations of narrative literature work. Since stories are representational, showing events and actions taking place over time, their translators must be seen as seeking to recreate the "world" as originally represented, rather than to convey the storyteller's intended message.

in essence he considers "versionings" as translation-*cum*-adaptation, rather than as imitations. By pointing out that early modern notions of imitation are different from modern ones (230), he draws a demarcation line and relegates imitation to the background. In any case, given the approach that he has adopted, his more accepting stance with regard to the departures from the source text can be readily appreciated. His contention that no "translational" evaluation of versionings is possible is grounded in the fact that faithfulness, as an ethical principle, becomes a secondary concern when adherence to the source is rendered unnecessary when target factors predominate. This concern with the reception aspects of rewritten texts also figures strongly in the history of imitative translations in East Asia, to which we now turn.

8

"New Wine in Old Bottles"

Two Sino-Japanese Traditions of Imitation

The history of translation as a transtextual activity in East Asia is inscribed within a context where imitation played a major role in mediating the contact between literatures of the countries at the periphery (Japan, Korea, and Vietnam) and China at the center. What Galin Tihanov said with reference to the West is hauntingly relevant, and it bears quoting before we proceed to examine several imitations in East Asia that illustrate Chinese-Japanese interaction through the centuries. According to Tihanov:

> Translation, in the modern sense in which we understand the term, is a fairly recent phenomenon. Its emergence is concomitant with the rising sense of intellectual property—and of the significance originality and imagination play in literature and in scholarship—that appears in the late eighteenth century. Before that, translation lives other lives: those of imitation, transposition, rendition, emulation, and recreation of the text. (2018: para. 2)

He attaches special significance to German Romantic theory, which lay behind the advent of modern notions of translation that occurred alongside the "transition from powerful cosmopolitan koines—Greek, Latin, Persian, Sanskrit—to a multitude of vernaculars, each of which insists on its own inimitable vocabulary, sensitivity, and plasticity" (2018: para. 3). The rise of national vernaculars also took place in East Asia, and it coincided with the growth of a sense of linguistic autonomy among countries on the fringes of the Sinosphere. The "incursion of the West" in the nineteenth century was conducive to the ascendancy of translation as a distinct field of human endeavor and the resultant simultaneous decline in the fortunes of imitation, as had already happened in the West.

But even as translation in its modern sense as faithful interlingual transfer to enable communication of information is a relatively recent concept introduced to East Asia, there have been attempts to prove that it was an indigenous concept datable to time immemorial. Joseph Allen (2019), however, has cast doubts on the "archaeological" attempts by scholars who mine various ancient sources to prove the native roots of translation in early China; he relates such an enterprise to the wish to prove the centrality of translation in Chinese culture, thereby finding common ground for Western and non-Western traditions. To Allen, as the title of his article suggests, "translation [did] not matter" in premodern China. Contrasting the myth of Cang Jie, the reputable inventor of the Chinese script, with the Biblical legend of Babel, in which (by God's decree) the builders of the tower were rendered incapable of communicating in a shared language, Allen asks if translation played as important a role in the past, as was asserted by some translation scholars. He not only reinterprets the early usages of the key Chinese term for translation (*yi*), but also suggests that even the Buddhist translation boom "did not produce . . . any wide-scale interest in translation itself, beyond the specific productions of Buddhist texts" (2019: 334). For him, it is transcription rather than translation that characterized mainstream Chinese intellectual life. A similar scenario, he argues, can be imputed to Japan and Korea. His conclusion that translation only played a secondary role in transtextual rewriting of the past lends some support to our view expressed here. He asks:

> What has all this to do with translation studies? First, it should challenge the assumption that high levels of literary production, whether measured in quantity or quality, are necessarily related to translation in any form. . . . How do transcription and its legacy in East Asia represent a fundamental humanistic concern with language that offers us another way of thinking about knowledge production? (Allen 2019: 142–3)

As will be further argued, it was imitation rather than translation which dominated textual transmission in the literary field in premodern times, till it was eclipsed by translation (in the sense that we know it today) in the late nineteenth century. While much of Chinese literature itself was derivative, with later works remodeled on earlier ones (see Kao 1985), it is the imitations that furnished a wide range of possibilities in premodern times for second-order writing.[1]

The present chapter will take a look at two premodern forms of imitation in the Japanese tradition, one in poetry and the other in prose fiction,

---

[1] Imitation also came in two varieties, the interlingual and the intralingual. In traditional times, while the former was prevalent in countries flanking China, the latter was widely practiced inside China itself, where the objects of imitation were earlier texts in the tradition.

both bearing a derivative relationship to antecedent Chinese texts. A preliminary word on similar situations in Korea and Vietnam is in order, if only to underline the fact that what happened in Japan was to a substantial extent replicated in these two other Asian traditions. The composition of Sino-Korean poetry reached a high peak during the Joseon dynasty (1392–1897), which adopted Confucianism as a state ideology. In such a context, the writing of poetry in literary Chinese flourished, the language viewed favorably as a vehicle for the expression of Confucian ideals. The object of imitation was almost predominantly Chinese poetry of the Song period (960–1279), with leading poets like Su Shi (1037–1101) providing the stylistic models for emulation. "Foreign" language writing was also facilitated by King Sejong's creation of the *hangul* alphabet, which made it easier than previously for a greater swathe of the educated population to read classical Chinese works. Judy Wakabayashi and Kang Ji-hae have also noted how Chinese texts became a popular object for translation after the widespread use of the *hangul*. For them, before that there were hardly any translations in the modern (or Western) sense to speak of; alternative forms of rewriting like imitations and adaptations, according to them, were rampant (2019: Introduction).

Similar imitative (Sino-Vietnamese) poetry was also avidly composed in Vietnam. Having experienced an equally long period of Chinese cultural influence as did Japan and Korea, Vietnam was as keen as both to rewrite literature from China (Yan 2014: 305). Facility with Chinese language there improved significantly with the prevalent use of *Chữ nôm*, the logographic writing system developed in the tenth century on the basis of Chinese characters. As seen in extant archival materials, *chữ hán* (writing in Chinese) was abundant: it was seen not just in literary composition, but also in official and legal areas. In poetry, the imitative impulse was underscored by the approximation of Chinese aesthetics, although changes were made to the form of seven-character regulated poetry originating in China in order to accommodate rhythms peculiar to the Vietnamese ear. Although there was much tampering with the original content (through the inclusion of local subject matter, for instance), it was the imitation of style that characterized imitative Chinese poetry in Vietnam.

Searching for (Dis)semblance: Sino-Japanese Poetry

The dominant mode of imitative translation in Japan involves Chinese literary texts; practiced up to the twentieth century, its best examples were Chinese-styled poetry and prose (*kanshibun*), especially the former, called *kanshi* ("Sino-Japanese poetry"). For centuries, classical Chinese was nothing less than the cosmopolitan written language in widespread use in premodern East Asia, and its use in the poetic compositions of Japanese men of letters was also shared by Korea, as a matter of course. As a written East Asian lingua franca, this hyperglossic language somehow united the peoples of East Asia, otherwise split by the plethora of spoken, local vernaculars. What is of interest is that those using it as a literary medium also strived to copy the styles of poetry writing in the country of origin, resulting in imitations par excellence where the end product is much closer to being a virtual replica of its source than is possible when there is a language barrier. As noted above, such acts of imitation are intralingual rather than interlingual.[2]

There has been no lack of studies of the imitation of Chinese poetry by Japanese *kanshi* poets, especially that of the Heian period, especially from the Japanese academia (e.g., Kojima 1962–2019; Ōsone 1998; Watanabe 1991). A welcome addition to the work done by David Pollack (1986) is a recent study in English of Meiji Sino-Japanese poetry. Matthew Fraleigh elucidates the nature and function of this genre, which was very much a part of traditional Japanese literature until the early twentieth century, even after Japan had successfully transformed itself into a major power. Noting how nationalistic considerations had caused some Japanese historians to relegate to obscurity this tradition of (re)writing at the same time as it moved literary production in the indigenous language to a central position, Fraleigh surveys the long-standing practice in which the imitation of Chinese models was the governing principle. The ideal state to be attained is revealed by the fact that "many Japanese *kanshi* poets aspired to write Chinese verse that was not linguistically or stylistically marked as the product of a Japanese hand" (Fraleigh 2016: 8). This pursuit of equivalence on two dimensions— language and style—is reflected in the belief that *kanshi* poetry would be commendable if they did not exude any "Japanese odor," a term that we saw earlier in the arguments raised by Lin Shaohua (see Chapter 3). Any trace of Japaneseness, seen in deviations from the Chinese lexicon, expressions, and rhyme schemes, was viewed as detracting from the imitator's achievement. The standards for evaluation, in other words, were set by Chinese poetry,

---

[2] The impact of this practice is seen on the linguistic level as well, as evidenced by the importation of Chinese vocabulary into the recipient languages. Many Sino-Japanese words entered the Japanese lexicon through the extensive practice of *kanshibun*. A similar situation obtained in Korea, resulting in the expansion of Sino-Korean vocabulary. In Vietnam, allegedly 75 percent of the modern Vietnamese lexicon consists of borrowings from the Chinese language (see Phan 2013), principally through writers writing in the regional lingua franca.

which was to be conscientiously copied. This shows how imitation was given pride of place in Japanese literary history under the rubric of a shared Sino-Japanese cultural and textual heritage.³ Nevertheless, the resistance against imitations became stronger and stronger as the modernization of Japan continued, eventually becoming a fad ("the Japanization of Chinese-styled poetry") in which originality was increasingly prized as a virtue, much as post-Romantic conceptions of literary worth had gained ground in the West.

While there was a strong desire—or an unspoken injunction—to replicate formal or stylistic properties in the Chinese original, as well as an expectation to see affinities in the derived product to its source, departures from the Chinese model are by no means non-existent. Brian Steininger highlights this other side to the Sino-Japanese imitations in question. He posits an interactive model whereby the boundaries between the two cultures are penetrable rather than hard and fast (Steininger 2017: 5–12). In this light, the *kanshi* imitations provided the chance for what was Chinese to be Japanized in spite of the strength of the non-indigenous elements coming from what was perceived to be a superior civilization. Imitation was a special mode of composition that still allowed for a degree of originality. According to Steininger, despite the borrowings on all levels (theme, language, and imagery) from Chinese poetic works, especially from the famous Chinese folk-poet Bai Juyi (772–846), the Japanese counterparts were never completely secondhand reproductions of their better Chinese sources, especially those in later periods. For instance, there are innumerable *kanshi* poems that exude a special Japaneseness in describing landscapes like Mount Fuji. There were thus two parallel movements: along with the efforts to emulate the Chinese originals, there were also strategies used to ensure that the foreign elements existed in hybridized juxtaposition with autochthonous features. For some time viewed derogatorily, "Japanese odor" became in this way associated with attempts at Japaneseness, especially in more recent times when it turned out to be a virtue rather than a defect. Despite the overwhelming presence of the Other, attempts were initiated to find some room for expressing the Self.⁴

---

³ Incidentally, sometimes pastiche was also a popular form deployed, especially where several Tang Chinese poets were imitated in one and the same *kanshi*.
⁴ For translations of *kanshi* which show how the Japanese poets adopt Chinese allusions, imagery, motifs, and conventions, and model themselves on poets from the Tang dynasty, see Bradstock and Rabinovitch (1997). The collection also contains examples of poets writing poems about specific places in Japan and focusing on Japanese rather than Chinese subjects while adopting a Japanese lexicon.

It may be relevant here to summarize the three phases in the gradual evolution of the Japanese (Sinological) approach to China—the ultimate Other—from early times till the twentieth century, as proposed by the Japanese philosopher and translator, Takeuchi Yoshimi (see Chan 2016):

(1) The Self is not distinguished from the Other (in complete identification);
(2) The Self is opposed to the Other, which is seen as a different, autonomous object; and
(3) The Self finds the Other in itself, so the Other is not just "out there" but also "within."

For Takeuchi, since the Other served as the medium through which the Self was reconstituted, China remained a primary frame of reference through the ages. In the first phase China was not the Other but part of Japan itself. This explains the heavy reliance on the imitation—even dutiful reduplication, as in most *kanshi*—of cultural products (especially literature) from the cultural neighbor. Such a scenario ended with the onset of the second phase. It has been argued that a "new" type of translation was triggered by the arrival of Westerners in Japan in the sixteenth century (Wakabayashi 2005b: 30). Finally, the twentieth century ushered in an era of fluctuating attraction-*cum*-repulsion in Japan's response to China, unsettling the older modes of thinking about China and their transtextual relationship.

The decline of the imitative mode can be roughly identified with the Sinologist-philosopher Ogyū Sorai, referred to earlier (see Sakai 1992). Sorai is famous for his denouncement of *kundoku* because of the "meaning confusion" it purportedly created, as well as his effort to raise awareness of the separateness between the two languages of Japanese and Chinese. The shift from "China as Self" to "China as Other" had fundamental consequences for a more intensified use of translation in the faithful mode, which gradually gained in importance until its heyday was reached with the country's opening to the West. Ironical as it may seem, the increasing awareness of Japaneseness brought with it an equally trenchant recognition of Chineseness. The story of Japan's cultural appropriation of China had taken a contorted course, and the changes in its view of China undergirded the choice—and then decline—of imitation as a rewriting practice. Of course, a final shift has occurred in contemporary Japan. Given the opportunities for play, parody, and emulation of the original, imitations have recently returned to serve different needs. Since drastic departures from the original are permissible in this mode, imitators have capitalized on their distinctive strengths to achieve new goals.[5]

Borrowing and Modeling: Japanese *Yomihon* Fiction

Kanshi poetry is an extreme example of the deployment of imitative translation in Japan, but it is by no means the only one. A comparable corpus exists in premodern fiction written in Japanese that "borrowed" plots, characters, and structural elements from Chinese historical records and fictional narratives, written in both literary and vernacular Chinese. Historically, once again it was at the time of Ogyū Sorai that momentous transformations occurred. At around the end of the seventeenth century Japan experienced a cultural fever in response to the massive importation into the country of full-length Chinese novels that became very popular with Japanese readers. The yearning for similar indigenous specimens followed the enthusiastic reception, resulting in a succession of adaptations and imitations of the major novels, especially of *Water Margin*—a story about the exploits of the 108 heroes who banded together at Mount Liang in present-day Shandong province. The appearance of imitations reflects an emerging concern with what is distinctly Japanese, as juxtaposed against the foreign (Chinese). It is from the imitations of *Water Margin*, which signal the gradual but determined replacement of the outside imports by indigenous products, that we can trace the development of the important Edo-period narrative genre called *yomihon* (books for reading).

In effect, through a comparison of these imitations with their source texts, we see "the separation of Japan from China," a process underscored by the imitations themselves. With regard to *Water Margin*, the chain of publication events started with its arrival: existing records show that copies of this book landed in Japan as early as 1639. While the novel was avidly imitated, it is clear that a certain trajectory can be discerned, with the history culminating in the monumental, multivolume work by Kyokutei Bakin (1767–1848), *Eight Dog Warriors* (1814–41). Seen by literary historians as

---

[5] Besides *kanshi*, there have been other subgenres like the *kudai waka* (Japanese topic poetry), whose compositional principle is the expansion or elaboration of selected (one or two) lines from Chinese poems, used as a "topic." The author is indebted to Xue Miaoling for her analysis of several poems by Ōe no Chisato (late ninth century), Jien (1155–1225) and Fujiwara no Teika (1162–1241), who took their "inspiration" from two lines in a poem by the Chinese poet Bai Juyi. For further discussion of this phenomenon, see Denecke (2007).

marking the maturity of the *yomihon* genre, which flourished first in Kyoto-Osaka and then in Edo (present-day Tokyo), this imitation used a Chinese storytelling format to tell a Japanese story with small doses of pseudo-historical detail. In this way, the Sinophilia seen in the initial receptivity to vernacular Chinese fiction finally gave way to a creative re-use of Chinese fictional form and content. An interesting comparison can be made to the evolution of the realist novel in mid-nineteenth-century Spain, where translations of French precedents led to a craze for imitations, resulting in the creation of an "inspired" genre with foreign roots (Martí-López 2002). Though often viewed pejoratively, imitative writing played a role in giving birth to autochthonous literary forms.

The chronology of texts spawned by *Water Margin* in Japan can be briefly summarized here. Modern archivists have discovered a *wakoku* version of the Chinese novel as imported via Nagasaki by Okajima Kanzan in 1728 entitled *Loyal Water Margin*, in which the insertion of annotations into the text facilitated comprehension of the reprinted Chinese text.[6] Okajima was a Confucian scholar and interpreter who promoted the learning of the vernacular language, which differed significantly from literary Chinese, and he wrote books explaining the vocabulary of the imported novels. Next came *Popularized Loyal Water Margin*, whose instalments were published from 1757 to 1790 (see Figure 8.1).[7] It must be noted, too, that while these versions of the novel appeared in print, a host of other Chinese works (like *Three Kingdoms* and *Journey to the West*), were also rendered into Japanese and eagerly read. A seismic shift—an "epistemological uncertainly" as William Hedberg calls it (2012: 24)—was occurring as Japan entered her early modern era.[8]

After these two versions, a flurry of imitations of *Water Margin* arrived on the scene, and in literary histories they are generally categorized as early

---

[6] The *wakoku* (lit., "Japanese woodblock carving") is a Japanese printing of the Chinese texts with additional *kana* inserted on the right-hand side that serve as an aid to the Japanese reader using the *kundoku* method of reading the original. For discussions in English of the *kundoku* method of reading Chinese texts, see Clements (2015: Chapter 3) and Semizu (2006: 283–95).

[7] *Tsūzoku* (in Figure 8.1) ("popular" in modern Japanese) meant "Japanese translation" in the Edo period. In contrast to the *wakoku* text, it has *kana* inserted in the main text (and not on the right); the text is re-organized according to Japanese word-order to make it even more readable—hence "popular."

[8] There were also many cases of intermedial adaptation in which the original Chinese story remains largely intact, not radically altered, as in the imitations to be considered below. Li Shuguo noted an orally adapted performance by Ogawa Kichitarō in Osaka in 1776 (1998: 204).They played a crucial part in popularizing the Chinese novel for the Japanese public, and fanned the craving for more vernacular Chinese novels as well as their imitative reproductions.

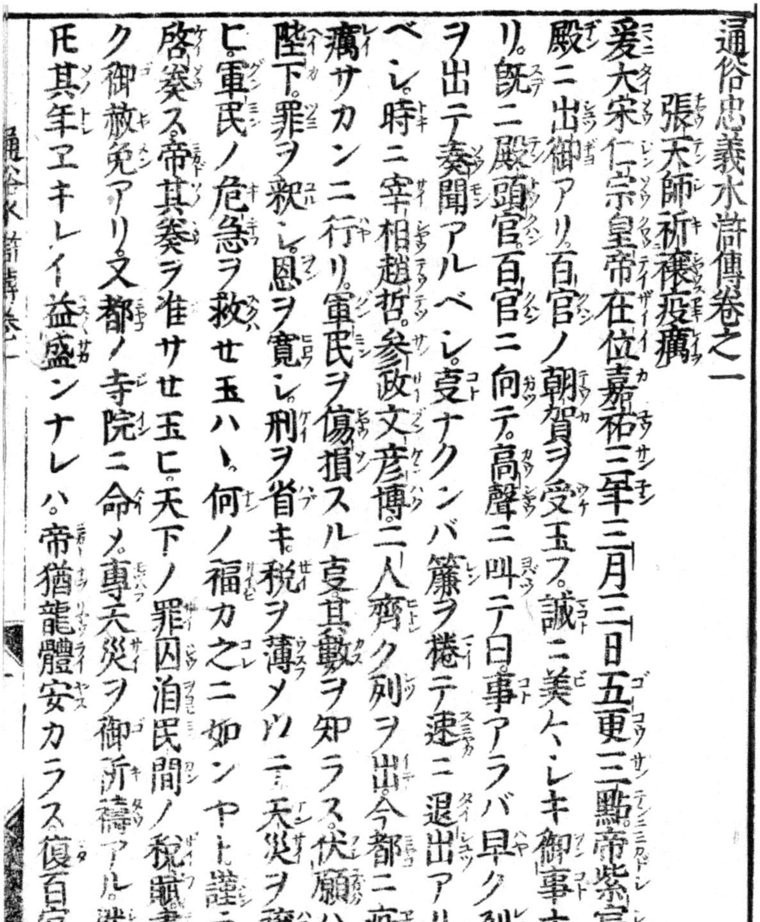

Figure 8.1 A "Popular" Version of *Water Margin*: *Tsūzoku chūgi suikoden* (Chapter 1).

yomihon. According to Ōtaka's classification, early *yomihon* appeared around 1750, while the late ones are those of the 1790s and later (2015: 539). In these stories the plots, characters, structures, and motifs were transposed. For those that were localized, bearing clear signs of adjustment, we can also see them as adaptations, depending on the viewpoint adopted. In *Water Margin in Our Realm* by Takebe Ayatari (1719–74) and published in 1774, the Chinese story was relocated to Japan in the Nara period, as were the characters and events. The novel begins like *Water Margin* with a legend about the celestial background of the 100 heroes. It introduces the villain, the crafty courtier who is the counterpart of Gao Qiu in the source novel. It then describes how individual characters were forced to flee to Mount Ibuki when prosecuted by the government, and adds to it the fabricated account of the Chinese Tang Emperor's consort Yang Guifei (719–756; Japanese: Yōkihi) who was not killed in the An Lushan Mutiny (755)—as the official histories have it—but fled to Japan. The language of the story is a hybrid Sino-Japanese. It has been said that the novel achieves "a problematization of the [Sino-Japanese] binary in the unique setting of the transnational travel and relocation" (Marceau 2016: 497). After *Water Margin in Our Realm*, other titles went further in the domestication direction: there was a version entitled *Water Margin in Japan* (1776) and another called *Female Water Margin* (1783). Emphasized in these two versions are, respectively, the Japanese setting and female warriors (instead of male ones).

Clearly, these versions straddle the borderline between adaptation and imitation. But the derived versions gradually shed their Chinese characteristics until, by the end of the eighteenth century, the only links are murky parallels or allusions, or features showing some structural resemblance to the source text. The late 1790s saw several late *yomihon*, most notably Bakin's *Ciphers of Takao* (1796), a pastiche that combines elements from a puppet play with the original Chinese story.[9] It would be misleading to consider this text as a pure imitation: besides plot and character parallels with the Chinese story, interspersed in the narrative are sentence-for-sentence, literal translations of parts of the original novel, so it should be termed a "trans-imitation." Bakin's patron and lifelong rival, Santō Kyōden, published another imitative work titled *Loyal Retainers' Water Margin* in 1799–1801.[10] Like Bakin, he fused two prior texts, and relocation is a key strategy in this derived story. He substituted the Akō Incident (1701–02) about the forty-seven *rōnin* who avenged the death of their master by seppuku, for that of the Mount Liang heroes who suffered injustices under a villainous high-ranking official of the Song dynasty. Also like Bakin, Kyōden used a *bōkun* style in which, to aid comprehension, *kana* was supplied on the right side of Chinese characters (as *okurigana*). Such a mode of hybrid mixing of the two languages is typical of the derivative *yomihon* at the time.

---

[9] For a biographical account of Bakin in English, see Zolbrod (1967), which also details the background to his composition of the story and analyzes at some length his best-known work, *Eight Dog Warriors*.

[10] Notably, *Loyal Retainers' Water Margin* has been praised for its ingenuity in using its sources (Devitt 264).

We will take a sustained look at Bakin's *Eight Dog Warriors,* the most freely imitative novel of Japan's early modern era that also represents the pinnacle of achievement of the genre. (For a chronological listing of the Japanese versions of *Water Margin* from 1728–1841, see Table 8.1.) Published in 106 volumes through a 28-year period from 1814 to 1841, this epic novel chronicles the adventures of eight samurai who exemplify the virtue of loyalty, which is also a core value of *Water Margin.* The eight "dogs" of the title in fact refers to the eight samurai whose surnames all contain the *kanji* for "dog." Focusing on events that took place in Awa (in present-day Chiba), the story is set against the Sengoku (Civil War) period of Japanese history (1467–1673). The plot centers round a princess who married a dog, while the eight samurai were born in different places, like the heroes of *Water Margin.* Each one of them had his own tragic destiny, but they were all forced to give up the comfortable lives they had led previously to become itinerant fighters, as in the Chinese novel. Through their adventures, the author conveys a message with Confucian and Buddhist connotations. The links between Bakin's tale and the Chinese classic are minimal at best, although no reader could have missed the imprint of the latter, or the interconnectedness between the two (see Li 1998: 207–8). This is indicative of Bakin's deep understanding of *Water Margin,* but a wide range of source texts also enter the imitation, much like the two novels mentioned in the last paragraph.

Comparison of *Eight Dog Warriors* with Bakin's earlier novels inspired by *Water Margin* reveals the creative nature of his textual transformations. Bakin's first attempt at imitating *Water Margin, Ciphers of Takao* (referred to above) is a simple layering of the Chinese novel on a kabuki and puppet theater story, *Precious Incense and Autumn Flowers of Sendai* (1777). Bakin's intention is demonstrated in the double-columned titles of the twelve parts of *Ciphers of Takao* where he clearly makes the connections to *Water Margin.* For example, the title of the first part reads "Hirouji Accidentally Opens Sanekata's Tomb," with the subtitle "That is the Chinese novel *Water Margin*"; this shows the borrowing from the opening chapter of *Water Margin.* All the other parts follow in a similar manner, each with a reference to a major plotline from *Water Margin,* as for instance, "Nine-Tattoo Dragon Shi Jin and His Martial Arts Teacher Wang Jin," "Instructor Lin Chong's Misfortune with His Wife," and "Wu Song on Jingyang Ridge and His Superhuman Strength." Bakin's next novel that bears a relationship to *Water Margin* is *New Illustrated Story of Water Margin* (1805). This is a faithful translation of the first ten chapters of *Water Margin* illustrated by the famous artist, Katsushika Hokusai. This text is almost identical to Okajima Kanzan's *Loyal Water Margin* but written in more readable Japanese with *kana* annotations (Takashima 2006: 191).

Table 8.1 Translations and Imitations of *Water Margin* in Edo Japan (Selected)

Year	Title	Author	Notes
1639	Earliest extant copy of *Water Margin* in Japan.		A *wakoku* version of the first ten chapters.
1728	*Chūgi suikoden* (*Loyal Water Margin*)	Okajima Kanzan	A translation of *Water Margin*. (The first ten chapters had also been translated by Bakin.)
1757, 1772, 1784	*Tsūzoku chūgi suikoden* (*Popularized Loyal Water Margin*)	Okajima Kanzan (attributed)	
1774	*Honchō suikoden* (*Water Margin in Our Realm*)	Takebe Ayatari	Use of historical material from the Nara period. Fifty chapters.
1776	*Nihon suikoden* (*Water Margin in Japan*)	Kyūtei Sanjin	The prologue and the ending in particular are similar to those of the source novel.
1783	*Onna suikoden* (*Female Water Margin*)	Itan Chin-en	Replaces the male characters with an all-female cast. Background moved to the North-South Dynasties period (1336–92).
1796	*Takao senjimon* (*Ciphers of Takao*)	Kyokutei Bakin	Combines a *jōruri* narrative, *Meiboku sendaihaki*, with the original Chinese story.
1799–1801	*Chūshin suikoden* (*Loyal Retainers' Water Margin*)	Santō Kyōden	Replaces the original story with the tale of the 47 *rōnin*.
1814–41	*Nansō Satomi hakkenden* (*Eight Dog Warriors*)	Kyokutei Bakin	Story of eight samurai sworn brothers "inspired" by the Chinese novel.

The third novel he published prior to *Eight Dog Warriors* is *Strange Tales of the Bow Moon* (1807–11), which also contains illustrations by Hokusai. Its second part is modeled on the Chinese *Sequel to The Water Margin* (1644), which tells of the life of Lee Jun after the tragic deaths and break-up of the Liangshan gang. In the conclusion, the story tells readers that Lee Jun sailed to Siam with a few remaining comrades and became king there. Bakin elaborated this plot about the exiled heroes to tell the fictitious tale of Minamoto no Tametomo becoming king of Ryukyu Island—although in history Tametomo was reportedly exiled to Izu Oshima Island after the Hōgen Rebellion of 1156. This is actually Bakin's first historical novel and hugely successful. It gave him the confidence to embark on the much more ambitious project of *Eight Dog Warriors*. Viewed in this broader context of Bakin's earlier novels, *Ciphers of Takao* can be seen as a trans-imitation; *New Illustrated Story of Water Margin*, as a strictly literal translation; and *Strange Tales of the Bow Moon*, as more of an adaptation. They are much shorter than *Eight Dog Warriors*, and may appear insignificant now in Japanese literary history. However, these preparatory exercises gave him a crucial opportunity to analyze and absorb the language and fictional elements of *Water Margin*, thoroughly internalize it, and re-create it as his own masterpiece (Takada 2005: 113).

The main difference between *Eight Dog Warriors* and other Edo era versions of *Water Margin* is Bakin's depth of understanding and capacity for "internalizing" borrowed content. Many other rewriters simply borrowed major plots and famous scenes, and transplanted them to Japan, falling short of creating their own style or conveying new messages. *Eight Dog Warriors*, too, contains simple transformations of plot details from *Water Margin*. An obvious example is the story of Wu Song's slaying of a tiger in Chapter 23 of *Water Margin*, which was transformed into a story of Inuta Kobungo's killing of a wild boar in Chapter 53 of *Eight Dog Warriors*. However, Bakin's intention was to create a novel as entertaining as *The Water Margin* but surpassing it in its philosophical content (Takashima 2006: 182). What really separates Bakin from his Edo counterparts is not just his talent as a novelist but his intellectual tenacity. He approached *Water Margin* both as a novelist and scholar of sorts. His tireless search for plots, language and techniques led him to explore a remarkable number of vernacular and classical novels plus a great range of source texts covering history, religion, mapping, folklore, war, astronomy, and astrology in both Chinese and Japanese. Having studied these, Bakin recast the plots from *Water Margin* and made them distinctive as well as complex. Cui Xianglan (2005: 15–19) lists Chinese and Japanese source texts that Bakin and other writers of his time rewrote for their *yomihon* novels. Her list contains novels that have used at most half a dozen sources; *Eight*

Dog Warriors references thirty-one, of which twenty-one are Japanese. What this reveals is that *Eight Dog Warriors* cannot be read as a straightforward adaptation of a Chinese novel, but a pastiched imitation, an amalgamation of multiple source texts from both China and Japan.

The most notable example of a complex use of materials for imitation concerns the introductory part of *Water Margin* where Marshal Hong released the 108 spirits who later resurfaced as the 108 outlaws gathered on Mount Liang. But Marshal Hong never appears in *Water Margin* again and the connection between this introductory episode and the rest of the Chinese novel is tenuous. Yet this plot is transformed in *Eight Dog Warriors* into the story of eight crystal balls released from the abdomen of Princess Fuse of the Satomi clan, who killed herself in front of her father and fiancé to prove her innocence. The eight crystal balls are later linked to the eight young warriors of the Satomi clan. The plot arrangement is used to launch the entire epic. Among Edo writers (who mostly composed short stories), Bakin was the one to recognize the importance of this plot in *Water Margin* and recreated it in his own novel as an episode to introduce questions that are solved later in the heroic chronicles—in the longest novel of the era (Ishikawa 2010: 199). This plot detail is symbolic to begin with, pointing to the release of suppressed evil spirits in *Water Margin*. But in *Eight Dog Warriors*, it is expanded and given added meanings relating to issues of human-animal marriage, virgin birth, lord-retainer (and father-son) and mother-son relationships, all of which originate in source texts other than *Water Margin*.

In addition to the innovative plot borrowings, Takashima Toshio notes that the literary quality of *Eight Dog Warriors* is to be found in its narrative style. To him the novel is "dark red blood endlessly gushing out of a large sewage pipe without changing the seven-and-five syllable rhythm except for occasional insertions of seven-and-seven syllables" (2006: 204–6). Takashima acknowledges the fact that some readers find the rather monotonous narrative style oppressive, but to him it is dynamic and appealing. Bakin's intensely dazzling expressions are, for him, made possible through his vast knowledge of Chinese and Japanese vocabulary. This kind of distinctive narrative style, together with complex plot transformations, characterize Bakin's efforts at imitative transcreation, the result of many years of searching for new ideas and practices from many literary genres. Indeed more imitations followed his to capitalize on its success.[11]

---

[11] What is worth noting is that imitations were not regarded at the time by readers as a lesser or inferior art form; they were enthusiastically embraced as reading matter for all and widely circulated in the main cities of Japan.

Seen in historical context, the surge of imitations, most notably those of *Water Margin,* signals a new phase in Sino-Japanese relations. Paradoxically, it also reveals an increased distance between the two countries. For centuries, in sharing a common Sinographic culture through the widespread use of literary Chinese, much as Latin was deployed as a cosmopolitan written language in premodern Europe, Japan had viewed herself as not distinguishable from the Other that was China. There had obviously been no strong need for making available Chinese texts in Japanese translation because of the strong linguistic affinities, and *kanji* had assisted many readers in comprehending Chinese texts. The cultural linkages fostered by similar philosophical and religious systems also helped, while the reading of *kundoku* texts obviated the need for anything like the source-text–bound translations that appeared later, even though only the better educated among the population had a mastery of the foreign language. But the terms of cultural and linguistic contact were already changing, as Japan entered her modern era.

The Decline of a Tradition

In their recent publications, Emanuel Pastreich (2011) and William Hedberg (2019) have written cogently on the Japanese reception of vernacular fiction like *Water Margin* from China, with special reference to the intellectual atmosphere of the era, especially the continuing fascination with Chinese culture. Nevertheless, imitation was not the focus of their interest, and sometimes the texts discussed above are referred to as adaptations. While, as noted earlier, the same texts could be placed in either category, some can be better analyzed as imitative, and others as adaptive. With regard to both Chinese inspired poetry and fiction in premodern Japan, the conclusions we have drawn are worth pondering from a broad historical context. While close, semantic translations could better bridge the two languages, it is in the imitations that one sees the strategy of "putting new wine in old bottles" used to great effect as a tool for mediating between cultures. They also show different views of a regional identity that was assumed by the countries in question. In Judy Wakabayashi's discussion of the material, semiotic, aesthetic, creative, and ideological uses of the script in premodern Japan, Korea, and Vietnam, she suggests, quite rightly, that the Chinese characters do not necessarily represent Chineseness, and can have "national overtones" for the three countries (2016: 185).

But in any case, the groundwork on which the East Asian classical tradition of imitation rested was being eroded even as a variety of imitations were produced. The disintegration of the traditional regional order had begun even when the production of *yomihon* continued unabated, and *kanshi* remained a favored mode of poetic composition for many even after Japan was opened up after the arrival of Commodore Perry in 1853—only twelve years after the last part of *Eight Dog Warriors* was published. In the decades that followed, the much diminished "borrowing" of Chinese textual elements indirectly bears witness to the way in which Japaneseness was foregrounded, in effect replicating the manner in which the smaller island country distanced herself from her all-powerful continental neighbor and asserted her new identity as she entered her modern era. Thus, the shared East Asian literary heritage, almost imperceptibly, underwent its most profound shake-up after its dominance for over a millennium. The "Sinographic cosmopolis" (a term adapted from Sheldon Pollock) began a process of re-ordering and re-constitution, as the age-old orientation toward the cultural center got undermined on all levels. For Japan, this opened the door to engagement with China on Japan's own terms, since China as a source of authority was no longer "an imagined or temporarily displaced locale" (Hedberg 2012: 89) and had to be confronted in reality. Much the same, of course, was happening in other countries in the Sinosphere, like Korea and Vietnam (see Wei 2017; Phan 2013).

It is easy to see the imitative *yomihon* as a case of literary "abduction" of a Chinese genre, just like the composition of imitative *kanshi* or even the use of allusions to Chinese verse in traditional Japanese poetry. We have seen the originality and creativity of *Eight Dog Warriors*, so to condemn imitations as literature of a lower order is out of place, reflecting nothing more than Romantic notions of literary worth. The re-use of Chinese literary models, the transfer of plots and motifs to a Japanese context, and the fusion of the "foreign" with the "native," though signaling an unequal relationship, were not viewed in eighteenth-century Japan with such distaste as they are by some modern literary historians, or by chroniclers of nationalistic literary histories. While the call for recognition of the fact that "China is China, Japan is Japan; the Past is Past, and Now is Now" (Hedberg 2012: 35) was voiced clearly and loudly in the early modern period, and the stage was set for interlingual translation to replace *kundoku* texts, the imitative mode was still going strong, as attested by the overwhelming popularity of *Eight Dog Warriors*.

Given the postmodern counterreaction against the entrenched concepts of originality and authenticity, it is perhaps time that the negative judgment on imitations be revamped, even reversed. In discussing the Spanish imitations of French novels called *misterios*, Elisa Martí-López counters the stigmatization of imitation by reading several Spanish specimens through the lens of appropriation, which, according to her, is "the conferring of meaning to another's word" (2002: 29). Not only does she argue for the importance of imitations, but through recourse to George Steiner's "hermeneutic motion," she also highlights the usefulness of appropriative imitations. As she puts it: "appropriation, as the literary practice of a decentered literary consciousness, does not represent the acceptance of one's alienation, but a different understanding of what constitutes identity" (2002: 31), which happens to be highly relevant as a comment on *Eight Dog Warriors*, one of the most impressive fictional imitations in Japanese literary history. As a whole, the Japanese imitative translation of classical Chinese fiction shows how Japanese writers appropriated a foreign literary model for their own use, while the readers of these fictional products experienced an emergent sense of Self (versus Other) that replicated what was happening in the real world.

In Wiebke Denecke's recent article concerning translation in East Asia (2017), she notes that in the Sinographic sphere of earlier times, "unlike in monolingual cultural sphere with phonographic scripts, translation was not needed" (Denecke 2017: 514)—that is, "translation" as it is popularly understood today. In discussing the Japanese *kundoku* strategy of reading Chinese texts, she disagrees somewhat with many translation studies scholars who published on the subject, saying that "*kundoku* is not translation in any conventional sense" and that "premodern Japanese were largely monolingual but did not perceive Chinese texts as foreign" (519).[12] Despite the majority view of scholars in the field that *kundoku* is a kind of translation, the debate on its nature is really inconclusive. Denecke also avers that it was not due to massive migration of peoples in the region, but to the "creative adaptation of Chinese cultural precedents" (516) that a shared cultural identity was fostered in East Asia. Among the most creative forms of adaptation is imitation. Notwithstanding the power of Chinese culture, it is the strong imitative strain that reveals how Chinese cultural items were received by her neighbors. Brilliantly conceived, Denecke's ideas can indeed be substantiated by transtextual evolutionary processes: by *kanshi* poetry through the ages as well as *yomihon* in the Edo era.

---

[12] Elsewhere Denecke also asked a question in this connection: "Did the absence of a necessity for translation create a type of intimacy among people from different East Asian countries that translation-mediated cross-cultural encounters did not allow?" (2014: 214).

9

Receptive Transcreation

Simulating James Joyce's Narrative Style

Imitations have long been researched in influence studies (otherwise named "source studies"), which focuses on how authors transpose subject matter and techniques from one culture to another. It is true that the hierarchical relationships set up by traditional influence studies do more harm than good, while the attribution of sources is often dubious. Among others, Mary Orr (2003) has argued for a different way of looking at influence, one which, among other things, acknowledges creative "interanimation" as taking place between texts across cultures. This provides an inspiration for the study of imitative translations, although, if the reception aspect is to be highlighted, it may be more appropriate to speak of "receptive transcreation." Rather than confining oneself to the surface similarities between the imitated text and the imitation, one should be alert to how the latter copies (and does not copy) from the former. According to Orr, "influence that openly recognizes different others . . . confounds any programmatic or even systematic mode of textual criticism, however socio-critical, interdisciplinary or formalist, and offers a site for cultural renewal" (2003: 87). Discovering divergences in the midst of similarities, and vice versa, and reading them in terms of their cultural significance, is therefore a key to the analysis of imitations.

The problem with some of the practitioners of the influence approach is that they rely too heavily on observed correspondences on just one level to determine the link between two texts, while divergences are downplayed. To cite one example: in his comprehensive study of James Joyce's impact on Spanish-American fiction, Robin W. Fiddian devotes too much attention to the thematic parallels between Joyce's novels and Spanish-American fiction from Jorge Luis Borges onward (Fiddian 1989: 23–39). Fiddian cites the themes shared by the works of Joyce and his imitators from Mexico and Argentina, including the search for identity in an alien environment, sexual initiation, anti-clericalism, rejection of Catholicism, and so on. He then compares *Ulysses* with four imitations, in particular Leopoldo Marechal's *Adán Buenosayres* (1948), the first "Argentinian *Ulysses*." Although some linguistic features (play on names, puns, verbal resonances) are also discussed, Fiddian's article is overdetermined by the emphasis on thematic borrowing as the basis for understanding imitations. While it is not as if Fiddian has neglected the microscopic level of analysis altogether, he does avoid coping on a linguistic level with his texts. The examples he quotes from Gustavo Sainz's imitation of Joyce show that his interest is in the conceptual rather than the verbal, a binary opposition that he introduces himself. Near the end of his article, Fiddian even denigrates Robert Martin Adam's view that "Joycean constants" are "technical innovations in the art of storytelling, and in the use of language" (Fiddian 1989: 36).

The thematic approach, however, is precisely what makes many influence studies so elusive and subjective. Unless the textual foundations of imitations are also demonstrated, the discussion of influence inevitably falls short. It is here that the insights of translation scholars are brought in and applied to the microlevel transformations in addition to broad-based similarities, to understand imitations better.[1] We can consider shared terminology to begin with. The convergences and divergences between the source text and its imitation are not different from the "correspondences" and "differences" between original and target texts in translation research. Direct borrowings from the preexistent text can be seen as "loanwords" and "calques." Also, features of transposition and appropriation, which reflect "influence," are akin to those of "acculturation" and "domestication," key conceptual tools in translational analysis. Imitations are, after all, textual testimonies of influence.

The role played by imitations in transforming literary taste in the receptor community is as important as that of more "faithful" translations. As attested by innumerable cases, imitations can move to central positions in a literary polysystem (Even-Zohar 1978), especially where they manage successfully to incorporate the foreign and give it an indigenous mold. Martí-López (2002), already referenced in previous chapters, has described how imitations played a crucial part in the development of the realist Spanish novel in the nineteenth century through the skillful transposition of mature French examples. This is perhaps similar to what happened to the stream of consciousness novel in twentieth-century China. Imitations not only assisted the source text in exerting an influence; they were also more palatable to the receptors—authors

---

[1] The critical literature on influence is voluminous, but for a recent critical appraisal of influence from the perspective of translation, see Bassnett (2007: 134–46). On the idea of influence operating both forward and backward, or "influence roundabout," see Manfredi (2001: 1–34). Instances of the difficulty in pinpointing precise influence in the Chinese case are aplenty; see Gálik (1968, 1990). Gálik's examples can similarly be reviewed from the perspective of translation studies.

as well as readers—in the target culture. They can, therefore, illustrate very well a special mechanism of influence. In twentieth-century China, many Western styles and genres were first experimented with through imitations before they were used in original writing, as one thing led to another.

A History of Imitations

The subject of the present chapter is the Chinese imitations of Joyce's *Ulysses* in the early 1960s in Hong Kong. Given that unabridged renditions of the novel only appeared toward the end of the twentieth century,[2] these imitations are among the first Chinese "translations" of the genre. They were partly meant as a means of introducing Joyce, especially his experimental narrative style, rather than the themes and content, to the Chinese readership. (In fact, because of the sexual descriptions, the novel was widely condemned in Mainland China later in the 1980s, when the country opened its door to foreign literary imports during the Cultural Fever.) The untranslatable character of this novel is seen in its being dubbed an "inscrutable book" (*tianshu*), a Chinese term frequently used for literary works that defy comprehension. Other imitations of Joyce's works and of stream of consciousness fiction had appeared in Shanghai in the 1920s and 1930s, so the history of the transmission of *Ulysses*, especially of the stream of consciousness technique, to China must be seen as one in which imitations preceded source-text–bound literal translations.

Interestingly, the works chosen for imitation first were Virginia Woolf's short stories: Xu Zhimo's "The Roulette" (1929), Lin Huiyin's "In Ninety-nine Degree Heat" (1934), and Ye Gongchao's "Trace on the Wall" (1932), a rendition of Woolf's "The Mark on the Wall." The second spate of imitations on the Mainland was published in Beijing some fifty years later, in the context of the controversial Subjectivity Debate (Tay 1984). This debate hinged upon a negative response at the time to the imitations. They were accused of having a corruptive impact on society; in particular, the narrative technique, in which the darker side of the individual consciousness is starkly presented, was seen as having a detrimental influence on morality. The imitative works

---

[2] Translations were published in 1993–95 and 1996, by Jin Di and Xiao Qian/Wen Jieruo, respectively. A third translation of the novel by Liu Xiangyu is forthcoming from the Shanghai Translation Press. Until the 1980s, there was only one partial and little noticed translation of the novel, by Zhu Nandu of the "Hades" episode (Zhu 1960). Incidentally, an even more audacious translation of *Finnegans Wake* into Chinese is being carried out by Dai Congrong; its first volume has already appeared in print (Dai 2013).

of Wang Meng, like "Sound of Spring" (1979) and "Eyes of the Night" (1979), were thus ostracized (see Tay 1984: 7–24), even though some critics did come to his support. Furthermore, some imitations showed up on the Taiwanese side: among these the most notable is "Hong Kong 1964" written by Bai Xianyong, generally regarded as the pioneer of the Modernist Movement on the island. Altogether, these show that the transplantation of high modernist literature into China was effected via attempts at imitating it on both sides of the Taiwan Strait, although the literary contexts behind these waves of imitations vary significantly.

Before looking at the *Ulysses* imitations from Hong Kong, we should note a diversity of definitions of "stream of consciousness." While, according to Monika Fludernik (1996), comparable methods of presenting characters' thought have been in use since the seventeenth century, the novelistic genre emerged only at the end of the nineteenth century. This genre signals what critics have called an "inward turn of narrative," which involves the shift of narrative emphasis from external action to mental activity. The method as used differed from author to author, but there is general consensus that Joyce is one of the method's best exemplars.[3] That an imitation of Joyce's best-known novel was undertaken by a dominant figure in the Hong Kong literary scene of the 1960s—Liu Yichang—underscores the perceived importance of the enterprise of transplanting Joyce. On the one hand, the imitations show the fascination on the part of young, aspiring writers with the possibility of transcreating Joyce's narrative style in Chinese. As Rosa Maria Bollettieri and Ira Torresi have put it, *Ulysses* "lends itself particularly well to recreation, since it is an open book in the sense that Umberto Eco gave in his theory of the *opera operta* (unlimited semiosis)" (2012: 43). On the other hand, it epitomizes an effort to introduce a new approach to fiction-writing to Chinese readers, who would find it unprecedented. It would not be an exaggeration to say, in hindsight, that twentieth-century Chinese fiction entered a new phase with the importation of Joyce and company.

Of course, there is also a more practical side to the multiple efforts at imitation of Joyce's novel: *Ulysses* is well known for his "unreadability" and "re-readability" (Bindervoet and Hankes 2012: 74). We have noted its unreadability above. Since Joyce was already "ahead" of his readers, how could he be made accessible to readers from a non-European cultural milieu? In addition to that, as the reader of the novel is amply rewarded when new layers of meaning are revealed at subsequent readings, how can there be a

---

[3] For that reason, major writers of the twentieth century have expressed interest in translating the novel into their own languages: Borges (into Spanish) and Nabokov (into Russian) (see Medina Casado 2010: 84–6).

perfect translation? The introduction of Joyce to Hong Kong in the 1960s has to be seen as having succeeded through a concerted effort: during the few years in which the three imitations to be discussed below were published, many scholarly essays on modernist techniques were also published in *Modern Literature*, a newly founded, avant-garde literary journal of the time.[4] They were meant to aid readers' comprehension of *Ulysses* as well as its experimental method as presented in the Chinese language. In turn, the imitation prepared readers for the "faithful" translations in the 1990s. By that time, *Ulysses* was already part of Chinese literary history and well-assimilated to a non-Western environment like that of China.

The Elusive Style of *Ulysses*: Translatability versus Imitability

The difficulty in imitating Joyce's narrative style in *Ulysses* in another language is proved by the story of the contorted course taken by the novel upon its entrance into China, via imitations first and faithful translations later. The stylistic incoherence and indirection of Joyce distinguish it from other modernist experimentalists. For instance, Joyce's stream of consciousness is seldom as controlled as Woolf's: in Woolf's novels words like "s/he thought" are just beneath the surface of the text, while in Joyce's work one often has difficulty deciding whether it is the narrator or the character that is doing the "thinking." This has given rise to the puzzlement and lack of comprehension that readers feel in reading *Ulysses*, although it is only by presenting thoughts as they come floating, uninterrupted and unstructured, into a character's mind that Joyce makes his stream of consciousness look authentic. Though the narrator does provide some guidance from time to time, hardly any allowances are made to ensure that the reader will grasp the content of Bloom's, Stephen's, and Molly's thought. Consequently, only at a second, or third, reading does the reader make sense of the story. Choosing a special lexicon and deploying rhythm to convey the characters' thinking styles, Joyce literally reinvents the English language. Tim Parks has drawn attention to Joyce's "determination to use every resource of the English language to create the worlds, atmospheres, mental states and even literary styles he wishes

---

[4] A special issue on James Joyce was featured in *Modern Literature* in September 1960 (no. 4). This was followed later by another on Virginia Woolf in January 1961 (no. 6). William Faulkner was the subject of a special issue in November 1961 (no. 11). The journal was Taiwan-based, but widely circulated in Hong Kong.

to evoke" (1998: 64). Guillermo Sanz Gallego rightly notes the two areas of difficulty—narratorial and linguistic—when he says that Spanish translators have to "pay attention to style in the form of prosodic elements, heterology and heteroglossia, as well as to the reproduction of the narrator's ideological voice" (2019: 275). To these we now turn.

First, Joyce makes greater use of interior monologue—the direct rendering of thought streams marked by the use of the first person—than, for instance, Woolf, where narrated monologue (or free indirect speech) largely predominates.[5] Both methods diverge from the more conventional mode of psycho-narration, in which an omniscient narrator tells the reader what goes on in a character's mind.[6] Interior monologue is, essentially, a direct quotation of thought in the first person, while narrated monologue, signaled by the use of the third person, features mediation by a narrator. While in both methods the actual words used in a character's mental discourse are ostensibly recorded, the stronger presence of the narrator in the latter leads to a more structured and orderly presentation. Because of Joyce's deliberate refusal to structure the characters' thoughts, in reading *Ulysses* one often has difficulty sorting out the separate "streams." In light of this, Weldon Thornton has perceptively suggested that Joyce aims to present collective, rather than individual, mentalities in *Ulysses* (Thornton 2001: 58-60). Woolf's stream of consciousness novels are easier to comprehend than Joyce's, and also more "translatable." The recourse to imitation is thus understandable: freed at least from the necessity to re-convey the content, the imitator can better focus on the transference, or duplication, of narrative style.

Second, there is the problem with Joyce's language: *Ulysses* has been praised for its "polyphonic dimension" (Baron 2010: 138), its "prosodic, musical and rhythmical aspects" (Sanz Gallego 2019), and its deployment of puns and echoes of Irish poetry (Boisen 1967: 166). On the level of word usage and sentence construction, the task of rendering *Ulysses* into Chinese is bedeviled not only by Joyce's game of words with special phonic qualities, but also his deliberate flaunting of syntactic rules. Both of these are more than purely linguistic tricks, of course. As an integral part of Joyce's presentation of mental processes, they reveal the way in which thoughts arise and subside according to the associative principles advanced by contemporary psychologists like

---

[5] Stream of consciousness techniques can be classified into: interior monologue, embedded dialogue, free indirect discourse, and objective descriptions. Dorrit Cohn (1978) has proposed a classification into psycho-narration, quoted monologue, and narrated monologue; Taraja Rouhiainen (2000), into free direct discourse vs. free indirect discourse.
[6] The tripartite division used here is suggested by Beeretz (1998: 21-7), although Cohn prefers "quoted monologue" to "interior monologue" (1978: 11-17).

William James and Sigmund Freud. Refracting the erratic and spontaneous nature of the flow of thought, words collide with one another and metamorphose into portmanteau words, compounds, and other neologisms. In *Ulysses* some sentences are truncated, others begin in medias res without a subject, and still others do without the main verb. Among the most daring feats of Joyce's linguistic experimentation is the final episode, "Penelope," where textual fragmentation shows the preverbal level of consciousness: the absence of punctuation and the free flow of random images replicate the workings of free association in Molly's mind.[7] Narratology and language are thus inseparable, and it is with some remarkable linguistic acrobatics that the style can be reproduced.

It is the failure to appreciate this that has led to highly questionable claims by some Chinese critics—those of the 1980s in particular—that the stream of consciousness technique has been used in classical Chinese literature, from medieval poetry to classical novels like *Dream of the Red Chamber*. While it is certainly true that the presentation of thought has not been altogether absent in the Chinese literary tradition, and techniques analogous to free indirect speech may be found in certain Chinese novels, one would be hard put to cite instances comparable to Joyce's in Chinese fiction prior to the twentieth century. The linguistic disparities between Chinese and English also mean that Joyce's strategies are distinctly non-Chinese. Unresolvable barriers to accurately rendering the novel have been noted by the likes of Enrico Terrinoni (who translated *Ulysses* into Italian), who bemoans the impossibility of adhering to the original: "One must admit that there is little room for faithfulness or unfaithfulness when we are asked to modify the cultural and linguistic horizons of a literary text" (2012: 117). That being the case, the barriers to successfully translating *Ulysses* adequately into a non-European language like Chinese are obvious, as is the reason why imitations dominated the scene for some seventy years after the novel's initial publication.

William Yip's "Ulysses in Taipei"

Published in 1960, William Yip's (1937–) short story "Ulysses in Taipei" boldly announces its indebtedness to Joyce's *Ulysses*. A prodigious translator of English poetry and an American-based university professor, Yip was very

---

[7] For accounts of the intractable problems that *Ulysses* presents to the Chinese translator, see the special issue of *James Joyce Quarterly* 35.1 (1997).

active on the Hong Kong literary scene of the 1960s. Through co-editing several leading literary journals, including the well-known *New Thought Currents* (*Xin sichao*), he did much to promote Western literary modernism, introducing T. S. Eliot, Marcel Proust, and Tennessee Williams through critical essays that he either wrote or translated. "Ulysses in Taipei" is about one day in the life of a university professor in Taiwan, strewn with an abundance of inconsequential details. It loosely imitates the story of Leopold Bloom's aimless wandering through the streets of Dublin on Bloomsday.

While completely departing from the original plot, Yip approximates Joyce's stream of consciousness method. The first sentence of his story is an instance of *catachresis*, with a disjunction between the noun and the verb: "armpit carrying a book toward the toilet"[8] can be corrected by rephrasing the sentence as "in his armpit he carries a book toward the toilet." The same device reappears eleven lines later, again in imitation of the verbal incoherence in *Ulysses*. The use of colons to string together phrases is also typically Joycean, a strategy meant to give readers an impression of unconnected thoughts arising in a sporadic manner. Examples are: "Paid the bill: two dollars fifty," "Waited for bus: twenty minutes already," and "Lunch: six dollars." Also transferred from *Ulysses* is the use of repetitions, as in "Why doesn't the bell ring?" The conversational exchanges that the professor (who is the protagonist) has with his students, and then his dialogue with the librarian, are embedded within the flow of his thought. Only in one way does Yip go beyond the mere transplantation of techniques to borrow Joyce's plot. The central portion of his story, where the professor teaches a poetry class, is re-created from the "Nestor" episode.

The expressive potentialities of the Chinese language are exploited to imitate Joyce's narrative technique. Since both past and present tenses are unmarked in the Chinese language, great chunks of "Ulysses in Taipei" can be read as either the narrator's (or the character's) after-event narration, or the unmediated representation of mental processes, in the past and the present respectively. The text thus remains ambiguous throughout, suspending time rather than making clear references to it. The past tenses in the first few sentences in the translation below are arbitrary, since the present tenses could have been used:

> (I/he) got off (my/his) bed, armpit carrying a book toward the toilet. (I/he) washed (my/his) face, brushed teeth. Put on clothes and trousers, socks and shoes; combed hair; picked up a bag of dirty laundry. Drank salted soya bean milk and ate a thin piece of pancake. Picked up a greasy

[8] The translations of all the Chinese texts discussed in this chapter are the author's.

paper: "Prime Minister Lumumba of Congo on the run"—*there's no desperate need to take such a course of action!* The supplement: "Nudity is an art?" Master Ha: "Lifelong Regret." (Yip 1960: 39; italics added)

The italicized sentence above shows the use of direct interior monologue, so it has to be translated with the present tenses in English.

This conflation of narrative time schemes is facilitated by the omission of the subject, which happens to be grammatical in a Chinese sentence, where it can be deduced. Hence the typically characteristic Joycean touch is undermined somewhat. The non-italicized portion quoted above can be read as either third-person/omniscient or first-person narration since it is not unusual for pronouns to be omitted in either spoken or written Chinese. The entire text, in fact, has characteristics of both first- and third-person narrative, even if it also contains vague stylistic indications that it might be coming from one and the same person. The ambiguity has been noticed by Joycean critics, who point out that the narrator in *Ulysses* has a tendency to adopt the idiom of the characters whose thoughts he is rendering.[9] It has been argued that the Chinese language is a better vehicle for free indirect speech (Liu 1994: 174–92), but judging from the above quote, it is also an apt medium for Joycean interior monologue. To sum up, the Chinese language is comparable to Slavic languages, which are characterized by topic–comment structures, flexible word-order, and liberal use of ellipsis, so that "longer chunks of text containing a fair amount of elided elements still appear coherent" (Bazarnik 2014: 38). The imitation, therefore, turns out to be more coherent than the original.

Lu Yin's "Armed Christ"

Unlike "Ulysses in Taipei," Lu Yin's (1935–) "Armed Christ" (1960) only simulates features of Joyce's style but does not take over plot elements. A co-founder of the Society of Modern Literature and Art in 1958, Lu actively contributed to the local journal *Repulse Bay*, and he is said to have been "responsible for the translation of stream of consciousness fiction into Chinese" (Li and Qin 2001: 842).[10] He served as editor for some popular literary and film journals before migrating to Canada in the 1970s. His "Armed Christ," published in *Xin Sichao*, is modeled after Molly's soliloquy.

---

[9] This is the well-known Uncle Charles Principle in Joyce scholarship (see Beeretz 1998: 33–8).
[10] Also see Li and Qin (2001) for a discussion of the translation scene of the 1960s in Hong Kong, especially the part played by journals in the introduction of modernist fiction.

Other than a dozen full stops, placed at the end of some paragraphs, and the frequent use of dashes, Lu dispenses with punctuation marks altogether, in simulation of Joyce's presentation of the ebb and flow of Molly's thought. Parenthetical statements are inserted sporadically—some of them to indicate external events and actions, others to allow the omniscient narrator to interpolate and add extra information.

The creative element of "Armed Christ" is seen in its allegorical use of the Biblical narrative of the persecution and killing of Jesus, whose counterpart in the story is Zhang Kang, a Malaysian triad member pursued by the police. After teaming up with twelve "sworn brothers" (the equivalent of the twelve disciples) in Hong Kong, he is betrayed by one of them and arrested. Three diegetic points of view are adopted—the narrator's, Zhang Kang's, and his wife Ah Xiang's—and used in turn. The first part of the story features Ah Xiang's interior monologue, in which she recalls the previous night when Zhang Kang made love to her (paragraphs 1–3). In the second, Zhang ruminates as he wanders aimlessly in the streets of Hong Kong (paragraphs 4–5). The third part narrates the couple's confrontation with the policemen who come to arrest Zhang (paragraph 6 to the end). Often a shift in point of view is captured in the conventional mode with an *inquit*-tag (like "he thought"), as in the fourth paragraph:

> Zhang Kang came out early in the morning thinking too of the night before even of the prostitute's room a year eight years ago he remembered clearly . . . as he walked he hoped he would not meet any Buddhist nuns. *He thought*: I will put an end to this he will end it as he did in Malaysia. (Lu 1960: 32; italics added)

However, in most places the shifts are unmarked, as at the end of the first paragraph, where the external narration changes into Ah Xiang's interior monologue rather abruptly (as indicated by a change in the subject). This has the effect of immersing the reader in the characters' streams of consciousness:

> . . . in the pictures *she* saw a bare-chested, mustached man placing his two outstretched hands on the log my Dad taught me this he is the God of Heaven the God of Heaven can give protection *I* am eighteen this year can do the laundry cook mend clothes when *I* have a kid . . . (Lu 1960: 30) (emphasis added)

As the story progresses, the various narrative modes crisscross and merge with increasing momentum. Near the climax of the story, just before the policemen break into Zhang Kang's apartment, Lu Yin mixes (a) external narration, (b) embedded conversations, (c) narrated monologue, and (d) interior monologue. In this hybridized mode, the story seeks to recreate Joyce's method in *Ulysses*. This is clear from the following passage:

> The sound of waves trembling Aladdin's oil lamp small boat afloat strolling onward Zhang Kang watched (a)—it's my business nothing to do with you (d) they will come they must come they want to fetch me I have washed my hands isn't that good (b) (he suddenly thought of death [c]) I opened all the windows I need more fresh air from the countryside I will have children Ah Xiang is healthy (d) . . . (Lu 1960: 34; parenthetical letters added)

Compared with "Ulysses in Taipei," "Armed Christ" comes closer in style to *Ulysses*, and it toys with Joyce's narrative twists and turns using a non-Western language—an obvious attempt to introduce the masterpiece to Chinese readers at a time when faithful renditions were not available. Understandably, in the earlier efforts at re-presenting the stream of consciousness novel, it was easier to simulate rather than translate literally. Lu's imitation bears a greater resemblance to Joyce's multilayered narrative than Yip's, and the amalgamation of narrative modes is more deftly handled. As an imitation, it poses a greater challenge to the reader than Yip's more one-dimensional approach. Furthermore, Lu is able to exploit more fully the resources offered by the experimental technique, while making some creative interventions of his own. His story is marked by a consistent pattern of Christian symbolism, with allusions to Christ's crucifixion, and by his structuring the events described in a Chinese (Hong Kong) cultural context. It is most exciting as a potpourri of elements East and West—with dragons, the First Emperor of China, Peng Lai (the Chinese island paradise), the Himalayas, and the Tibetan plains on the one hand and Christ, Eden, Adam and Eve, Noah's ark, the Cross, the twelve disciples, and God on the other.

Liu Yichang's *The Drunkard*

Published less than three years after "Ulysses in Taipei" and "Armed Christ," and now renowned as a modern classic, Liu Yichang's (1918–) novel *The Drunkard* (1962–63) is yet another Chinese imitation of *Ulysses* in Hong Kong. Even on the surface, *The Drunkard* exhibits a rather thorough use of Joycean narrative strategies, including: disjointed, elliptical sentences; syntactical contortions; cinematic devices like zooming and cutting; leitmotifs and repetitions; and suggestive imagery and symbolism. In spite of this, Liu once denied during an interview that he "imitated either *Ulysses* or *The Sound and the Fury* or *The Waves*" (Huoyi 1995: 118), claiming that the style he used was "his own." The debasement of imitations at his time may well have led to his reluctance to acknowledge his indebtedness to Joyce. On yet another occasion, most tellingly, Liu spoke of his feeling "uncomfortable" about the stream of consciousness technique in *The Drunkard* (Houyi 1995: 192), which indirectly reflects his negative attitude toward imitations. It is paradoxical, then, that on the basis of this novel he has been honored as "an institution" in Hong Kong literary history (Pollard 1995: vii). Recently, his fame was further catapulted when the novel was adapted into *In the Mood for Love* (2000), the award-winning movie by Wong Kar-wai.

Significantly, in critical articles published over the past three decades on *The Drunkard*, the novel's technical accomplishment has often been emphasized. It has been argued that it skillfully combines a traditional narrative method with the modernist mode (Huoyi 1995: 183). It has also been said to be an experimental success as lyrical fiction or as metafiction (Huoyi 1995: 217, 238). But even as most critics choose to read it as an "original," there is no denying the ties that it bears to *Ulysses*, so the designation of "imitation" is unavoidable despite its pejorative connotations. To be sure, there is loss, rather than gain, if one reads the novel without reference to the Joycean hypotext. Partly owing to its length, it showcases a greater range of stream of consciousness techniques as used in *Ulysses* than the above-mentioned stories by Yip and Lu. Other than a means of reporting what goes on in the conscious mind, the interior monologue becomes a vehicle for presenting the memories, daydreams, fantasies, and sensory impressions of the nameless protagonist, whose prototype is none other than the author himself. Serious about his vocation as a writer but forced by poverty to churn out low-brow swordsman and pornographic fiction, he is much given to drinking bouts and constantly inebriated. Perhaps to facilitate comprehension by the uninitiated reader, Liu Yichang often separates his protagonist's internal thoughts from the external narration by putting them within parentheses. This is seen in the following extract from Chapter 8, when the protagonist is confined to the hospital after being beaten up by some ruffians:

> He left.
> (He walks like a pigeon, I thought.)
> The nurse also left.
> (She walks as if she were doing a rumba, I thought.)
> I continued to recline in bed. . . .
> (Who has the power to reverse the passage of time, so that the past can
>   be substituted for the future? The smile under the Bodhi tree causes

the murderer to withdraw his knife; the frown on the cross is greeted by peals of thunder . . .) (Liu 1993: 41–2)

Liu Yichang also painstakingly imitates other devices used by Joyce. The unpunctuated paragraphs below from Chapter 10 (B) show how wordplay, repetitions, and omission of punctuation infiltrate the protagonist's hallucinations:

With the steps of a traveler I enter 1992
The Great War is over the entire earth is burnt only the oceans have not been dried
Even the wind has been polluted by nuclear dust
Lazily blowing the green smoke from the burnt earth
Cannot find cockroaches cannot find tadpoles cannot find mosquitoes cannot find ants cannot find earthworms cannot find lizards cannot find dragonflies cannot find bats cannot find eagles cannot find pigeons cannot find crows cannot find carp . . . (Liu 1993: 57)

The Joycean repetition of words and phrases occurs elsewhere too, as in "the wheels keep turning" (Chapter 4), "one glass, two glasses" (Chapter 5), "I would like to take a space shuttle . . ." (Chapter 6), and "Sima Li wearing . . ." (Chapter 11). Compounded with imagistic references to "thought running wild like an unreined horse/ like the wind/like the rain/like a tram" (Liu 1993: 41, 42, 43, 67) and "swimming in a glass of wine" (Liu 1993: 2, 26), they create a kind of rhythmic intensity, with recurrent patterns of motifs. Mogens Boisen, the Danish translator of *Ulysses*, has described the book's style as similar: "there are thousands of [leitmotifs], often only a word, but it must be repeated some 700 pages later, and repeated either in the identical form or in some significant variation" (1967: 166).

In the protagonist's digressions on literary topics, one notices his high evaluations of Western modernist literature, condemnation of a consumer society where the arts have no place, and laments on the miserable predicament of Hong Kong intellectuals in the 1960s. His characterization of Hong Kong as a "capitalized, commercial hub of Chinese culture, 'lacking in culture'" (Larson 1993: 89) shows why Liu Yichang was drawn spiritually to Joyce, and allows us to see the imitation as providing a context for paying homage to the master. He calls Joyce "one of the greatest literary talents of the twentieth century" who "has a key to opening the door of modern literature" (Liu 1993: 41). With some exaggeration, he even points out that "thousands of books have been written on *Ulysses* and *Finnegans Wake*" (41). Liu's denial of any influence by the greatest English novel of all time is well-nigh unwarranted. The itinerant wanderings of the *flaneur*-like protagonist in the city of Hong Kong easily remind us of Leopold Bloom cruising in Dublin on June 16, 1904.

Emulation versus Apprenticeship in Imitation

In considering what imitating *Ulysses* meant for the Chinese writers who attempted it, one may seize upon the classical Western model of imitation that emphasizes the motive of emulation. In this model, literary works chosen for imitation are landmarks of tradition, to be renewed or transcended by its successors. Imitations are thus carried out against a context of veneration for the originals. While this may apply to a certain extent to the cases considered above, it does not appear to be an ideal explanation for what happened. The polysystems framework may also be relevant here: the imitations can reflect a desire to incorporate a foreign genre into the target literary system, where anything loosely comparable is lacking (see Even-Zohar 1978). The Chinese imitations of *Ulysses* were undertaken with an awareness of the "superiority" of Joyce's novel, and imitating it becomes an opportunity to take advantage of the new technique, and re-apply it to subject matter from a different culture. As seen in the three examples considered above, the primary and persistent interest for the imitators of *Ulysses* was its narrative style—given that the transfer of content from the source texts is seldom a principal motivation.

Literary historians in the West can point to numerous examples of imitations that are achievements in their own right, in some cases even surpassing the texts they imitate. The poems of Augustan authors like Alexander Pope and Samuel Johnson are illustrative, while more recent successes are the imagist poems of Pound, inspired by Chinese and Japanese lyrical poetry. The same does not hold true for two of the three Chinese imitations in question, if one were to judge by the critical and popular reception.[11] Yip's and Lu's imitations of *Ulysses* in Hong Kong have virtually been consigned to obscurity; they are now of interest only as documenting an almost lost chapter in Hong Kong's literary history. They may have participated in a trend of experimentation with stream of consciousness techniques in fiction in China's periphery in the 1970s and 1980s, but they are not deemed worthy of serious critical exegeses in themselves. It is as if, after having helped transplant a foreign literary genre, they can be shelved

---

[11] China has its own imitation theory too: the terms used are *mofang* (see Kao 1985) and *linmo* (Henningsen 2010).

and forgotten. *The Drunkard* did become a classic, but interestingly, critics care little for it as an imitation, especially given Liu's denial. It is obvious that he borrowed Western modernist narrative techniques for his own use, but the acclaim *The Drunkard* received has apparently little to do with its being an imitation.

There is yet another side to the coin, however, if things are viewed from a receptionist perspective. It can be said that the imitators aimed not to emulate but to learn their craft from a foreign maestro. A theory of apprenticeship has probably more relevance in modern East Asia than a theory of emulation. Subtle motives underlie the desire to acquire literary techniques and genres from another system via imitation, but our examples document the "learning" that had taken place along with the creative experimentation. William Yip zeroed in on the skill with which Joyce presented the inner mental thoughts of a character, and took over the latter's use of a narrow temporal and spatial frame—everything takes place in one day, on a university campus. Lu Yin borrowed Joycean strategies for narrating multiple consciousnesses while imposing a consistent pattern of Biblical allusions, much as Joyce had drawn Homeric parallels in *Ulysses*. Liu Yichang explored the full range of Joyce's idiosyncratic techniques for presenting varied states of consciousness, and engaged with them in the much larger scope offered by a full-length novel. There was nothing comparable from the indigenous tradition at the time, and thus the practice was pedagogically sound.

With regard to the cases in point, one needs to consider the possibility that the imitators may have based their imitations on more than one source text. In the imitation of particular styles or genres of writing the use of pastiche is rampant. Rather than working exclusively with one original text, the imitator can build on an ensemble of texts encountered in reading, including some recollected from memory. Because of the central position occupied by *Ulysses* in the stream of consciousness tradition, it can be designated as the Urtext for imitations like those mentioned above as well as others to appear later, although this suggestion is not entirely unproblematic. In any case, the three Hong Kong imitators may have used more than one stream of consciousness text besides Joyce's. Those of other modernists like Marcel Proust, William Faulkner, and Woolf may have been sources of inspiration as well.

Imitation, Reception, and Transcreation

While imitations of stream of consciousness fiction served many Chinese writers of the twentieth century who sought to learn from (if not emulate)

Western models, they also facilitated the reception of the genre by the general readership. At least before the unabridged translations came along, they were all that was available. That *Ulysses* resists literal or "faithful" translation there can be no doubt, with Joyce's transgressive use of the English language being the biggest obstacle. His radical experimentation with his own mother tongue entailed nothing less than a complete reconstruction, a re-representation, of "the linguistic world" as his contemporaries knew it. Rendering *Ulysses* in another language has been a nightmare for generations of translators,[12] but the irony is that the linguistic demands placed by *Ulysses* even on native English readers are immense.[13] Imitations are somewhat kinder to the reader. Imitators can navigate the linguistic and cultural obstacles when strict adherence to the source text is not the prime concern. Since it is not mandatory that they stay close to either the verbal texture or the subject matter of the hypotext, there is allowance for greater flexibility. The linguistic provocations may still be there, but the shock is cushioned. While some modernist novelists, like Virginia Woolf, sought to speak more directly to the "common reader," it remains true that many modernist novels—*Ulysses* in particular—have chosen to deliberately keep a distance. To say the least, then, the three early imitations in Chinese at least managed better to speak to a wider range of readers, creating the grounds for a more general receptivity to Joyce that could make the full translations, when they finally appeared, perhaps more quickly digestible.

Ben Jonson brilliantly summed up what he understood to be the nature of imitation as a generic category when he called it a "middle composition" between translation and original writing. In this way he hinted at the creative element in imitative translations. The significant alterations permitted in imitations are evidenced by all three examples in the present chapter, but particularly so with the last two. Thus, other than the one obvious contribution that the Chinese imitations have made—namely, that they paved the way for the "real Joyce" when *Ulysses* finally "landed" in China in the 1990s—these imitations also enabled the three authors in question to express what they felt in a novel manner, as described above.

Late twentieth-century developments in translation studies have seen scholars seeking to expand the territory within which the phenomenon of imitation can be placed. Susan Bassnett and André Lefevere (1990) have

---

[12] For discussions of the difficulty of translating *Ulysses* into other languages, see Senn (1991); into Japanese, see Matsuoka (1988–89).

[13] Owing to the work of scholars like Don Gifford and Robert Seidman who tracked down such references and supplied readers with copious annotations, reading the original novel has become easier—perhaps easier than reading the translation.

offered a more inclusive definition for "translation." For them, critical commentaries, movie versions, and so on, are all "translations," and their famous statement, "translation is a rewriting of an original text," implies that imitations are translations too. There are those, of course, who sought to impose some limits. Armin Paul Frank, for instance, states categorically that "it is not helpful to redefine 'translation' in a way which includes responses within the same language, discursive (journalistic, critical, scholarly) responses, and inter-medial transpositions" (Frank 1992: 370). Still, with that proviso, he proceeds to define translation as "receptive re-creation," thus opening the possibilities for considering imitation as a translational activity. Perhaps it will be more apposite to call imitations acts of "receptive transcreation." Anthony Pym offers yet another perspective on the problem of how to handle the dazzling array of transformed texts, the relations among which present a perennial problem. For him, one needs to apply inclusive definitions first and exclusive definitions only afterwards, permitting the textual materials that one is examining to reveal their true nature when placed next to each other (Pym 1998: 58). As we have seen, incorporating imitations into a broader framework of translation, and applying close textual analysis to these works, generates insights that may reorient thinking about the cross-cultural transplantation of a genre, a narrative technique, and a masterpiece. The case of the imitative translations of *Ulysses* in Hong Kong in the early 1960s shows how they effectively played a role in introducing not only a new genre but also novelty in literary composition that cultural polysystems are constantly searching for.

10

The Aggregate Monkey

Parody and Pastiche in Japanese Manga

The premodern history of imitation in Japan includes many cases of rewritten Chinese classical fiction, in a way that parallels Western imitations of Greek and Roman classics from the Renaissance onward. Given that the history of Sino-Japanese cross-cultural interaction is often documented by Japanese imitations of Chinese canonical texts they are virtually a barometer of the Japanese response to China over time. The situation can be seen as analogous to the way in which Augustan imitations linked English literature and culture to classical antiquity. In Chapter 7 we analyzed the reinvention, emulation, and modernization impulses behind the major Western imitations. In the last chapter we crossed the East-West divide and examined how imitations transposed the characteristic style of Western high modernism to a Chinese context. If the imitations of Hong Kong authors are meant as homage to Joyce's *Ulysses,* then those of a canonical Chinese novel by Japanese manga artists in the 1990s show a new twist to the centuries-long reverence for things Chinese. If it is not to be interpreted simply as a deconstructionist move, then how does it reflect a shift in the Japanese attitude toward a cultural neighbor?

At the same time, the Romantic disparagement of imitation as theft, especially when the indebtedness to the source is not specified, has for some time held sway under the banner of originality. If we take a closer look at the enormous body of theory built around imitation for centuries, especially with respect to its openness to the practice of parody, perhaps it is easier to understand how it can be resurrected and re-energized for an age that boldly reasserts the legitimacy of derivative rewriting. In the following sections, I will first take issue with Gérard Genette's "restricted definition" (1997: 73) of imitation and offer an alternative view, namely that the parody and the pastiche are both forms of imitation. This will be followed by an account of the historical evolution of Japanese manga imitations of Chinese fiction in the twentieth century. The core of the chapter will be the analysis of one example from the 1990s, *Journey to the Extreme,* a manga that borrows only a modicum of structural and plot elements from the classical Chinese novel *Journey to the West* but succeeds in creating a vastly different narrative universe through a combination of visual and verbal means. I will conclude with speculations on how imitation, while linked to prototypical forms of translation as a transtextual activity, differs from them by virtue of its capacity for subverting the source text. It does precisely what "normal" translations will not even attempt, wreaking havoc with the text that it imitates and completely reconfiguring the source content and style.

Imitation, Parody, and Pastiche

A convenient starting point for understanding imitation as a transtextual act is Gérard Genette's arbitrary division, in *Palimpsest*, between parodies and pastiches: the former is said to belong to the category of transformations and the latter, to that of imitation.[1] For him, "*it is impossible to imitate a text* [and] *one can imitate only a style: that is to say, a genre*" (1997: 83; italics in the original). Genette is correct in distinguishing imitation from copying on grounds that it is a creative act, unlike mere reproduction (as in the replication of earlier paintings). But then he thinks that imitation should deal only with the style or genre of the original text(s). This leads him to classify parodies as "transformations" because they take on texts(s), but never a genre—imposing changes on the hypotext in either a limited or systematic manner (1997: 84). This binary classification, which underlies his entire book, is problematic. In view of the current discussions of parody by scholars (see below), especially the preference for a broader definition of imitation, it may be best to begin with a slightly revised version of Genette's formulation (see Table 10.1) (cf. Genette 1997: 28):

In this table, Genette's category of "transformation" is removed from the left column. Of course, Genette's other categories are still useful, especially his emphasis on the way derivative texts can be differentiated in terms of function: playful (for parodies and pastiches), satirical (by travesties and caricatures), and serious (by transpositions and forgeries). This model has informed many subsequent elaborations, such as Richard Dyer's (2007) "signaled" versus "unsignaled" imitations (depending on whether the imitators choose to identify the sources they have used). Of immediate

---

[1] More precisely, as Genette puts it in his opening chapter, his book is about hypertextuality (the relation between hypotexts and hypertexts, or source and target texts in translational parlance), one of five kinds of transtextuality (1997: 5).

Table 10.1 Categories of Imitations (Revised from Genette 1997)

Imitation	playful	parody
		pastiche
	satirical	travesty
		caricature
	serious	transposition
		forgery

relevance to our discussion in the present chapter, however, is Genette's idea of "playful" imitation (as contrasted with "serious" parody), which clearly shows his sensitivity to functional distinctions. He notes the "onerous confusion" caused by "parody," which is "called upon to designate at times playful distortion, at times the burlesque transposition of a text, and on other occasions the satirical imitation of style" (1997: 24). As an improvement, he defines the contemporary parody more broadly as that "which only takes [the hypotext] as a model or template for the construction of a new text which, once produced, is no longer concerned with the model" (1997: 27). This effectively turns it into a kind of imitation.

Within this framework, we can identify some of the key issues that pertain to our analysis of playful imitations (in opposition to the "serious" ones studied in our last chapter). One interesting feature of Genette's classificatory system is that he moves parody from the "satirical" category that it used to occupy and places it squarely within the "playful" category—he calls this a "correction." In his functional approach, the parody "aims at a sort of pure amusement or pleasing exercise with no aggressive or mocking intention," and so it displays only the ludic mode (1997: 27). Later, he further notes that the boundaries between the different genres are not hard and fast, and between them some intermediary modes can be imagined. He adds three other functions: the ironic, the humorous, and the polemical. This loosens up the strict demarcation of boundaries, and contests a narrow definition of what is "playful." Genette clearly recognizes the taxonomic and terminological obfuscations that are an intrinsic part of his subject. He rightly points out that one can see the terms as conceptual tools, bearing in mind that they cross over to one another in a circular system where "each mood would have a point of contact with the two others" (1997: 29).

Still, there is the problem of distinguishing between parody and pastiche, both playful imitations. In his book, Genette notes that while a parody plays with one original text, a pastiche can involve playing with more than one "original." (Elsewhere, Genette also makes another distinction by saying that "pastiche plain and simple would refer to the imitation of a style without any satirical intent" [1997: 25], whereas parodies are directed against a work rather than a style.) By its very name, the pastiche is a collage, a hodgepodge, or a potpourri. With an etymological meaning of "mixing," it is a hybrid mode, in which textual elements taken over from various sources are blended. Yet there is no reason why the parody cannot be based on a body of works related by theme, manner of expression, style, or genre; the "one hypotext" requirement is perhaps unnecessarily restrictive. Seymour Chatman, in his essay on "Parody and Style" (2001: 25–39), has discussed the parodying of a style shared by many works. For him, "style" is "the constellation of idiosyncratic practices" (2001: 26) of an author, so a whole group of texts by one author can be parodied at the same time. The job of the literary critic is to study the changes occurring to individual "stylemes."[2]

Linda Hutcheon has chosen not to make a distinction between parody and pastiche, extending the meaning of "parody" so that it encompasses virtually the full range of imitative practices—even all kinds of intertextual relations. In this formulation, parody is also more or less coterminous with imitation. In Margaret Rose's definitions of parody (1993), mockery is emphasized as an indispensable element. In disagreement, Hutcheon uses a more inclusive definition in which ridicule is not made an essential ingredient when it comes to deciding whether a literary work is a parody. This allows her to include in *A Theory of Parody* (1985) discussion of postmodern specimens, such as metafiction, video games, film, opera, and even amusement parks. It seems fair enough to say that a less restrictive definition perhaps makes better sense since it is often impossible to decide whether a certain imitative text is jokey or serious. To stipulate a contrast between the disrespectful parody and the celebratory pastiche, too, is a position not universally supported by known examples.[3]

For a working definition of parody that can be used to analyze our Japanese imitations, I would like to quote Nil Korkut. According to him, a parody is "an intentional imitation—of a text, style, genre, or discourse—which includes an element of humor and which has an aim of interpreting

---

[2] Incidentally, John Melling makes yet another distinction between parody and pastiche: "A parody is a burlesque imitating some serious work; a pastiche is usually a serious imitation in the exact manner of the original author" (Melling 1996: 1). This differs from both Genette's and our own definitions, as presented above.

[3] The functions of parodies are more wide-ranging than those we have covered here. Ingeborg Hoesterey focuses on the emulation (rather than the mockery) aspect of parody as a transtexual mode, saying that in parody the writer "rewrites a model to triumph over it" (2001: 95).

its target in one way or another" (Korkut 2009: 21). The emphasis given to playing with the source becomes a signpost in the discussion that ensues. As for a working definition of pastiche, I would like to reference Luke Kuhns, who has highlighted three subcategories. First, there are traditional pastiches, in which elements from the original text are elaborated or reinforced with additional information (as in sequels and prequels). A second group consists of pastiche crossovers, in which source text materials are enmeshed in a new genre or a different historical period, even in the imagined future. The last category is made up of conversions into another (usually visual) medium (Kuhns 2014: 55–6). Whether parody or pastiche, however, from a translational perspective, the ingredient that really defines imitation is "freedom in rendition," with an inclination toward the free rather than the literal end.

Parodic Imitation in Translation

In Chapter 7, we already surveyed some premodern Western approaches to imitation as translation from the Renaissance onward. The proliferation of modern views on the subject, however, measures up to the richness of the earlier theoretical tradition. This is especially so when we deal with the concept of parodic imitation as it relates to translation. According to John Melling (1996), the term "parody" was first used in 1598, derived from the Greek word *paroidia* (meaning: distortion), while "pastiche," a derivative of *pasticcio* in Italian (meaning: medley), made its first appearance much later, in 1878. We will make some use of this basic semantic distinction while bearing in mind the broader use of the term "parody." As an intertextual move, parody works in very much the same way as translation, in that it rewrites a prior text. But unlike the case of translations, which are normally read by those who have no linguistic access to the original, the objective intended by the parodist will be lost to the reader who is unfamiliar with the imitated text. The parodist succeeds when the text is read with a double vision, and the source text is re-presented, or a tribute is paid to the original author. In Augustan times, the connotations of "parody" were much less fixed than they are today: the term was used indiscriminately to refer to both translation and imitation (see Weinbrot 1966: 442–50). It was a time when educated readers had the ability to recognize the original model and appreciate the similarities and discrepancies between the imitated text and its imitation. In fact, such a mode of reading was even facilitated by the printing of the source and target texts on opposing pages, often Latin against English.

Parodists were then highly regarded, unlike plagiarists. Howard Weinbrot draws the conclusion that "[Augustan imitation] in its most significant form is the offspring not only of a theory of free translation, but of the Restoration parody as well" (1966: 447).

Obviously the territory occupied by imitations needs to be clearly charted if translation's distinctive identity is to be established. One modern translation studies scholar who has discussed it at length is André Lefevere (1975), who singles it out as an essential strategy in poetry translation. With reference to the English translations of Catullus's sixty-fourth poem published between 1870 to 1970, he analyzes and critiques seven strategies used by translators—phonemic, literal, metrical, verse to prose, rhymed, blank/free verse, and interpretive—with the last being identical with imitation (or version). To him, in imitating a predecessor poet, the translator "produces a poem of his own."

Theo Hermans has also addressed the subject, saying that imitation can be used in two senses: first, as a looser, freer method of translation, diametrically opposed to verbatim translation; and second, as the creative emulation of previous models, a kind of rewriting, comparable to what was done in Europe during Renaissance times by the writer who sought to learn the styles of his Greek and Latin predecessors (Hermans 1992: 95–116). Hermans demonstrates how, during the earlier period, the two senses dovetailed with one another—quite unlike the contemporary preference for separation of the two. He further advances the idea that the free method of translation only became established when a subsequent generation of translators justified it by making use of the discourse traditionally associated with imitation in the second sense. For Hermans, even when imitators did not have specific, identifiable source texts to work on, some "source" there obviously was, for without it their literary works could not have come into existence. It is the processes of the "digestion, transformation and grafting" of prior literary sources from outside the indigenous tradition that made them "translations" at the same time as they are "imitations." The combination of two elements—free translation and deployment of earlier models, native or foreign—clearly define the legacy that the Renaissance imitators bequeathed to the modern world, and provide the basis for incorporating imitation in the present study of modes of translation.

To conceptualize imitations as translations, one can benefit from negative as well as positive evaluations of the former. In discussing the French *belles infidèles* tradition, Corinne Lhermitte makes a clear distinction between adaptation and imitation, but while approving of the former's contribution to human knowledge (*l'appétit du savoir*), she does not regard the latter very highly because, for her, the translator's ability to communicate cultural materials appropriately is more important than "cloning" (2004: sec. 16). By contrast, as is well known, Harold Bloom privileges imitation in his theory of the "anxiety of influence" (1973). For him, imitators seek to either overcome their belatedness with respect to other poets in the tradition, or emulate the achievements of their predecessors, so the value of appropriative works must be judged differently. Without considering imitations to be of less value than authentic works, or equating them with copying or plagiarism, we propose an objective model for analyzing imitations as translations. Imitation is not just mimicry, because many mechanisms of imitation (including exaggeration, deletion, distortion, recontextualization, etc.) enable the transformation of a source text. With reference to "paratextual, contextual and textual" factors (Dyer 2007: 47), we can evaluate the liberties taken by the translator who imitates. Also, by categorizing the elements of likeness and deformation, we can be in a position to define the imitator's attitude toward the original—parodic, admiring, tongue-in-cheek, or mocking, as the case may be. The old-school requirement of faithfulness is clearly irrelevant.

Of special interest in this connection are the discussions of Reuben Brower (1974) and Andrew Reimer (2010) on "radical translation." Both scholars have sought to theorize the relationship between translation and parodic imitation. Brower notes that, whether working with the style or thought of the original, parodies invariably involve "playing" in a constructive (showing admiration) or destructive (embodying rivalry) sense. His examples are the "translations" of the Classics (*The Iliad*, Ovid, Lucan, and Vigil) by Dryden, Shakespeare, and Chapman. But for him, while both the parodist and the translator can have impure motives, "no translator sets out to parody (in the critical sense) the author he has chosen to translate, in a work publicly offered as a translation" (1974: 5). We can qualify this statement by noting that the translation he refers to here is the "faithful" variety. For Brower, the parodist strives for freedom; the translator, for fidelity. Parody, in other words, is practically impossible in translation proper, so to speak. It is often seen, however, in extremely free forms of translation like imitation. Because of the room allowed for manipulation, amplification, and recreation, the parodic imitation is a favored mode for those for whom fidelity is not a concern. Reimer (2010: 43) also discusses parodic translations, a practice prevalent in the seventeenth and eighteenth centuries and exemplified by the English example of Samuel Johnson's free re-renderings of Greek and Latin originals. While alterations to the original text can be made to conform to cultural assumptions of the target audience, for Reimer there is another possibility: changes can be made where the translator sees certain hidden potentials in the text that can be explored or exploited. The Japanese manga artists to be considered below, in imitating *Journey to the West*, can be viewed as creative manipulators—and their imitations of the Chinese novel, as radical translations.

Japanese Pastiches and Genetic Mutation

While the tradition of parodic imitation is a vibrant one in our time, it is the pastiche that is currently gaining great traction, in particular through its connection to the emergence of a subculture of fan-fiction writers. With the proliferation of self-published fictional works (primarily on the Web), imitation turns out to be a dominant form of rewriting whereby literary works from the past are given new iterations. In these cases, alterations made to the originals are substantial, and the source text may not even be easily identified. Ironically, this practice is not so dissimilar to what Renaissance critics said about the daring modernizing efforts at imitating classical authors in their own time. Turning East, and to examples of the twenty-first century, we note a deluge of Japanese fan productions called *dōjinshi*, which appear in the forms of manga, anime, and fiction. As the counterpart of fan fiction in the West, these products represent mostly the effort of Japanese fans (*otaku*) who work either individually or in collaboration with fellow enthusiasts, reaching out to potential readers via unconventional channels of publication and distribution. The impact this practice has on the text reproduction scene is apparent in the fact that, following the example of successful amateur manga artists, even professional ones use similar publication methods (Azuma 2009: 25). The link between imitation and manga composition is a particularly strong one in contemporary Japan, which provides us with some excellent examples to illustrate the complex issues of parodic imitation.

Generally speaking, two categories of source texts are preferred by imitators: classics (e.g., Greek and Latin literature) and bestselling fiction (e.g., the *Harry Potter* novels and *The Lord of the Rings*). The better known a literary work is, the more attractive it is to imitators. In Japan innumerable pastiches have been produced on the basis of the sixteenth-century Chinese novel *Journey to the West*. A lengthy list of some 103 manga versions based on the novel is given in "Mansaidana's Blog" (http://members.jcom.homee.ne.jp/mocca/ saiyuki_x/man_ saku.html), showing the great number of imitations inspired by the Chinese "father text" to varying degrees. For better focus, in the next section we will look at an enormous success—*Journey to the Extreme* —as an example of a postmodern imitation of a premodern novel. The mode of ludic play in this manga remains similar to that of early times in the West: an older, authoritative text is rewritten in the imitation, which re-presents it to a new breed of readers who have grown up under rather different cultural circumstances. On a temporal plane, too, the past of the original novel is appropriated for present purposes, for the manga offers a comment on the contemporary Japanese scene. The method is essentially one of appropriation, defined by Paul Ricoeur as "the process by which the revelation of new modes of being . . . gives the subject new capacities for knowing himself" (qtd. Lianeri 2006: 144). New meanings supersede those of the originary tale about the Chinese monk on a mission to obtain the Buddhist scriptures from India with the help of three disciples.

The Chinese story needs to be briefly recounted. *Journey to the West* opens with brief past histories of the four main characters: Tripitaka (Japanese: Sanzō), Monkey (Son Gokū), Pigsy (Chu Hakkai), and Sandy (Sha Gojō).[4] After a description of the past history of the rebellious Monkey, we are told that Tripitaka is approached by the bodhisattva Guanyin, who entrusts him with the mission of retrieving the Buddhist scriptures from India so that the Chinese people may be enlightened. He proceeds to recruit the other three pilgrims, and, as he does so, the reader also learns of the lackluster pasts of the lazy and lascivious Pigsy and the careless and indecisive Sandy. In the journey itself, the four pilgrims encounter eighty-one "catastrophes" when demons abduct Tripitaka so they can devour his flesh, which is said to confer immortality on those who partake of it. While Monkey is able to fend off some of the demons, in many cases it is the intervention of Guanyin (Japanese: Kannon) and other deities (like Red Boy) that saves the day. The most famous episodes include those of the Ox-Demon King, the Iron-Fan Princess, the White-Bone Spirit, and so on. The sequence of events is somehow presented as having taken place in actual geographical locations in Turkistan, Afghanistan, and Kyrgyzstan, but these are no more than fantasy re-creations of places along the Silk Road. In the end, the pilgrims reach their destination, obtain the scriptures, and are welcomed into the Buddha's palace.

Among the many imitation manga published, six can be described here to give an idea of how imitators have rewritten the Chinese novel, with special reference to departures from the original plot, characters, setting, and historical details:

1. Probably best-known among Western readers is Toriyama Akira's *Dragon Ball* (1984), a *shōnen* (young boy) manga. Its link to the source Chinese text is superficial, with only the borrowing of the major characters, although Monkey plays a somewhat leading role. He accompanies the young girl Bulma on her journey to recover the lost Dragon Balls. Quite differently portrayed than his counterpart in the Chinese story, he has been so successful with readers that he completely replaces the original character in the Japanese popular imagination.

---

[4] The English translations of the four names have been made famous by Arthur Waley's landmark translation of the novel—*Monkey*. However, for better focus, this chapter will keep the name "Monkey" while using transliterations for the other three names.

Xavier Minguez-López (2014) discusses how *Dragon Ball* plays havoc with the source text, playing with Chinese cultural items (e.g., Chinese oolong tea, Shaolin monks, and Mao suits) while elements of Japanese religion and customs are randomly incorporated into the story.

2. Yamamoto Atsuji's *Maiden Team* (1989) is another *shōnen* manga about three girls (one of them a reincarnation of Monkey) who help Sanzō obtain new sutras in order to establish a Department of Buddhology at Daitō Bunka Daigaku (Tang Culture University). They are failures at school but choose to assist the monk, a mountain-climber, in his quest. An attempt to subvert gender roles, the narrative takes place in a campus setting, where demons have been let loose. All three girls are tomboyish, and one is shown as lusting after men.

3. In *Marvelous Adventures of Monkey King* (1998), which marks the high point of Terada Katsuya's career, Sanzō is sadistically treated by Monkey as they journey west. She (not he) is an unclothed Buddhist nun accompanied by Monkey, who is a bully intimidating others and inspiring fear wherever he goes. The other two disciples are villainous characters who assist Monkey in his evil acts. The gruesome depictions appear to have appealed to certain groups of readers and the series is widely acclaimed for its shocking reinvention of the Chinese story.

4. Matsubara Chinami's *Saiyūki* (1997) is a "school" *shōjo* (young girl) manga in which the heroine, Kusano Misora, is an outstanding student. She is, however, transformed into Monkey whenever she lets fall her long hair and removes her spectacles. Wielding the Golden Cudgel, she beats up evildoers at school, forcing them to swear that they will follow the teachings of the Buddha. Often she is rescued at the last minute by her handsome boyfriend, who protects her like Gautama Buddha, the only one powerful enough to restrain Monkey in the original Chinese tale. The story's links with *Journey to the West* are extremely tenuous.

5. Tanaka Kanako's *Three Beast-men* (2000) is marketed in the *shōnen* category. The manga artist is adept at transforming historical material from China for her manga.[5] In *Three Beast-men*, Monkey is a new incarnation of the Monkey King, wearing a cowboy's hat that gestures toward the Western (though the settings for the action are identifiably Chinese, taking place in cities like Kaifeng). Both Monkey

---

[5] Another of Tanaka's well-known works is based loosely on the Chinese novel *Water Margin*, and it describes the exploits of female bandits gathered round the son of the gang-leader featured in the Chinese novel.

and Gojō wield guns, a full range of which figures in the manga. Plot-wise, the three "bounty hunters" make the trip to India in search of hidden treasures and fight a multitude of demons, some of them bearing names of Chinese historical and fictional personages. As for the characters, male figures are presented as macho guys, with exaggerated muscles and exposed buttocks, while female ones are invariably sexualized, scantily dressed and striking seductive poses. Sanzō is a big-bosomed woman whom it is the duty of the three Beast-men to protect.

6. Maya Mineo's *Patariro Journey to the West* (2000) is a Boys' Love (BL) manga with fantasy and science fiction elements. It is not immediately apparent whether Sanzō, with long, blonde hair, is male or female. The male bodhisattva Banko Rakan takes Sanzō to bed the first time they meet, and the story then narrates Sanzō's competition with Banko's "wife" (Third Prince in the Chinese original) for his affections. A number of sex scenes are depicted in the story. Monkey is the naughty trickster, although he no longer plays a central role.

As the number of *Journey to the West*–based manga keeps growing, with manga artists making forays into the various subgenres that cater to specific consumer groups and adjusting to the demands of different readerships, one can see why there are increasingly outrageous departures from the original novel.

Journey to the Extreme: Imitation and Sino-Japanese Contrasts

Minekura Kazuya's *Journey to the Extreme*, published in *G-Fantasy* (a "beautiful men" magazine) from 1997 to 2002, imitates *Journey to the West* while giving it a postmodern setting. Hugely popular with readers, it was followed by two sequels, two prequels, and an anime adaptation. Framed by a battle between demons and human beings, the story is somewhat thematically linked to *Journey to the West*, but its plot departs substantially from the latter, and like most imitations of the novel, it makes use of the episodic, almost picaresque, quest structure to digress at will. It narrates the journey of four antiheroes (the monk Sanzō, Monkey, the half-swine Hakkai, and the water-demon Gojō) to India, not to secure the Buddhist scriptures as in the Chinese version, but to halt the impending resurrection of Gyūmaō, the Ox-Demon King of *Journey to the West* who is upstaged to become the manga's main villain although he appears in only one of the eighty-one encounters with demons in the Chinese story. On the way, the foursome is assaulted by all kinds of evil beings and faces unpredictable mishaps, but unfazed by the trials and tribulations, derives much fun from the experience.[6]

Notable features signal the extent to which *Journey to the Extreme* strays from the classic novel—most prominently seen in the postmodernist "feel" that it exudes. Twenty-first-century gadgets appear in the story, and the landscape drawn by the manga artist contrasts markedly with that of the original text: the colorful adventures taking place in Central Asian deserts are replaced by events in the more surreal settings out of this world. The characters are completely reinvented, not just in character but in outward appearance, which is highlighted visually in manga format. Under the orders of the androgynous goddess Kannon, the monk Sanzō gathers together his three disciples for the journey to India, coming across demonesses who want to eat him up, like the Spider Lady. Particularly noteworthy is the monk's less-than-pious nature, which reflects a negative attitude toward Buddhism that contradicts the original. He is no longer the merciful religious man, but an ordinary person much given to smoking and drinking. He changes his temper easily and is prone to use expletives at moments of crisis. Laurie Cubbison points out that Minekura seems to be questioning Buddhist notions through her depiction of Sanzō, especially when he is seen in contrast to the childlike Monkey, presented as good-hearted and naïve throughout (Cubbison, n.d.).

The transformation of the three disciples' character also shows Minekura playing fast and loose with the acknowledged Chinese classic. Monkey is a teenager wearing a flashy headband, a replica of the diadem in the original story that gives him severe pain in the head whenever his master chants a mantra, though it no longer serves that function. Rather than all-invincible, he is a kid who is constantly asking for more food, unlike even the Monkey in more "faithful" manga versions before the 1990s. Hakkai is the suave and attractive "beautiful boy" (*bishōnen*) and a heavy drinker.[7] Gojō is nicknamed lustful "River-boy" (i.e., Kappa) who gambles excessively and engages in promiscuous sex with bare-breasted female characters. With Sanzō, the three disciples drive around in a Jeep, which substitutes for the White Dragon in the original. The relationship between the four pilgrims is nothing like that

---

[6] For fuller descriptions of the plot, the reader is referred to the following webpages: (1) http://www.answers.com/ topic/saiyuki-manga; and (2) http://www.radford.edu/ lcubbiso/personal/ research/Variations%20on%2 0the%20Monkey%20King.htm ("Variations on the Monkey King").

[7] For studies of the "beautiful boy" phenomenon in contemporary East Asia and its link to the boy bands, see Jung (2009). The subject has also been discussed in Chapter 6 of the present study.

in the Chinese text, and none of the disciples even address Sanzō as their "master." A lighthearted tone is also maintained through the verbal jostling between the three disciples, who at times even go so far as to insult their master. When they are not engaged in fighting the demons, they live in a rather cavalier manner, indulging in a range of leisure activities, although as soon as there is trouble they are quickly united.

Journey to the Extreme contains a hybrid mix of diverse cultural elements, thrown together as in a melting pot. The Chinese background is registered through the references to items of material culture (like food and mahjong), while the temples and interiors of buildings shown throughout are recognizably Chinese. There is an occasional use of English like "thank you," which underscores the playfulness of the rewritten version. Even more provocatively, in the visual presentation of the major characters we observe an amalgam of Chinese, Japanese, and Western fashions. Sanzō wears a white robe that is in part religious attire, together with gloves and wooden Japanese clogs; Monkey, a wristband, a fluttering cape and a modish headband; Gojō, a tight-fitting, sleeveless sweater (to accentuate the muscles) and long, trendy boots; and Hakkai, a monocle, earrings, and a Chinese-styled cloak (see Figure 10.1). The furthest departure from the "father text" is seen in the deployment of the East Asian trope of the beautiful boy, represented most aptly by Hakkai, who smiles and smokes ceaselessly. The pilgrims all have youthful, punkish looks, sporting wavy hair, fancy accessories, and colorful outfits that readers can immediately associate with the stereotypical "decadent" figures in Japanese manga. Perhaps it is not too far-fetched to see some resemblance between the four "boys" and the hugely successful boy bands in contemporary Japan like SMAP and Arashi.[8]

As regards the reception of Japanese manga in general, two factors are crucial: genre and readership. Manga products are always neatly compartmentalized in fixed categories (science fiction, gag manga, robot manga, fantasy, sports tales, homosexual romances, erotica, etc.) that are marketed to separate groups, like children, young men, young girls, and adults. These frameworks indirectly determine the way a manga is produced, even for those that are imitative of Chinese (or Western) models. Accordingly, *Demonic Journey to the West* and *Saiyūki* are meant to be read as romances for young girls, while *Dragon Ball* and *Journey to the Extreme* are adventure

---

[8] Created in 1998, SMAP has had a successful decades-long career and is the prime example of a boy band making its mark on the various genres of Japan's entertainment industry. Arashi, another band with five boy members, debuted in 1999 and has since taken the Japanese popular music scene by storm. With the addition of the White Dragon as a fifth "pilgrim" in *Journey to the West*, the parallels with the boy bands are complete.

Figure 10.1 (From left) Sanzō, Monkey, Gojō, and Hakkai. Copyright permission: Ichijinsha.

tales for teenage boys. The textual changes and the visual reconfigurations, showing derivations from the source text, have significance within the generic and readership contexts. There is little doubt that readers, all familiar with the centuries-old Chinese tale, can appreciate the play of difference between the imitations and the text imitated, for it is continually highlighted through the lens of the genre in question. The superimposition of the characteristics of Japanese adventure manga on the borrowed Chinese story, which is already familiar even to the ordinary person through centuries of retelling, is used to great effect by the manga artists, resulting in hybridized Sino-Japanese compositions. Some pleasure is derived from the awareness of Chinese-Japanese cultural differences, but it is primarily the juxtaposition of the two texts that delights the reader: the discrepancies between the "predecessor text" and the "successor text" impact strongly on the reading experience. In this connection, Tereko Chin has pointed out that "parallel worlds" exist for the readers of *Journey to the Extreme*: in the context of the well-known Chinese story, links are nevertheless built with the contemporary scene through such trivia as tobacco and credit cards. As a result of these creative manipulations, the reader can approach the manga from the perspectives of both an "outsider" and a "participant" (Chin 2013: 228).

Eckart Voigts-Virchow's brilliant article on "proliferating textualities" (2014: 63), which discusses the many contemporary versions of Lewis

Carroll's *Alice's Adventures in Wonderland*, demonstrates the processes at work behind the creation of an "Aggregate Alice." A similar situation occurs with regard to Monkey's many reincarnations in Japanese manga imitations at the turn of the twentieth century.[9] Voigts-Virchow's subject is ostensibly adaptations, but in view of the polytexts that end up constructing an Aggregate Alice, he could well have been talking about imitations. He notes the usefulness of the term "meme," borrowed from British evolutionary biologist Richard Dawkins's genetic theory to explain the range of textual transformations undergone by the Alice story in the past two centuries. This echoes our characterization of imitation in terms of genetic mutation in Chapter 1. The simple dictionary definition has it that "memes" are elements of culture passed on from one individual to another genetically through imitation. As Dawkins puts it in his first book, *The Selfish Gene* (1976), a meme is "a unit of cultural transmission, or a unit of *imitation*" (italics mine). By the same logic, the factors that have facilitated the inexhaustible imitations of Monkey in *Journey to the West* in Japan can be understood as equivalent to those that have generated the many serializations of Alice. The memes are transmitted from China to Japan, but radically transformed on the way. Voigts-Virchow's special insight is that, in the multiple transformed versions of Alice, even essential or core features of the originary narrative may be tampered with, so that imitation becomes more than just copying, and very few of the elements are transferred intact. Through a process of radical translation, we are left not with "the cat with a grin," but only "the grin without a cat," as Voigts-Virchow puts it.

What emerges clearly from the above discussion is the extreme radicalness of imitation: almost all of the less central plot details, and almost every trait of the characters in the original Chinese novel, have been ruthlessly removed from the postmodern *Journey to the Extreme*. Minekura has certainly gone to an extreme herself, but so have the authors of *Dragon Ball*, *Maiden Team*, *Three Beast-men*, and other manga mentioned above. In the case of *Dragon Ball*, its departures from the Chinese novel which "inspired" it are most blatant: as the story unfolds from 1984 to 1995 in 519 chapters and 42 volumes, whatever is derived from *Journey to the West* slowly gets eclipsed and the manga virtually takes on a life of its own, although a central character, Monkey, is still there. How these imitations reflect the cultural relationship between the two Asian powers is an intriguing, but relevant, question. Two brief observations can be made here. First, the relationship between China

---

[9] For the many transformations of the Aggregate Monkey in Japan, see the entry on "Goku" at: http://en.wikipedia.org/wiki/Goku.

and Japan must be seen to underlie the "polytexting" of a Chinese novel in a Japanese context, and this should be a factor in the interpretation of imitative strategies. Second, while it can be argued that the intrinsic features of *Journey to the West* (like its episodic structure) have enhanced its "iterability," it must be emphasized that, ultimately, the parodies are a deconstructive act against a canonical Chinese text. For that reason, the waves of Chinese anger directed in 2007–08 against the manga imitations of *Journey to the West* are, to a certain extent, justified.[10]

Imitative Translation in a Postmodern Context

Many modern Western writers deliberately "signal" the imitative nature of their works. For example, Robert Lowell entitled his controversial poetry collection *Imitations* (1962) to underscore the liberties that he had taken with the originals. Through the title of "Homage to Sextus Propertius" (1919) Pound also indicated that his poem was meant as a tribute to the Roman author, and not a literal rendition of the original. Pound also freely imitated some Chinese classical poems in his *Cathay* (1915); in the process he not only modernized but also falsified them (see Preda 2001: 77).[11] In text-bound, literal translations, derivations from the original are generally kept within limits, but in imitations, changes made to the (acknowledged or hidden) source text can be so radical that some readers conversant with the original might voice objections. What is particularly irksome to readers of this category are disrespectful imitations. With those imitations that are performed with the goal of learning from, or paying homage to, an eminent master, the infidelities are pardonable. Such is the case of the imitations by Lowell or Pound, who were also luminaries in their own time. When hitherto familiar objects are toyed with under the defensive umbrella of "imitation," readers may react strongly. What makes things worse is that, currently, there is a (postmodern) tendency to shift from the objective of "learning from the masters" to that of "playing with textual potentialities."[12]

---

[10] For a discussion of the Chinese reaction against the Japanese "meddling" (*egao*) with their cherished classics in 2007–08, especially *Journey to the West*, see Chan (2017), Li (2013), and Gong and Xin (2010).

[11] It is perhaps noteworthy that imitation as a method of rewriting is often associated with poetry and not narrative literature (see Luo 2012).

[12] Studies of fandom and fan rewriting in imitation of their favorite authors have increased exponentially in recent years. See, for instance, Busse (2017), Leong (2010) and Moraru (2001).

One characteristic shared by the manga texts considered above is that of play (as Genette calls it) on the part of not just imitators but also readers. In our age, cultural production (e.g., composing a manga of one's own) has increasingly come to be viewed as something undertaken "for fun." While commercial and instrumental motives continue to impact literary and artistic production, they are no longer sufficient, or primary, considerations. Alluding to the comparison that Freud draws between the creative writer and the child at play, Cranford says that "the desire to inhabit imagined fantastical worlds is . . . rooted in the satisfaction of infantile fantasy as much as it is in the shared infancy of our pre-modern past" (Cranford 2014: 69). Imitating the classics is above all a creative engagement (by *otaku*) with works of the past (by their forebears) that demand renewal or rejuvenation after having been around for centuries. There has also emerged a trend toward rewriting noncanonical works, as the possibilities for playing with the canon diminish, and imitators turn their attention to works published more recently. The abundance of *dōjinshi* in Japan and slash fiction in the West (e.g., those that borrow characters and plot-lines from the Harry Potter novels) testifies to the extensiveness of the phenomenon. Of course, on the consumer side there is a voracious readership with incessant demands for more imitations. The pleasure they derive from the imitations cannot be divorced from an experience of the familiar as unfamiliar, of the commonplace transformed into the unrecognizable.

Changing views on authorship is a factor contributing to the proliferation of imitative translations of the kind examined above. Before the Augustan period drew to a close, much acclaim had been attached to works which proudly displayed their lineage, declaring their link to works previously published—works classified as imitations in the present study. But with the advent of Romantic notions of authorship, when the value of "originality" was highlighted and the imagination foregrounded, "literature in the second degree" lost out. New conceptions of literary creation—seen more and more as an individual rather than a communal event but also as an individual act—have since determined critical perception of what constitutes literary value. With the Romantic glorification of the author, the re-use (however creatively) of fellow writers' productions is denigrated, at the same time as it comes under severe attack by laws on copyright protection. Such laws in the West have made borrowing vulnerable, and the legal risk that accrues to the composition and publication of imitations adds further to their stigmatization. Even with copyrighted translations, the contracts issued by publishers, which give translators legal permission to translate, ironically work against them by affirming the dependency and subordination of the translated text to the original. If the notion of copyright forces the translator to translate as literally and faithfully as possible, it does not bode well for the imitator who copies—unfaithfully.

Interestingly, it is fan-fiction writing that gives room, even as the legal ropes tighten, to the practice of imitation in recent decades, allowing it to grow and prosper, especially when it is carried out online.[13] One consequence is that the "autonomous text" has lost some ground. In fact, given the ubiquity of intertextuality as enunciated by a generation of deconstructionist scholars, "literature in the first degree" may not even exist.[14] Along this line of analysis, we may ask: In the postmodern era, when forms of pastiche—especially those involving the creative reworking of elements from another culture—have assumed such prominence, can we not expect imitations to occupy a more central position, although it has been de-centered in the English-speaking world since the days of the great Augustan imitators? Some of the negative terms used in the discourse on imitation, like borrowing, appropriation, manipulation, and mutilation, reflect the unpleasant legacy bequeathed to us by the nineteenth-century theorists of originality. Contemporary imitations need to be viewed in a more positive light, rather than being made synonymous with stagnation or regression.

In Japanese manga imitations, we see the attempts of a fan subculture to "strive to stand out from the mainstream culture, employ different cultural products for their own purposes [and] conquer their own space" (Lehtonen 2000: 147). The commingled, hybrid elements in pastiches create a textual bricolage that reveals the imitators' desire to carve a niche of their own, forging new meanings through interventions into the canonical texts of a cultural neighbor whose global power has been increasing by the day. The examples we have looked at show how manga artists tear apart *Journey to the West*, and then collect and reassemble the broken pieces in a new (visual) format. It will be difficult to pinpoint with confidence the precise motive of each Japanese imitator. However, rather than paying homage to the classical novel, whose impact has for centuries extended beyond Chinese shores, they seem to have preferred to make fun of elements of established cultural significance. The preceding analysis has highlighted the element of play in the imitative translations of a masterwork from Chinese into Japanese, seen against the shift from a high-brow (the novel) to a low-brow medium (manga). The re-inflection of meanings, the updating of period elements,

---

[13] One notes, in this connection, J. K. Rowling's decision to withdraw the suit she initially brought against the Harry Potter online translators. There are comparable cases in Anglo-America, most notably the legal proceedings taken against the sequels and prequels (i.e., pastiches) based on *Gone with the Wind* (see Gómez-Galisteo 2011).

[14] Another factor that works against the idea of the autonomous text is the attack on single authorship made with reference to the collaborative text.

and the piecing together of interpretations are indeed the most fascinating aspects of contemporary imitative translations. Theories of fan fiction and *dōjinshi*, so enthusiastically explored in Western and Asian contexts, can be applied fruitfully to imitations. As Mikko Lehtonen has remarked, imitations have special value since each of them constitutes "a new entity put together out of ideas and excerpts gathered from here and there, thus gaining new meanings" (2000: 149).

We can now return to the question we began this chapter with: Why has imitation failed to attract greater attention from contemporary translation studies, when it already figured so prominently in early modern (Western) thinking about translation, and was expatiated upon at such length by eminent theorists like Dryden? After all, imitation is widely recognized as an inescapable part of the postmodern condition, its centrality confirmed in both the East and the West by such philosophers as Azuma Hiroki (2009) and Jean Baudrillard (1981), in particular, through their conceptualizations of the simulacrum. If betrayal of the original text is the crux of the issue, certainly translation studies scholarship in recent decades has done much to show that departures from the source are unavoidable no matter how literally one wants to translate a text. Perhaps it is due to the persistent view of imitations as repugnant acts of borrowing, plagiarism, and theft, relatable to copying and aping, and hence of a lower order than authentic works (see Henningsen 2010: 18–32)? Whatever it is, it is hoped that the above discussion has revived the idea of "imitative translation" by referencing examples from the East and the West, in addition to tracing a delicate terminological shift from parody to pastiche in its history.

Conclusion

In Chapter 1 of the present study, the groundwork was laid by bringing adaptation and imitation within a more inclusive definition of translation. That makes possible a revisionist approach whereby translations are not judged on the basis of how faithfully they represent their originals. While the concern with fidelity—which legitimizes the study of prototypical forms of translation—has come under attack in recent decades and now deviations from the original are generally seen as the rule rather than the exception, a cloud of suspicion still hangs over attempts to theorize on the "free forms," seen perhaps most radically in connection with imitation, an extreme form of adaptation. The preference for compartmentalization of different kinds of human activities, which is reflected by institutional developments in academia, has extended to modes of translation, but it is a hurdle to be overcome in our case too. The "family" relationship (defined whether in terms of siblings or triplets) that exists between translation, adaptation, and imitation provides the ground for a more holistic view that opens up new avenues for exploring transtextual rewriting and widening the horizons of the field of translation studies as well.[1] This reconfiguration is especially timely: we are already witnessing the growing interest in nonliterary translation, technology-enhanced translation, and commissioned practical translation, most of which either call for greater adherence to fidelity, or make this goal more attainable.

One advantage of our approach, the seeds of which have already been planted by certain sectors of the Western scholarly community, is that it encourages a new perspective on translation activities in the non-West, especially in historical terms. The abundance of research published on translation among, into, or from European languages has alerted scholars in the field to the ill-advised tendency to be more Eurocentric than necessary. The focus, in the present study, on translation in its liberal forms—with a wealth of examples from Sino-Japanese transtextual rewriting—is an encouragement to highlight relatively neglected contexts that can perhaps proffer insights of benefit to the field of translation studies as a whole. We have

---

[1] It might be said that the broadened definition of translation proposed in the present study is constructed on the basis of narrowed redefinitions of "adaptation" and "imitation," but that is as it should be.

made incidental forays into some Korean reworkings of Chinese texts, even Vietnamese re-versions of Chinese texts (though strictly speaking, Vietnam is part of Southeast, rather than East, Asia), as well as two case studies of Chinese translations from English, but in each of the three parts of the present study the climax is reached with a detailed analysis of a significant moment in the transference of textual material from/to China and Japan, viz. the major novels of a contemporary Japanese novelist freely rendered into Chinese, several Chinese TV drama adaptations of a bestselling young girls' manga, and the spate of Japanese imitations of a masterwork of Chinese fiction.

The question may be asked as to whether our case studies are meant to challenge existing Western paradigms by offering an alternative, or if they are merely non-European examples that use theories already developed in a European context. Perhaps the simple answer is that existing Western theory enriches our understanding of these cases, but only with a more comprehensive model of translation can we explain some of the subtleties of translational interaction between China and Japan, especially that of the premodern era. Even acknowledging the differences between Chinese-Japanese, Chinese-Korean, and Japanese-Korean transtextual relationships, and that generalizations are invalid beyond a certain point, we can see that the more restrictive model—what we may call the "translation proper" model—limits our understanding of East Asian translation traditions. It may be thought, for instance, that both Chinese and Japanese translators had put up "weak" performances, or were hardly comparable to their counterparts in richer traditions. Or it may be thought that, in the case of China, the only phenomena worth talking about are the renditions of Buddhist sutras in medieval times and of Western scientific and technical writings in the seventeenth century. In Japan, translation, in the sense of literal rendering of a source text into the target language, may be thought of as a secondary activity before the early modern period (unless the much debated practice of *kanbun kundoku* is recognized as a form of translation).[2] Rebekah Clements has pointed out the reasons for an increase in more literal translations in Tokugawa times, including the rise of popular print industry, increasing literacy rates, and a market of readers who wanted access to classical texts but did not have the level of education necessary to read the original unaided

---

[2] The debate on whether *kundokubun* (text for *kundoku* reading) are translations is not easily resolvable because those who argue for and against it do not have shared assumptions. For Clements, the existence of the *kundoku* method, made possible by the close relationship between Japanese and Chinese forms of writing, at least partly filled the gap that would have been taken up by faithful forms of translation as they existed in the West (with commentary filling a good part of the rest of it) (personal communication).

(Clements 2015: 47–59). The expectation that translations should be done with the goal of achieving the greatest source-target semblance appears to be largely unfulfilled until late in the histories of both countries. Especially in the case of Japan, it is often forgotten that adaptive and imitative translation of Chinese works had its field day over a long historical time-span. In this light, Claudine Salmon could be seen as having moved in the direction of greater openness by devoting an entire section to "Translations and Adaptations" in her Introduction to her landmark anthology (2013: 18–22), where several contributors survey translations in Asia alongside adaptations and imitations, such as Jacques Népote and Khing Hoc Dy (2013: 199–217) and Kim Dong-uk (2013: 39–57).

With respect to the cases of Chinese-Japanese transtextual rewriting analyzed in the foregoing chapters, it must be noted that they have been chosen because of their relevance to our concern with the many-faceted character of "translation." They may not be the most representative instances showing the full range of practices in the two histories concerned, but they illustrate clearly specific norms that govern the use of free translation, adaptation, and imitation in the Sino-Japanese linguistic and cultural context. The Murakami Phenomenon, the pan-Asian transmission of *Boys over Flowers*, and the dozens of manga that exploit the parodic possibilities of *Journey to the West* are indicative of certain approaches to dealing with well-known or canonical texts from "the other side"—the relationship between the two countries has been encapsulated in the proverbial saying, "separated only by a narrow strip of water" (*yiyi daishui*). These cases are also exemplary to a certain extent because they reflect similar practices adopted across a wide range of transtextual productions. For instance, it may be argued that there are only about a dozen manga imitations parodying *Journey to the West*, but the subversive tendencies identified in our examples can also be seen in the filmic and TV versions, revealing what is worth examining as a transcultural phenomenon. What is more, comparable transformative use of other classic Chinese novels, like *Three Kingdoms* and *Water Margin*, shows that our case study is in some ways representative of certain predispositions on the part of postmodern Japanese manga rewriters.

Special note must be made of the fact that media specificity is a factor constraining the extent to which generalizations can be made of the cases studied. The materials for the present investigation, which comprise not just conventional texts but also less conventional media forms like TV dramas and manga, pose the issue of whether the coverage is perhaps a little indiscriminate. Nevertheless, as our focus lies not on Sino-Japanese relationships but also on the applicability of an enlarged definition of "translation" to East Asia, an effort has been made to explore the full range of source-target ruptures through a wider, rather than a narrower, sampling. To sidestep complications that can arise as a result of purely intermedial shifts, we have chosen to examine only modifications to source-text content or style from the perspective of interlingual and cross-cultural transfer, and not alterations necessitated by the specific target medium. One may add, too, that the methodology applied throughout is one that pertains in particular to literary, rather than nonliterary, productions. In contradistinction to nonliterary translations serving communicative functions, literary and quasi-literary translations (like films, TV dramas) have been selected with the aim of showing how representational functions are manipulated with. In terms of the dichotomy set up in this book, whereas faithful translations aim to recapture the "world" as originally conceived, free, adaptive, and imitative translations seek not to represent the characters, events, actions, emotions, and so on, as they were in the original.

There is, then, the issue of spatial specificity. We have placed the discussion of Sino-Japanese translation (as illustrative of East Asian translation) within a Western theoretical framework, if only for the simple reason that there has been a paucity of Chinese and Japanese translation theories, both traditional and modern, that can be usefully deployed. The strong reluctance among some contemporary Chinese translation theorists to consider adaptation and imitation as forms of translations contrasts sharply with the (somewhat) greater openness in Western theorizations. In the present study, other than discussions of the three modes of translation as seen in Aesop's fables, Wilde's *Dorian Gray*, and Joyce's *Ulysses*, all freely rendered into Chinese, the main focus of attention has been pivotal cases that reveal the dynamics of cultural and literary interaction between China and Japan. The texts studied are, in every case, preceded by surveys of discourses about translation originating in the West. Of course, the use of Western conceptual apparatuses should not obscure the fact that the two East Asian traditions of practice should be of interest in their own right. Most importantly, transtextual relations in that region must be understood against the background of the Chinese Cultural Sphere, which had existed for millennia and is still a force very much in existence (despite the upheavals of the mid-nineteenth to the mid-twentieth century). That being the case, it is natural that translations undertaken in the two directions differ markedly, even while Sino-Japanese cultural affinities traceable to Confucian and Buddhist beliefs may have facilitated reception at either end. The lens of our three-pronged approach reveals a significant degree of "Sinicization" in translations from Japan, and "Japanization" in those from China. In terms of the strict redefinitions of adaptation and imitation as enunciated in Chapter 1, we can say that accommodationist and genetic impulses configure the less-than-faithful forms of Sino-Japanese translation, although directionality determines the specific way in which this is played out.

This brings us, finally, to a question regarding temporal specificity: What does the triad of free, adaptive, and imitative translation tells us about the history—and, on that basis, the nature—of Sino-Japanese translational interaction? The first, and important, observation is that the modern scenario differs from the premodern. After (roughly) the mid-nineteenth century, more faithful, source-oriented practices increased exponentially, especially in translations of texts outside the East Asian sphere, while Western discourses of translation (like Alexander Tytler's, which is understood to have impacted Yan Fu) gained greater currency. The increasing number of texts translated from Japanese after China's defeat in the Sino-Japanese War of 1894, and the corresponding decrease in translation in the opposite direction, signals not just a quantitative change, but a different mode in which translations are to be undertaken. That makes 1894 a watershed in Sino-Japanese translation history. If, prior to "the rise of Japan," East Asian translation had been affected seriously by the dominance of Chinese cultural power (which has been erroneously equated with cultural colonialism in much current scholarship), the arrival of Western "modernity" unleashed what is tantamount to a revolution in transtextual relationships in the region. More succinctly put, nationalism replaced regionalism, resulting in a splintering of the centuries-old, shared pan-Asian culture in which China, Japan, and Korea were the participants. Translation began to be played out in a context where China was no longer firmly placed at the center, and shifts of balance occurred to the tripartition, most strongly in the years before, and then after, the Second Sino-Japanese War. This is the historical background against which the "competition" between the literal and liberal modes of translation is to be understood.

Our study of premodern Japanese adaptive and imitative translations of Chinese texts should have made evident the fact that literalism—the faithful translation, that is—must not be seen uncritically as the foremost mode of transtextual rewriting in the premodern Sino-Japanese context. This is not even true of the Sino-Korean case: Claudine Salmon might have implied as much when she noted that Korea "seems to be the country where [prose adaptations] achieved the greatest success, especially during the nineteenth century among the less educated" (2013: 22). One can also cite the huge volume of Sino-Korean poetry to support this view. Literalism, as either strategy or attitude, was not a major orientation behind the premodern Japanese renditions of Chinese texts. This can be attributed to several factors, among them the borrowing of the Chinese script into Japanese, the widespread use of classical Chinese as "the language of literature, scholarship and officialdom" (Wakabayashi 2005b: 24) in Japan, and the ability of educated Japanese readers to decipher original texts in Chinese. Only by arguing that *kundoku* rendition is a form of translation could one muster enough support for the case that literal translation was a predominant part of the Japanese tradition. The reason is obvious: *kundoku* "translation" is a form of extreme literalism; one could not have been more faithful, except perhaps by just copying the source text word for word.

Given the unique configuration of cultural relations in premodern East Asia, one can reasonably expect translation history in China to reflect a response to its own superiority. With its cultural supremacy, China had little need for "translating Japan," whether literally or freely.[3] Even masterworks like *The Ten Thousand Leaves Collection* and *The Tale of Genji* never got completely translated into Chinese until the modern age. A reversal occurred, as we have noted above, in the first half of the twentieth century, when relay translations from Japanese of Western scientific texts, followed later by direct translations of Japanese literature, showed up in abundance in China. As the center of the East Asian order, China had "faithfully" translated Buddhist sutras from the Indian subcontinent. The same was done, in the seventeenth century, to scientific texts from the West. Yet the original texts in both cases came from outside the Sinosphere in East Asia. While some translation studies scholars have eulogized the rich Chinese tradition on the basis of the "Two Waves," the case remains unclear as to whether much will be lost if literalism is seen as the overriding mode of its transtextual practice—and whether other modes at other times are taken adequately into consideration.[4]

It seems appropriate to end our discussion with a note on the contemporary scene. It may fairly be said that the three modes of nonliteral translation have continued to assume importance in our time, although the weakening hold of the center and the rebalancing of politico-economic powers point to a "new" East Asian regionalism that is less stable than the one that went before. In the free translations of Murakami Haruki's novels, which found favor with a Mainland readership at a time when Sino-Japanese diplomatic relationships were strained, and in the adaptive reworkings of the manga *Boys over Flowers*, we see a Chinese receptivity to things Japanese that would have

---

[3] This is succinctly expressed by Judy Wakabayashi: "A feature of text selection in China before the twentieth century was the general lack of interest in foreign literature and philosophy, which were regarded as inferior to that of China" (2005b: 43).
[4] It is worth noting that adaptations and imitations in premodern China have often been undertaken with respect to predecessor texts in the indigenous tradition. This means, in effect, that intralingual forms were prioritized over interlingual forms.

been inconceivable, say, two centuries ago. In translation studies parlance, in premodern times Chinese texts had virtually been the only "source texts" for Japan, but that is no longer true. While the Taiwanese versions of Murakami Haruki and Kamio Yōko could have served as intermediaries easing their transmission to the Mainland, it is equally true that significant changes were made in the Mainland versions to Sinicize the originals to enhance Chinese reception. That takes us to the real meaning and significance of "unfaithful" forms of transtextual rewriting. They all are means of intervention into non-indigenous texts, attempts to make the Other palatable to the local readership and/or audience. That applies as much to the Japanese rewriting China in premodern times as to the Chinese rewriting Japan now. Interestingly, Claudine Salmon has pointed out that most Asian writers "had no sense of the inviolability of a text and had few qualms about borrowing from other works, so it is difficult to separate loose translations from adaptations" (2013: 22). That says a good deal about the prevalence of the modes of translation that are the subject of the present study.

On the Japanese side, the modes of unfaithful translation operate according to this same rationale, and the cases we have studied—including the cluster of adaptations of "The Peony Lantern," imitations of *Water Margin*, and manga versions of *Journey to the West*—provide useful evidence in this regard. As a general rule, the eradication of foreignness is a staple feature of free renderings: although complete elimination of Otherness is not possible, the Other can at least be comfortably accommodated. That, however, points to a paradox in all forms of translation, literal or liberal. Bearing in mind that each case must be viewed on its own terms, we can still see that the free forms, while removing some of the distance between the two cultures, also encrypt the unbridgeable gap between two. In the Japanese manga imitations of *Journey to the West*, for instance, certain elements from the source Chinese text do not just disappear; they remain as traces in the target text. Even the slightest of traces can signify the genetic connection to the parent text. This reminds us that faithful and free translations are not polar opposites but relational categories. And by redefining three key words—"translation," "adaptation," and "imitation"—the present study makes a case for the relevance of Western theory as applied to phenomena from peripheral, non-Western traditions, like those from East Asia.

Bibliography

Abrams, Meyer H. [1981] 1999. *A Glossary of Literary Terms*. 7th ed. Fort Worth: Harcourt Brace College Publishers.

Adams, Suzi, and Michael Janover. 2009. "Introduction: Theorizing the Intercultural." *Journal of Intercultural Studies* 30.3: 227–31.

Allen, Joseph R. 2019. "The Babel Fallacy: When Translation Does Not Matter." *Cultural Critique* 102: 117–50.

Alvstad, Cecilia. 2019. "Children's Literature." In *The Routledge Handbook of Literary Translation*. Eds. Kelly Washbourne and Ben van Wyke. New York: Routledge, 159–63.

Amorim, Lauro Maia. 2009. "Translation and Adaptation: Differences, Intercrossings and Conflicts in Ana Maria Machado's Translation of *Alice in Wonderland* by Lewis Carroll." At: http://brasillewiscarroll.blogspot.com/2009/08/translation-and- adaptation.html

Angélil-Carter, Shelley. 2000. *Stolen Language? Plagiarism in Writing*. London: Longman.

Arrojo, Rosemary. 1994. "Fidelity and the Gendered Translation." *TTR: Traduction, Terminologie, Redaction* 7.2: 147–63.

Azuma, Hiroki. 2009. *Otaku: Japan's Database Animals*. Trans. Jonathan E. Abel and Shion Kono. Minneapolis: University of Minnesota Press.

Baer, Brian J. 2014. "Translated Literature and the Role of the Reader." In *A Companion to Translation Studies*. Eds. Sandra Berman and Catherine Porter. Oxford: John Wiley & Sons, 333–45.

Bakhtin, Mikhail. [1979] 1986. "Toward a Methodology for the Human Sciences." In *Speech Genres and Other Later Essays*. Eds. Caryl Emerson and Michael Holquist. Austin: University of Texas Press, 159–72.

Barnett, George A., and D. Lawrence Kincaid. 1983. "Cultural Convergence: A Mathematical Theory." In *Intercultural Communication*. Ed. Deborah A. Cai. Vol. 4. Los Angeles: Sage Publications, 1–22.

Baron, Scarlett. 2010. "'The Place Where Bloom Is in the Restaurant': French Translations of the 'Scarlett' Passage of *Ulysses*." *Scientia Traductionis* 8: 134–46.

Barry, Raymond W., and A. J. Wright. 1966. *Literary Terms: Definitions, Explanations, Examples*. San Francisco: Chandler.

Barthes, Roland. 1977. *Image-Music-Text*. Trans. Stephen Heath. London: Fontana.

Bassnett, Susan. 2007. "Influence and Intertextuality: A Reappraisal." *Forum for Modern Language Studies* 43.2: 134–46.

Bassnett, Susan, and André Lefevere. 1998. *Constructing Cultures: Essays on Literary Translation*. Clevedon: Multilingual Matters.

Bassnett, Susan, and André Lefevere, eds. 1990. *Translation, History, and Culture*. New York: Pinter Publishers.

Bastin, Georges. 2014. "Adaptation, the Paramount Communication Strategy." *Linguaculture* 1: 73–87.

Bastin, Georges, and Hugo Vandal-Sirois. 2012. "Adaptation and Appropriation: Is There a Limit?" In *Translation, Adaptation and Transformation*. Ed. Laurence Raw. London and New York: Continuum, 21–41.

Baudrillard, Jean. [1981] 1994. "The Precession of Simulacra." In *Simulacra and Simulation*. Trans. Sheila Faria Glaser. Ann Arbor: University of Michigan Press, 1–42.

Bazarnik, Katarzyna. 2014. "Excavatory Notes on the Style of Interior Monologue in the Polish Translation of Joyce's *Ulysses*." In *Continuity in Language: Styles and Registers in Literary and Non-literary Discourse*. Ed. Ewa Willim. Krakow: Krakow University, 35–47.

Beebee, Thomas C. 2012. *Transmesis: Inside Translation's Black Box*. Basingstoke: Palgrave Macmillan.

Beeretz, Sylvia. 1998. *'Tell Us in Plain Words': Narrative Strategies in James Joyce's "Ulysses."* New York: Peter Lang.

Belle, Marie-Alice. 2011. "Critical Introduction to Dryden's Preface (Ovid's Epistles)." *Textes théoriques sur la traduction*. At: http://ttt.univ-paris3.fr/spip.php? article9&lang=fr

Benjamin, Walter. [1923] 1992. "The Task of the Translator." In *Selected Writings*. Eds. Marcus Bullock and Michael W. Jennings. Trans. Harry Zohn. Cambridge, MA: Harvard University Press, I: 253–63.

Bernstein, Charles. 2010. "De Campos Thou Art Translated." At: http://poemsandpoetics.blogspot.com/2010/09/Charles-Bernstein-de-Campos-Thou-Art.html

Bhatti, Anil. 2014. "'Cultural Similarity Does Not Mean That We Wear the Same Shirts': Similarity and Difference in Culture and Cultural Theory." *Word and Text: A Journal of Literary Studies and Linguistics* 4.2: 13–23.

Biguenet, John, and Rainer Schulte, eds. 1992. *Theories of Translation: An Anthology of Essays from Dryden to Derrida*. Chicago: University of Chicago Press.

Bindervolt, Erik, and Robbert-Jan Henkes. 2012. "Why We Needed a Third Dutch Translation of *Ulysses*." *Scientia Traductionis* 12: 72–87.

Blackham, Harold J. 1985. *The Fable as Literature*. London: The Athlone Press.

Bloom, Harold. 1973. *The Anxiety of Influence: A Theory of Poetry*. New York: Oxford University Press.

Bluestone, George. 1957. *Novels into Film*. Berkeley: University of California Press.

Boase-Beier, Jean. 2006. *Stylistic Approaches to Translation*. Manchester: St. Jerome Publishing.

Boisen, Mogens. 1967. "Translating *Ulysses*." *James Joyce Quarterly* 4.3: 165–9.

Boldt, Leslie, Corrado Federici, and Ernesto Virgulti, eds. 2010. *Rewriting Texts, Remaking Images: Interdisciplinary Perspectives*. New York: Peter Lang.

Bollettieri, Rosa Maria, and Ira Torresi. 2012. "Re-foreignizing the Foreign: The Italian Retranslation of James Joyce's *Ulysses*." *Scientia Traducionis* 12: 36–44.

Bradstock, Timoty R., and Judith N. Rabinovitch. 1997. *An Anthology of Kanshi by Japanese Poets of the Edo Period*. Lewiston: Edwin Mellon Press.

Branchadell, Albert. 2005. "Introduction: Less Translated Languages as a Field of Inquiry." In *Less Translated Languages*. Eds. Albert Branchadell and Margaret West. Amsterdam: John Benjamins, 1–27.

Bridgman, Elijah, and Samuel W. Williams. 1840. *The Chinese Repository*. Vol. 9. Canton: Publisher unknown.

Brodovich, Olga I. 1997. "Translation Theory and Non-standard Speech in Fiction." *Perspectives: Studies in Translatology* 5.1: 25–32.

Brower, Reuben A. 1974. *Mirror on Mirror: Translation, Imitation, Parody*. Cambridge, MA: Harvard University Press.

Brower, Reuben A. 1959. *Alexander Pope: The Poetry of Allusion*. Oxford: Clarendon Press.

Bruhn, Jørgen. 2016. *The Intermediality of Narrative Literature: Medialities Matter*. New York: Palgrave MacMillan.

Busse, Kristina. 2017. *Framing Fan Fiction: Literary and Social Practices in Fan Fiction Communities*. Iowa City: University of Iowa Press.

Cattrysse, Patrick. 2018. "Adaptation Studies, Translation Studies, and Interdisciplinarity: Reflections on Siblings and Family Resemblance." *Adaptation* (advanced articles). At: https://doi.org/10.1093/adaptation/apy011

Cattrysse, Patrick. 2014. *Descriptive Adaptation Studies: Epistemological and Methodological Issues*. Antwerpen: Garant.

Chakrabarty, Dipesh. 2000. *Provincializing Europe: Postcolonial Thought and Historical Difference*. Princeton: Princeton University Press.

Chamberlain, Lori. 2000. "Gender and the Metaphorics of Translation." In *The Translation Studies Reader*. Ed. Lawrence Venuti. New York: Routledge, 314–29.

Chan, Leo Tak-hung. 2017. "Transgenderism in Japanese Manga as Radical Translation: *The Journey to the West* Goes to Japan." In *Queering Translation, Translating the Queer: Theory, Practice, Activism*. Eds. Brian Baer and Klaus Kaindl. New York: Routledge, 96–111.

Chan, Leo Tak-hung. 2016. "Japanization and the Chinese 'Madman': Triangulating Takeuchi Yoshimi's Philosophy of Translation." *Translation Studies* 9.1: 1–16.

Chan, Leo Tak-hung. 2010. "The Poetics of Recontextualization: Intertextuality in a Chinese Adaptive Translation of *The Picture of Dorian Gray*." *Comparative Literature Studies* 41.4: 464–81.

Chan, Leo Tak-hung. 2004. *Twentieth-Century Chinese Translation Theory: Modes, Issues and Debates*. Amsterdam: John Benjamins.

Chan, Leo Tak-hung. 1995. "Chinese Animal Fables of the Eighteenth Century: Translations from Shen Qifeng's *Words of Humor from an Ancient Bell*." *Asian Culture Quarterly* 23.1: 29–36.

Chatman, Seymour. 2001. "Parody and Style." *Poetics Today* 22.1: 25–39.
Chen, Richard Rong-bin. 2012. "Chongdu *Du Liankui*: Jianzhushi Wang Dahong yu fanyi (xiaoshuo) jia Wang Dahong de duihua" [Rereading *Du Liankui*: Wang Dahong's Transwriting of *The Picture of Dorian Gray* and His Identity as an Architect]. *Zhongwai wenxue* 41.3: 161–89.
Chesterman, Andrew. 2017. *Reflections on Translation Theory: Selected Papers, 1993–2014*. Amsterdam: John Benjamins.
Chesterman, Andrew. 2014. "Beyond the Particular." In *Translation Universals: Do They Exist?* Eds. Anna Mauranen and Pekka Kujamäki. Amsterdam: John Benjamins, 33–49.
Chesterman, Andrew, and Emma Wagner. 2002. *Can Theory Help Translators? A Dialogue between the Ivory Tower and the Wordface*. New York: Routledge.
Chesterman, Andrew, Helle V. Dam, Jan Engberg, and Anne Schjoldager. 2003. "Bananas—On Names and Definitions in Translation Studies." *Hermes* 31: 197–209.
Chin, Teroko, 2013. "Nitchū ni okeru Chūgoku yondai meicho no manga hikaku kenkyū: *Sangokushi* to *Saiyūki* o chūshin ni" [A Comparative Study of the Manga Based on the Four Classical Chinese Novels in Japan and China, with a Focus on *The Three Kingdoms* and *The Journey to the West*]. PhD dissertation, Doshisha University, Japan.
Chin, Teroko. 2012. "Nihon ni okeru no saisōsaku gaikyō: Manga bun'ya o chūshin ni" [Re-creation of *Journey to the West* in Japan: Focusing on the Field of Comics] 27: 71–96.
Cho, Heekyoung. 2016. *Translation's Forgotten History: Russian Literature, Japanese Mediation, and the Formation of Modern Korean Literature*. Cambridge, MA: Harvard University Asia Center.
Cho, Younghan. 2011. "Desperately Seeking East Asia amidst the Popularity of South Korean Pop Culture in Asia." *Cultural Studies* 25.3: 383–404.
Choo, Kukhee. 2008. "Girls Return Home: Portrayal of Femininity in Popular Japanese Girls' Manga and Anime Texts during the 1990s in *Hana yori Dango* and *Fruits Basket*." *Women: A Cultural Review* 19.3: 275–96.
Chua, Beng Huat. 2008. "Structure of Identification and Distancing in Watching East Asian Television." In *East Asian Pop Culture: Analysing the Korean Wave*. Eds. Beny Huat Chua and Koichi Iwabuchi. Hong Kong: University of Hong Kong Press, 73–89.
Chua, Beng Huat, and Iwabuchi Koichi, eds. 2008. *East Asian Pop Culture: Analysing the Korean Wave*. Hong Kong: University of Hong Kong Press.
Clej, Alina. 1997. "The Debt of the Translator: An Essay on Translation and Modernism." *Symploke: A Journal for the Intermingling of Literary, Cultural and Theoretical Scholarship* 5.1–2: 7–26.
Clements, Rebekah. 2015. *A Cultural History of Translation in Early Modern Japan*. Cambridge: Cambridge University Press.
Clifford, James. 1997. *Routes: Travel and Translation in the Late Twentieth Century*. Cambridge, MA: Harvard University Press.

Cohn, Dorrit. 1978. *Transparent Minds: Narrative Modes for Presenting Consciousness in Fiction*. Princeton: Princeton University Press.

Compton, Robert. 1971. "A Study of the Translations of Lin Shu, 1852–1924." PhD dissertation, Stanford University.

Constandinides, Costas. 2010. *From Film to Post-celluloid Adaptation: Rethinking the Transition of Popular Narratives and Characters across Old and New Media*. New York: Continuum.

Cotter, Sean. 2004. "Living through Translation: Lucian Blaga, T. S. Eliot, and the Cultural Politics of Translation in Modernism." PhD dissertation, University of Michigan.

Couling, Samuel. 1917. *Encyclopaedia Sinica*. Shanghai: Kelly and Walsh.

Cranford, Jonathan. 2014. "Sherlock Holmes, Fan Culture and Fan Letters." In *Fan Phenomena: Sherlock Holmes*. Eds. Tom Ue and Jonathan Cranfield. Chicago: Intellect Books, 67–78.

Cubbison, Laurie. n.d. "Goku's Journeys: The Monkey King in *Dragon Ball* and *Saiyuki*." At: http://www.radford.edu/~cubbison /personal/research/Goku. htm

Cui, Baoguo. 2010. "Japanese TV Drama in China." At: http://www.jamco.or.jp/ 2010_symposium/006/index.html

Cui, Xianglan. 2005. *Bakin yomihon to Chūgoku kodai shōsetsu* [Bakin's Yomihon and Traditional Chinese Fiction]. Hiroshima: Keisuisha.

Dai, Congrong, trans. 2013. *Fennigen de shoulingye* [Finnegans Wake]. Vol. 1. Shanghai: Shanghai renmin chubanshe.

Daly, Lloyd W., trans. 1961. *Aesop without Morals: The Famous Fables, and a Life of Aesop*. New York: A. S. Barnes.

Davis, Kathleen. 2001. *Deconstruction and Translation*. Manchester: St. Jerome Publishing.

Davis, Paul. 2008. *Translation and the Poet's Life: The Ethics of Translating in English Culture, 1646–1726*. Oxford: Oxford University Press.

Dawkins, Richard. 1976. *The Selfish Gene*. Oxford: Oxford University Press.

De Geest, Dirk. 1992. "The Notion of 'System': Its Theoretical Importance and Its Methodological Implications for a Functionalist Translation Theory." In *Histories, Systems, Literary Translations*. Ed. Harold Kittel. Berlin: Erich Schmidt, 32–45.

Delabastita, Dirk. 2008. "Status, Origin, Features: Translation and Beyond." In *Beyond Descriptive Translation Studies: Investigations in Homage to Gideon Toury*. Eds. Anthony Pym, Miriam Shlesinger, and Daniel Simeoni. Amsterdam: John Benjamins, 233–46.

Denecke, Wiebke. 2017. "Shared Literary Heritage in the East Asian Sinographic Sphere." In *The Oxford Handbook of Classical Chinese Literature (1000 BCE–900 CE)*. Eds. Wiebke Denecke, Li Wai-yee, and Tian Xiaofei. Oxford: Oxford University Press, 510–32.

Denecke, Wiebke. 2014. "World without Translation: Premodern East Asia and the Power of Character Scripts." In *A Companion to Translation Studies*. Eds.

Sandra Bermann and Catherine Porter. New York: John Wiley and Sons, 204–16.
Denecke, Wiebke. 2007. "'Topic Poetry Is All Ours': Poetic Composition on Chinese Lines in Early Heian Japan." *Harvard Journal of Asiatic Studies* 67.1: 1–49.
Deppman, Hsiu-Chuang. 2009. "Made in Taiwan: An Analysis of *Meteor Garden* as an East Asian Idol Drama." In *TV China*. Eds. Ying Zhu and Chris Berry. Cambridge: University of Cambridge, 90–101.
Derrida, Jacques. 1981. *Positions*. Trans. Alan Bass. Chicago: University of Chicago Press.
Devitt, Jane. 1979. "Santō Kyōden and the *Yomihon*." *Harvard Journal of Asiatic Studies* 39.2: 253–74.
D'hulst, Lieven. 2018. "Transfer Modes." In *A History of Modern Translation Knowledge*. Eds. Lieven D'hulst and Yves Gambier. Amsterdam: John Benjamins, 135–42.
Diamond, Catherine T. C. 1993. "The Role of Cross-cultural Adaptation in the 'Little Theatre' Movement in Taiwan." PhD dissertation, University of Washington.
Dicecco, Nico. 2015. "State of the Conversation: The Obscene Underside of Fidelity." *Adaptation* 8.2: 161–75.
Dollerup, Cay. 1999. *Tales and Translation: The Grimm Tales from Pan-Germanic Narratives to Shared International Fairytales*. Amsterdam and Philadelphia: John Benjamins.
Dong, Lan. 2011. *Mulan's Legend and Legacy in China and the United States*. Philadelphia: Temple University Press.
Dong, Shaoyan. 2012. "Cong *Yiqi laikan liuxingyu* kan neidi zizhi ouxiangju de fazhan" [The Development of Indigenized Idol Drama in Mainland China: A View from *Let's Go Watch the Meteor Shower*]. *Chuanmei luntan*, no. 330.
Dryden, John. 1680. "Preface to *Ovid's Epistles*." At: bartleby.com/204/207.html
Dyer, Richard. 2007. *Pastiche*. New York: Routledge.
Eco, Umberto. 1985. "'Casablanca': Cult Movies and Intertextual Collage." *Substance* 14.2: 3–12.
Elleström, Lars. 2014. *Media Transformation: The Transfer of Media Characteristics among Media*. New York: Palgrave Macmillan.
Espagne, Michel, and Michael Werner, eds. 1988. *Transferts: Les relations interculturelles dans l'espace franco-allemand (XVIIIe-XIXe siécles)*. Paris: Ed. Recherche sur les civilisations.
Even-Zohar, Itamar. 1978. "The Position of Translated Literature within the Literary Polysystem." In *Literature and Translation: New Perspectives in Literary Studies*. Eds. James S. Holmes, José Lambert, and Raymond van den Broeck. Leuven: Acco, 117–27.
Fan, Shengyu. 2016. "Fanyi shi xiugai de yishu" [Translation is the Art of Revision]. *Translation Quarterly* 79: 47–95.

Fiddian, Robin W. 1989. "James Joyce and Spanish-American Fiction: A Study of the Origins and Transmission of Literary Influence." *Bulletin of Hispanic Studies* 66: 23–39.

Fludernik, Monika. 1996. "Linguistic Signals and Interpretative Strategies: Linguistic Models in Performance, with Special Reference to Free Indirect Discourse." *Language and Literature* 5.2: 93–113.

Foley, John M. 1995. *The Singer of Tales in Performance*. Bloomington: Indiana University Press.

Ford, Andrew. 2002. *The Origins of Criticism: Literary Culture and Poetic Theory in Classical Greece*. Princeton: Princeton University Press.

Fraleigh, Matthew. 2016. *Plucking Chrysanthemums: Narushima Ryūhoku and Sinitic Literary Traditions in Modern Japan*. Cambridge, MA: Harvard University Press.

Frank, Armin Paul. 1992. "Towards a Cultural History of Literary Translation: 'Histories,' 'Systems,' and Other Forms of Synthesizing Research." In *Histories, System, Literary Translations*. Ed. Harald Kittel. Berlin: Erich Schmidt, 369–87.

Frus, Phyllis, and Christy Williams. 2010. "Introduction: Making the Case for Transformation." In *Beyond Adaptation: Essays on Radical Transformations of Original Works*. By Phyllis Frus and Christy Williams. London: McFarland and Company, 1–18.

Frye, Northrop. 1957. *Anatomy of Criticism: Four Essays*. Princeton: Princeton University Press.

Fujii, Shōzō. 2009. "Murakami Haruki no Chūgoku goyaku: Nihon bunka no dochakuka to Chūgoku hondo bunka no henkaku" [The Chinese Translation of Murakami Haruki: The Expropriation of Japanese Culture and the Transformation of Indigenous Chinese Culture]. *Nihongo no gakushū to kenkyū* 1: 111–17.

Fujii, Shōzō. 2007. *Murakami Haruki no naka no Chūgoku* [China in Murakami's World]. Tokyo: Asahi shinbunsha.

Fung, Anthony. 2007. "Inter-Asian Cultural Flow: Cultural Homologies in Hong Kong and Japanese Television Soap Operas." *Journal of Broadcasting and Electronic Media* 51.2: 265–86.

Gálik, Marián. 1990. *Interliterary and Intraliterary Aspects of the May Fourth Movement 1919 in China*. Bratislava: The Slovak Academy of Sciences.

Gálik, Marián. 1968. *Milestones in Sino-Western Literary Confrontation 1898–1979*. Wiesbaden: Otto Harrassowitz.

Gambier, Yves. 2003. "Introduction: Screen Tradaptation, Perception and Reception." *The Translator: Studies in Intercultural Communication* 9.2: 171–89.

Ge, Baoquan. 1992a. "Jin sibainian lai Zhongyi *Yisuo yuyan*" [Aesop's Fables in Chinese Translation in the Last 400 Years]. In *Fanyi xinlunji* [A New Collection of Essays on Translation]. Ed. Liu Ching-chih. Hong Kong: Shangwu yinshuguan, 84–109.

Ge, Baoquan. 1992b. "Mingdai Zhongyi *Yisuo yuyan* shihua" [*Aesop's Fables* Translated into Chinese in the Ming Dynasty]. In *Zhongwai wenxue yinyuan: Ge Baoquan bijiao wenxue lunwenji* [The Marriage of Chinese and Foreign Literatures: Essays on Comparative Literature by Ge Baoquan]. Beijing: Beijing chubanshe, 375–436.

Genette, Gérard. [1982] 1997. *Palimpsests: Literature in the Second Degree*. Trans. Channa Newman and Claude Doubinsky. Lincoln: University of Nebraska Press.

Gentile, Paola, and Luc van Doorslaer. 2019. "Translating the North–South Imagological Feature in a Movie: *Bien-venue chez les ch'tis* and Its Italian Versions." *Perspectives* (advanced articles). At: http://doi.org/10.1080/0907676x.2019.1596137

Gentzler, Edwin. 2017. *Translation and Rewriting in the Age of Post-Translation Studies*. New York: Routledge.

Gentzler, Edwin. 2008. *Translation and Identity in the Americas: New Directions in Translation Theory*. New York: Routledge.

Giles, Herbert A. 1935. *A History of Chinese Literature*. New York and London: D. Appleton-Century Company.

Gillespie, Stuart. 2011. *English Translation and Classical Reception: Towards a New Literary History*. London: Wiley-Blackwell.

Gómez-Galisteo, M. Carmen. 2011. *The Wind Is Never Gone: Sequels, Parodies and Rewritings of* Gone with the Wind. Jefferson: McFarland.

Gong, Haomin, and Xin Yang. 2010. "Digitized Parody: The Politics of *Egao* in Contemporary China." *China Information* 24.1: 3–16.

Gottlieb, Henrik. 2005. "Multidimensional Translation: Semantics Turned Semiotics." In *MuTra 2005: Challenges of Multidimensional Translation: Conference Proceedings, Saarbrücken, 2–6 May*, 1–29. At: www.euroconferences.info/proceedings/2005_Proceedings/2005_proceedings.html

Greene, Thomas A. 1982. *The Light in Troy: Imitation and Discovery in Renaissance Poetry*. New Haven: Yale University Press.

Ha, Kim-lan. 2001. "Texte, Translation, Readability, Scriptability and Transmitability." *Hanxue yanjiu tongxun* 20.3: 16–26.

Hamilton, Donna B. 1990. *Virgil and* The Tempest: *The Politics of Imitation*. Columbus: Ohio State University Press.

Handford, S. A., trans. 1954. *Aesop's Fables*. London: Puffin Books.

Hanying cidian Group, ed. 1981. *Hanying cidian* [A Chinese-English Dictionary]. Beijing: Shangwu yinshuguan.

Harmon, Coy L. 1985. "Ch'u Yu's *Chien-teng hsin-hua*: The Literary Tale in Transition." PhD dissertation, University of Arizona.

Härter, Pia. 2014. "Generatio(n): The Concept of Genealogy as a Form of Cultural Mobilization in Francis Meres' Honoring of Shakespeare, Sir Philip Sidney's *Defence of Poesie*, Ben Jonson's *Timber, or Discoveries Made upon Men and Matter*." *Word and Text: A Journal of Literary Studies and Linguistics* 4.2: 50–63.

Hartmann, Charles. 1986. "Yu-yen." In *Indiana Companion to Traditional Chinese Literature*. Ed. William Nienhauser, Jr. Bloomington: Indiana University Press, 946–8.

He, Yonghai. 2005. "Women zhenyang kangju Hanliu?" [How Can We Resist the Korean Wave?] In *Zhongguo funu bao* 22.6.

Hedberg, William C. 2019. *The Japanese Discovery of Chinese Fiction: The Water Margin and the Making of a National Canon*. New York: Columbia University Press.

Hedberg, William C. 2012. "Locating China in Time and Space: Engagement with Chinese Vernacular Fiction in 18th-century Japan." PhD thesis, Harvard University.

Heep, Hartmut. 1996. *A Different Poem: Rainer Maria Rilke's American Translators Randall Jarrell, Robert Lowell, and Robert Bly*. New York: Peter Lang.

Henningsen, Lena. 2010. *Copyright Matters: Imitation, Creativity and Authenticity in Contemporary Chinese Literature*. Berlin: Wissenschafts.

Hermans, Theo. 1999. *Translation in Systems: Descriptive and System-Oriented Approaches*. Manchester: St. Jerome Publishing.

Hermans, Theo. 1992. "Renaissance Translation between Literalism and Imitation." In *Histories, Systems, Literary Translations*. Ed. Harald Kittel. Berlin: Erich Schmidt, 95–116.

Hermans, Theo, ed. 1985. *The Manipulation of Literature: Studies in Literary Translation*. London: Croom Helm.

Hill, Forbes I. 2003. "Aristotle's Rhetorical Theory." In *A Synoptic History of Classical Rhetoric*. Eds. James J. Murphy and Richard A. Katula. Mahwah: Lawrence Erlbaum Associates, 29–126.

Hill, Michael G. 2013. *Lin Shu, Inc.: Translation and the Making of Modern Chinese Culture*. Oxford: Oxford University Press.

Hillenbrand, Margaret. 2007. *Literature, Modernity, and the Practice of Resistance: Japanese and Taiwanese Fiction, 1960-1990*. Leiden: E. J. Brill.

Hoenselaars, Ton. 2004. *Shakespeare's History Plays: Performance, Translation and Adaptation in Britain and Abroad*. Cambridge: Cambridge University Press.

Hoesterey, Ingeborg. 2001. *Pastiche: Cultural Memory in Art, Film, Literature*. Bloomington: Indiana University Press.

Hu, Gengshen. 2003. "Translation as Adaptation and Selection." *Perspectives: Studies in Translatology* 11.4: 283–91.

Huang, Zhonglian. 2009. "Shiying yu xuanze: Yan Fu fanyi sixiang tanyuan" [Adaptation and Selection: The Origins of Yan Fu's Translation Thought]. *Shanghai Journal of Translation*, no. 4: 7–11.

Huang, Zhonglian. 2002. *Bianyi lilun* [A Theory of Translation Variation]. Beijing: Zhongguo duiwai fanyi chuban gongsi.

Huoyi bianjibu [Editorial Group, Huoyi Publishers], eds. 1995. Jiutu *pinglun xuanji* [*The Drunkard*: Selected Critical Essays]. Hong Kong: Huoyi chuban shiye.

Hutcheon, Linda. 2006. *A Theory of Adaptation*. New York: Methuen.
Hutcheon, Linda. 1985. *A Theory of Parody: The Teachings of Twentieth-Century Art Forms*. New York: Routledge.
Inggs, Judith. 2019. "Fairy Tales and Folk Tales." In *The Routledge Handbook of Literary Translation*. Eds. Kelly Washbourne and Ben Van Wyke. New York: Routledge, 146–58.
Inoue, Yuhiko, ed. 2012. *Kanryū and Karyū rimeiku dorama* [Drama Remakes: Korean and Chinese Waves]. Tokyo: Tatsumi Publishing Co.
Ishikawa, Hidemi. 2010. "Edo no *Suikoden* to shite no *Nansō Satomi hakkenden*" [*Eight Dog Warriors* as *Water Margin* of the Edo Period]. In *Suikoden no shōgeki, Higashi Ajia ni okeru gengo sesshoku to bunka juyō* [The Impact of *Water Margin*: Linguistic Contact and Cultural Reception in East Asia]. *Ajia Yūgaku* 131: 194–204.
Iwabuchi, Koichi, ed. 2004. *Feeling Asian Modernities: Transnational Consumption of Japanese TV Dramas*. Hong Kong: Hong Kong University Press.
Jakobson, Roman. [1959] 2000. "On Linguistic Aspects of Translation." In *The Translation Studies Reader*. Ed. Lawrence Venuti. New York: Routledge, 113–18.
Jameson, Frederic. 2011. "Afterword: Adaptation as a Philosophical Problem." In *True to the Spirit: Film Adaptation and the Question of Fidelity*. Eds. Colin Maccabe, Kathleen Murray, and Rick Warner. Oxford: Oxford University Press, 215–32.
Jia, Chang'an, trans. 1972. *Maitian bushou* [The Catcher in the Rye]. Taibei: Chenzhong chubanshe.
Jiang, Xiaohua. 2009. "Yizhe de xuanzexing shiying yu shiyingxing xuanze: Ping *Mudanting* de sange Yingyiben" [The Translator's Selective Adaptation and Adaptive Selection: On Three Translations of *The Peony Pavilion*]. *Shanghai Journal of Translation*, no. 4: 11–15.
Jin, Di, trans. 1993–96. *Youlixisi* [Ulysses]. 2 vols. Beijing: Renmin wenxue chubanshe.
Jonson, Ben. 1985. *Ben Jonson*. Ed. Ian Donaldson. Oxford: Oxford University Press.
Joyce, James. [1922] 1990. *Ulysses*. New York: Vintage International.
Jung, Sun. 2013. "K-Pop beyond Asia: Performing Trans-nationality, Trans-sexuality, Trans-textuality." In *Asian Popular Culture in Transition*. Eds. Lorna Fitzsimmons and John A. Lent. New York: Routledge, 108–30.
Jung, Sun. 2010. "Chogukjeok Pan-East Asian Soft Masculinity: Reading *Boys over Flowers*, *Coffee Prince* and *Shinhwa* Fan Fiction." In *Complicated Currents: Media Flows, Soft Power and East Asia*. Eds. Daniel Black, Stephen Epstein, and Alison Tokita. Melbourne: Monash University Press, 8.1–8.16.
Jung, Sun. 2009. "The Shared Imagination of *Bishōnen*, Pan-East Asian Soft Masculinity: Reading DBSK, Youtube.com and Transcultural New Media Consumption." *Intersections: Gender and Sexuality in Asia and the Pacific* 20. At: http://intersections.anu.edu.au/issue20/jung.htm

Kamio, Yōko. 1992-. *Hana yori dango* [Boys over Flowers]. Tokyo: Shūeisha.
Kao, Karl S. Y. 1985. "Aspects of Derivation in Chinese Narrative." *Chinese Literature: Essays, Articles, Reviews* 7.1-2: 1-36.
Kim, Dong-uk. [1987] 2013. "The Influence of Chinese Stories and Novels on Korean Fiction." In *Literary Migrations: Traditional Chinese Fiction in Asia*. Ed. Claudine Salmon. Beijing: International Culture Publishing Corporation, 39-57.
Kim, Tae-bum [Jin, Taifan]. 2000. "Hanguo dui *Sanguo yanyi* de xishou he zhuanhua" [The Absorption and Transmutation of *The Three Kingdoms* in Korea]. PhD dissertation, Tung-hai University, Taiwan.
Klingberg, Gote, Mary Owig, and Stuart Amor, eds. 1978. *Children's Books in Translation: The Situation and the Problems*. Stockholm: Almqvist and Wiksell International.
Kojima, Noriyuki. 1962-2019. *Jōdai Nihon bungaku to Chūgoku bungaku: Shuttenron o chūshin to suru hikaku bungaku teki kōsatsu* [Early Japanese Literature and Chinese Literature: Comparative Literary Considerations with a Focus on Source Theory]. 4 vols. Tokyo: Hanawa shoten.
Korkut, Nil. 2009. *Kinds of Parody from the Medieval to the Postmodern*. Frankfurt am Main: Lang.
Krebs, Katjia. 2012. "Translation and Adaptation: Two Sides of an Ideological Coin?" In *Translation, Adaptation and Transformation*. Ed. Laurence Raw. London: Continuum, 42-53.
Kuhns, Luke B. 2014. "Doyle or Death? An Investigation into the World of Pastiche." In *Fan Phenomena: Sherlock Holmes*. Eds. Tom Ue and Jonathan Cranfield. Chicago: Intellect Books, 66-79.
Kyokutei, Bakin. 1807-11. *Chinzei Hachirō Tametomo gaiden*: Chinsetu yumiharizuki [Chinzei Hachirō Tametomo's Sequel: *Strange Tales of the Crescent Moon*]. Edo: Hirabayashi shogoro.
Kyokutei, Bakin. 1805. *Shinpen* Suiko *gaden* [New Illustrated *Water Margin*]. Vol. 1, 10 chapters. Edo: Kadomaruya jinsuke.
LaMarre, Thomas. 2000. *Uncovering Heian Japan: An Archaeology of Sensation and Inscription*. Durham: Duke University Press.
Lambert, José. 1991. "In Quest of Literary World Maps." In *Interculturality and the Historical Study of Translations*. Eds. Harald Kittel and Armin Paul Frank. Berlin: Erich Schmidt, 133-44.
Larson, Wendy. 1993. "Liu Yichang's *Jiutu*: Literature, Gender, and Fantasy in Contemporary Hong Kong." *Modern Chinese Literature* 7: 89-103.
Lathey, Gillian. 2016. *Translating Children's Literature*. New York: Routledge.
Lee, Dong-Hoo. 2004. "Cultural Contact with Japanese TV Dramas: Modes of Reception and Narrative Transparency." In *Feeling Asian Modernities: Transnational Consumption of Japanese TV Dramas*. Ed. Iwabuchi Koichi. Hong Kong: Hong Kong University Press, 251-74.
Lee, Peter H. 1986. "Chinese Literature in Korean Translation." In *An Indiana Companion to Traditional Chinese Literature*. Ed. William H. Nienhauser, Jr. Vol. 1. Bloomington: Indiana University Press, 305-6.

Lefevere, André. 1975. *Translating Poetry: Seven Strategies and a Blueprint*. Assen: Van Gorcum.

Lefevere, André. 1992. *Translation, Rewriting, and the Manipulation of Literary Fame*. New York: Routledge.

Lehtonen, Mikko. 2000. *Cultural Analysis of Texts*. London: Sage Publications.

Leitch, Thomas. 2009. *Film Adaptation and Its Discontents: From* Gone with the Wind *to* The Passion of the Christ. Baltimore: Johns Hopkins University Press.

Leong, Jane Ying Yieng. 2010. "Selling the Sweatdrop: The Translation of 'Japaneseness' in Manga and Anime Fan Fiction." PhD thesis, University of Western Australia.

Leung, Y. M. Lisa. 2004. "An Asian Formula? Comparative Reading of Japanese and Korean TV Dramas." At: http://www.jamco.or.jp/2004_symposium /en/ lisa/index.html

Lhermitte, Corinne. 2004. "Adaptation as Rewriting: Evolution of a Concept." *Revue LISA* 11.5: 26–44.

Li, Sher-shiueh. 1990. "Xila yuyan yu Mingmo tianzhujiao dongchuan: Jinian Liu Shouyi jiaoshou" [Greek Fables and the Eastern Transmission of Catholicism in the Late Ming: Commemorating Professor Liu Shouyi]. *Zhongwai wenxue* 19.1: 131–57.

Li, Shuguo. 1998. *Riben duben xiaoshuo yu Ming Qing xiaoshuo* [Japanese Yomihon and Chinese Fiction of the Ming and Qing Dynasties]. Nankai: Tianjin renmin chubanshe.

Li, Xiu, and Qin Linfang, eds. 2001. *Ershi shiji Zhongwai wenxue jiaoliushi* [History of the Twentieth-Century Interaction between Chinese and Western Literatures]. Shijiazhuang: Hebei jiaoyu chubanshe.

Li, Zeng. 2013. "Adaptation as an Open Process: *Dahua* Fandom and the Reception of a Chinese Odyssey." *Adaptation: The Journal of Literature on Screen Studies* 6.2: 187–201.

Lianeri, Alexandra. 2006. "The Homeric Moment? Translation, Historicity, and the Meaning of the Classics." In *Classics and the Uses of Reception*. Eds. Charles Martindale and Richard F. Thomas. Oxford: Blackwell Publishing.

Lim, Bliss Cua. 1999. *Translating Time: Cinema, the Fantastic, and Temporal Critique*. Durham: Duke University Press.

Lin, Shaohua. 2006. *Luohua zhi mei* [The Beauty of Falling Petals]. Beijing: Zhongguo gongren chubanshe.

Lin, Shaohua. 2005. *Chunshang cunshu he tade zuopin* [Murakami Haruki and His Works]. Yinchuan: Ningxia renmin chubanshe.

Lin, Shu, Yan Peinan, and Yan Ju, trans. 1938. *Yisuo yuyan* [Aesop's Fables]. Changsha: Shangwu yinshuguan.

Lin, Wenyue, trans. 1973–79. *Yuanshi wuyu* [Genji monogatari]. Taipei: Hongfan shuju.

Littau, Karin. 1997. "Translation in the Age of Postmodern Production: From Text to Intertext to Hypertext." *Forum for Modern Language Studies* 33.1: 82–96.

Liu, Lydia He. 1995. *Translingual Practice: Literature, National Culture, and Translated Modernity—China, 1900-1937*. Stanford: Stanford University Press.

Liu, Lydia He. 1994. "Butouming neixin xushi: Youguan fanyiti he xiandai Hanyu xushi moshi de ruogan wenti" [Non-Transparent Inner Narration: On Some Questions Related to Translation Styles and Narrative Models in Modern Chinese]. *Jintian*, no. 3: 174-92.

Liu, Shih-shun, trans. 1975. *Vignettes from the Late Ch'ing: Bizarre Happenings Eyewitnessed over Two Decades*. Hong Kong: Chinese University of Hong Kong Press.

Liu, Yichang. [1962-63] 1993. *Jiutu* [The Drunkard]. Hong Kong: Jinshi tushu.

Lowell, Robert. 1961. *Imitations*. New York: Farrar, Straus, Giroux.

Lu, Yin. [1960] 1998. "Peiqiang de Jidu" [Armed Christ]. In *Liushi niandai Xianggang xiaoshuo xuan* [Selected Short Stories from Hong Kong in the Sixties]. Ed. Ye Si. Hong Kong: Tiandi tushu, 29-37.

Luo, Shiwei. 2006. "Taibei yuyan: Wang Dahong zai *Du Liankui* zhong de xiandaixing zaishuxie" [Taipei Fable: Wang Dahong's Modernist Rewriting in *Du Liankui*]. In *Wang Dahong*. Ed. Lin Zhisong. Taipei: Jianzhushi quanlianhui zazhishe, 34-9.

Luo, Xinzhang, ed. 1984. *Fanyi lunji* [Collected Essays on Translation]. Beijing: Shangwu yinshuguan.

Luo, Xuanmin. 2012. "Yanyi: Shige fanyi de niepan" [Imitative Translation: The Nirvana of Poetry Translation]. *Waiyu jiaoxue lilun yu shijian* no. 2: 60-6.

Ma, Hongjun. 2006. *Cong wenxue fanyi dao fanyi wenxue: Xu Yuanchong de yixue lilun yu shijian*. [From Literary Translation to Translated Literature: Xu Yuanchng's Theory and Practice of Translation]. Shanghai: Yiwen chubanshe.

Malinowska, Anna. 2014. "Cultural Transplantation and the Problems of Transferability." *Word and Text: A Journal of Literary Studies and Linguistics* 4.2: 24-36.

Malmkjaer, Kirsten. 2000. "Adaptation." In *Encyclopedia of Literary Translation into English*. Ed. Olive Classe. London: Fitzroy Dearborn Publishers, 2-3.

Manfredi, Paul. 2001. "The Influenced Text: Modern Chinese Symbolist Poetry." *Journal of Modern Literature in Chinese* 4.2: 1-34.

Marceau, Lawrence. 2016. "*Bunjin* (Literati) and Early *Yomihon*: Nankaku, Nankai, Buson, Gennai, Teishō, Ayatari, and Akinari." In *The Cambridge History of Japanese Literature*. Eds. Haruo Shirane, Tomi Suzuki, and David B. Lurie. Cambridge: Cambridge University Press, 488-502.

Marranca, Bonnie, and Gautam Dasgupta, eds. 1991. *Interculturalism and Performance: Writings from PAJ*. New York: PAJ Publications.

Martí-López, Elisa. 2002. *Borrowed Words: Translation, Imitation, and the Making of the Nineteenth-Century Novel in Spain*. Lewisburg: Bucknell University Press.

Matsubara, Chinami. 1997. *Sai-yū-ki* [West-Travel-Record]. Tokyo: Jitsugyū no Nihon sha.

Matsuoka, Naomi. 1988–89. "Japanese–English Translation and the Stream of Consciousness." *Tamkang Review* 19.1–4: 537–45.
Maya, Mineo. 2000–2004. *Patariro Saiyūki!* [Patariro *Journey to the West!*]. Tokyo: Hakusensha.
McFarland, Thomas. 1985. *Originality and Imagination*. Baltimore: Johns Hopkins University Press.
Medina Casado, Carmelo. 2010. "The Earliest Translations of Joyce's *Ulysses*." *Papers on Joyce* 16: 81–91.
Melehy, Hassan. 2003. "Spenser and Du Bellay: Translation, Imitation, Ruin." *Comparative Literature Studies* 40.4: 415–38.
Melling, John K. 1996. *Murder Done to Death: Parody and Pastiche in Detective Fiction*. Lanham: Scarecrow Press.
Miller, J. Scott. 2001. *Adaptations of Western Literature in Meiji Japan*. New York: Palgrave.
Milton, John. 2009. "Translation Studies and Adaptation Studies." In *Translation Research Projects 2*. Eds. Anthony Pym and Alexander Perekrestenko. Tarragona: Intercultural Studies Group, 51–8.
Milton, John. 2007. "Between the Cat and the Devil: Adaptation Studies and Translation Studies." *Journal of Adaptation in Film and Performance* 2.1: 47–64.
Minekura, Kazuya. 1997–2002. *Saiyūki* [Journey to the Extreme]. Tokyo: Enikkusu.
Minguez-López, Xavier. 2014. "Folktales and Other References in Toriyama's *Dragon Ball*." *Animation: An Interdisciplinary Journal* 9.1: 27–46.
Minier, Márta. 2014. "Definitions, Dyads, Triads and Other Points of Connection between Translation and Adaptation Discourse." In *Translation and Adaptation in Theatre and Film*. Ed. Katjia Krebs. New York: Routledge, 13–35.
Moraru, Christian. 2001. *Rewriting: Postmodern Narrative and Cultural Critique in the Age of Cloning*. Albany: State University of New York Press.
Mori, Yoshitaka. 2008. "*Winter Sonata* and Cultural Practice of Active Fans in Japan: Considering Middle-Aged Women as Cultural Agents." In *East Asian Pop Culture: Analysing the Korean Wave*. Eds. Chua Beng Huat and Iwabuchi Koichi. Hong Kong: University of Hong Kong Press, 121–47.
Mowry, Hua-yuan Li. 1984. "The Wolf of Chung-shan." *Tamkang Review*, 139–59.
Munday, Jeremy. 2014. "Using Primary Sources to Produce a Microhistory of Translation and Translators: Theoretical and Methodological Concerns." *The Translator* 20.1: 64–80.
Munday, Jeremy. 2013. "The Role of Archival and Manuscript Research in the Investigation of Translator Decision-Making." *Target* 25.1: 125–39.
Murakami, Haruki. 2002. *Murakami Haruki zensakuhin 1990–2000* [The Complete Works of Murakami Haruki]. Vols. 1–4. Tokyo: Kōdansha.
Murakami, Haruki. 1991. *Murakami Haruki zensakuhin 1979–1989* [The Complete Works of Murakami Haruki]. Vols. 1–8. Tokyo: Kōdansha.

Murakami, Haruki. "Murakami and the Beatles." Undated. At: goosky.com/norwood/bbs/dispbbs.asp?boardid=1&replyid=22970&id=1934&page=1&skin=0
Nakamura, Yukihiko. 1968. "Hon'yaku, chūshaku, hon'an" [Translation, Original Writing, and Adaptation]. In *Nihon kangaku (Chūgoku bunka sōsho)*. Eds. Mizuta Norihisa and Rai Tsutomu. Vol. 9. Tokyo: Taishūkan shoten, 260–7.
Nakano, Yoshiko. 2002. "Who Initiates a Global Flow? Japanese Popular Culture in Asia." *Visual Communication* 1.2: 229–53.
Naremore, James. 2000. *Film Adaptation*. New Brunswick: Rutgers University Press.
Népote, Jacques, and Khing Hoc Dy. [1987] 2013. "Chinese Literary Influence on Cambodia in the Nineteenth and Twentieth Centuries." Trans. Noel Castelino. In *Literary Migrations: Traditional Chinese Fiction in Asia, Seventeenth to Twentieth Centuries*. Singapore: Institute of Southeast Asian Studies.
Nguyen, Nam. 2005. "Writing as Response and as Translation: *Jiandeng xinhua* and the Evolution of the *Chuanqi* Genre in East Asia, Particularly in Vietnam." PhD dissertation, Harvard University.
Ning, Xi. 1992. *Zhongguo yuyan wenxueshi* [A History of the Literature of the Fable in China]. Kunming: Yunnan renmin chubanshe.
Nord, Christiane. 1991. *Text Analysis in Translation: Theory, Methodology, and Didactic Application of a Model for Translation-Oriented Text Analysis*. Amsterdam: Rodopi.
Nöth, Winfried. 1990. *Handbook of Semiotics*. Bloomington: Indiana University Press.
Oberstebrink, Christina. 2010. "Plagiarism and Originality in Painting: Joshua Reynolds's Concept of Imitation and Enlightenment Translation Theory." In *Cultural Transfer through Translation: The Circulation of Enlightened Thought in Europe by Means of Translation*. Ed. Stefanie Stockhorst. Amsterdam: Rodopi, 45–59.
Oittinen, Riitta. 2000. *Translating for Children*. New York: Garland Publishing.
Ōki, Yasushi, and Ōtsuka Hidetaka. [1987] 2013. "Chinese Colloquial Novels in Japan—Mainly During the Edo Period." In *Literary Migrations: Traditional Chinese Fiction in Asia*. Ed. Claudine Salmon. Beijing: International Culture Publishing Corporation, 106–39.
Orr, Mary. 2003. *Intertextuality: Debates and Contexts*. Cambridge: Polity Press.
Orvell, Miles. [1989] 2014. *The Real Thing: Imitation and Authenticity in American Culture, 1880–1940*. Chapel Hill: University of North Carolina Press.
Ōsone, Shōsuke. 1998. *Nihon kanbungaku ronshū* [Collected Essays on Sino-Japanese Literature in Japan]. Tokyo: Kyūko shoin.
O'Sullivan, Emer. 2012. "Children's Literature and Translation Studies." In *Routledge Handbook of Translation Studies*. Eds. Carmen Millán and Francesca Bartrina. New York: Routledge, 451–63.

Ōtaka, Yōji. 2015. "Development of the Late *Yomihon*: Santō Kyōden and Kyokutei Bakin." In *The Cambridge History of Japanese Literature*. Eds. Haruo Shirane, Tomi Suzuki, and David B. Lurie. Cambridge: Cambridge University Press, 539–50.

Palmer, R. Barton, and David Boyd. 2011. "Introduction: Recontextualizing Hitchcock's Authorship." In *Hitchcock at the Source: The Auteur as Adaptor*. Eds. R. Barton Palmer and David Boyd. Albany: State University of New York Press, 1–9.

Papusha, Olga. n.d. "Translation as Adaptation: The Winnie-the-Pooh Stories as Children's and Adult Reading." At: http://liternet.bg/publish15/o_papusha/translation.htm. Accessed December 17, 2010.

Parks, Tim. 1998. *Translating Style: The English Modernists and Their Italian Translations*. London: Cassell.

Pastreich, Emanuel. 2011. *The Observable Mundane: Vernacular Chinese and the Emergence of a Literary Discourse on Popular Narrative in Edo Japan*. Seoul: Seoul National University Press.

Pavis, Patrice. 1996. "Introduction: Towards a Theory of Interculturalism in the Theatre?" In *The Intercultural Performance Reader*. Ed. Patrice Pavis. New York: Routledge, 1–26.

Pavis, Patrice. 1989. "Problems of Translation for the Stage: Interculturalism and Post-modern Theatre." In *The Play out of Context: Transferring Plays from Culture to Culture*. Eds. Hanne Scolnocov and Peter Holland. Trans. Loren Kruger. Cambridge: Cambridge University Press, 25–44.

Phan, John Duong. 2013. "Lacquered Words: The Evolution of Vietnamese under Sinitic Influences from the 1st century B.C.E. through the 17th Century C.E." PhD dissertation, Cornell University.

Piette, Adam. 2008. "Pound's 'The Garden' as Modernist Imitation: Samain, Lowell, H. D." *Translation and Literature* 17: 21–46.

Pigman, III, G. W. 1980. "Versions of Imitation in the Renaissance." *Renaissance Quarterly* 33: 1–32.

Pollack, David. 1986a. "Chinese Literature in Japanese Translation." In *An Indiana Companion to Traditional Chinese Literature*. Ed. William H. Nienhauser, Jr. Vol. 1. Bloomington: Indiana University Press, 302–5.

Pollack, David. 1986b. *The Fracture of Meaning: Japan's Synthesis of China from the Eighth through the Eighteenth Centuries*. Princeton: Princeton University Press.

Pollard, David, ed. 1995. *Cockroach and Other Stories*. Hong Kong: Renditions.

Preda, Roxana. 2001. *Ezra Pound's (Post)modern Poetics and Politics: Logocentrism, Language and Truth*. New York: Peter Lang.

Puurtinen, Tiina. 1991. "Dynamic Style as a Parameter of Acceptability in Translated Children's Books." In *Translation Studies: An Interdiscipline*. Eds. Mary Snell-Hornby, Franz Pochhacker, and Klaus Kaindl. Amsterdam: John Benjamins, 83–90.

Pym, Anthony. 2010. *Exploring Translation Theories*. New York: Routledge.

Pym, Anthony. 2004. *The Moving Text: Localization, Translation, Distribution.* Amsterdam: John Benjamins.

Pym, Anthony. 1998. *Method in Translation History.* Manchester: St. Jerome Publishing.

Raphals, Lisa. 1992. *Knowing Words: Wisdom and Cunning in Classical Traditions of China and Greece.* Ithaca: Cornell University Press.

Raw, Laurence, ed. 2012. *Translation, Adaptation and Transformation.* New York: Continuum.

Raw, Laurence. 2009. "Two New Adaptation Studies Journals." *Literature/Film Quarterly* 37.1: 72–4.

Reider, Noriko. 2002. *Tales of the Supernatural in Early Modern Japan:* Kaidan, Akinari, Ugetsu monogatari. Lewiston: Edwin Mellon Press.

Reimer, Andrew. 2010. "Translation, Imitation, Parody." *Australian Journal of French Studies* 47.1: 36–45.

Riftin, Boris. 2007. "Qu You's Short Story Collection, *New Stories Written While Trimming the Wick* and the Effect Abroad." *Chengda Zhongwen xuebao* 17: 31–42.

Rippl, Gabriele. 2015. *Handbook of Intermediality: Literature, Image, Sound, Music.* Berlin: De Gruyter.

Rose, Margaret. 1993. *Parody: Ancient, Modern, and Post-modern.* Cambridge: Cambridge University Press.

Rouhiainen, Taraja. 2000. "Free Indirect Discourse in the Translation into Finnish: The Case of D. H. Lawrence's *Women in Love*." *Target* 12.2: 109–26.

Sakai, Naoki. 1992. *Voices of the Past: The Status of Language in Eighteenth-Century Japanese Discourse.* Ithaca: Cornell University Press.

Salmon, Claudine, ed. [1987] 2013. *Literary Migrations: Traditional Chinese Fiction in Asia, Seventeenth to Twentieth Centuries.* Singapore: Institute of Southeast Asian Studies.

Sanders, Julie. 2006. *Adaptation and Appropriation.* New York: Routledge.

Sanz Gallego, Guillermo. 2019. "Retranslating Joyce's *Ulysses* into Spanish: An Interview with Francisco García Tortosa and María Luisa Venegas Lagüéns." *Cadernos de Tradução* 39.1: 275–8.

Sayols Lara, Jesús. 2015. "Translating as Transculturating: A Study of Dai Wangshu's Translation of Lorca's Poetry from an Integrated Sociological-Cultural Perspective." PhD dissertation, Hong Kong Baptist University.

Semizu, Yukino. 2006. "Invisible Translation: Reading Chinese Texts in Ancient Japan." In *Translating Others.* Ed. Theo Hermans. Manchester: St. Jerome Publishing, 283–95.

Senn, Fritz. 1991. *Joyce's Dislocutions: Essays on Reading as Translation.* Ann Arbor: University Microfilms International.

Shen, Fei. 1985. "*Yuyue wuyu* yu *Jiandeng xinhua*" [*Tales of Moonlight and Rain* and *New Tales of Trimming the Wick*]. *Riyu xuexi yu yanjiu*, no. 1: 45–9, 44.

Shi, Zhecun, ed. 1991. *Zhongguo jindai wenxue daxi: Fanyi wenxue 3* [A Compendium of Early Modern Chinese Literature: Translated Literature 3]. Shanghai: Shanghai shudian.

Shi, Zhiwu. 2010. "Zhong Ri sanpian *Mudang dengji* de duibifenxi" [A Comparative Study of Three Chinese and Japanese Versions of "The Chronicle of the Peony Lantern"]. *Riyu xuexi yu yanjiu*, no. 3: 115–22.
Shirane, Haruo, ed. 2002. *Early Modern Japanese Literature: An Anthology, 1600–1900*. New York: Columbia University Press.
Shyu, Ming Song. 2007. *A Guide to Wang Da Hong's Architecture*. Taipei: Muma wenhua shiye.
Sitter, Zak. 2008. "William Jones, 'Eastern' Poetry, and the Problem of Imitation." *Texas Studies in Literature and Language* 50.4: 385–407.
Sowerby, Robin. 2000. "Imitation." In *Encyclopedia of Literary Translation into English*. Ed. Olive Classe. Chicago: Fitzroy Dearborn, 700–1.
Spariosu, Mihai. 1984. "Editor's Introduction." In *Mimesis in Contemporary Theory: An Interdisciplinary Approach*. Ed. Mihai Spariosu. Vol. 1. Amsterdam: John Benjamins, i–xxiv.
Stam, Robert, ed. 2005. *Literature through Film: Realism, Magic, and the Art of Adaptation*. Oxford: Blackwell Publishing.
Stam, Robert. 2000. "Beyond Fidelity: The Dialogics of Adaptation." In *Film Adaptation*. Ed. James Naremore. London: Athlone Press, 54–76.
Stam, Robert, and Ella Shohat. 2009. "Transnationalizing Comparison: The Uses and Abuses of Cultural Analogy." *New Literary History* 40.3: 473–99.
Starrs, D. Bruno. 2006. "A Queer New World: Adaptation Theory and the Zeugma of Fidelity in Derek Jarman's *The Tempest*." *AMERICAN@*: 4.1: 71–92.
Steiner, George. 1975. *After Babel: Aspects of Language and Translation*. Oxford: Oxford University Press.
Steiner, T. R. 1975. *English Translation Theory 1650–1800*. Amsterdam: Van Gorcum.
Steininger, Brian. 2017. *Chinese Literary Forms in Heian Japan: Poetics and Practice*. Cambridge, MA: Harvard University Press.
Su, Heyun. 2013. "Miaoxie yixue xia *Jiandeng xinhua* Chaoxian chaoyiben yanjiu" [A Study of the Korean Translations of *Trimming the Wick* from the Perspective of Descriptive Translation Studies]. *Dongbeiya waiyu yanjiu* 2: 92–7.
Sun, Junyue. 2004. "Goyaku no naka no shinri: Chūgoku ni okeru *Noruwei no mori* no hon'yaku to juyō" [The Truth in Mistranslation: The Translation and Reception of *Norwegian Wood* in China]. *Nihon kindai bungaku* 71: 147–9.
Sun, Yingcun. 2009. "Zhang Guruo yu 'shiying' 'xuanze'" [Zhang Guruo and Adaptation/Selection]. *Shanghai Journal of Translation*, no. 4: 1–6.
Susam-Sarajeva, Şebnem. 2006. *Theories on the Move: Translation's Role in the Travels of Literary Theories*. Amsterdam: Rodopi.
Tabbert, Reinhert. 2002. "Approaches to the Translation of Children's Literature: A Review of Critical Studies since 1960." *Target* 14.2: 303–51.
Tachikawa, Kiyoshi. 1999. *Botan dōrō no keifu* [The Genealogy of "The Peony Lantern"]. Tokyo: Benseisha.

Takada, Mamoru. 2005. Kanpon Hakkenden *no sekai* [The World of *Eight Dog Warriors*: Full Version]. Tokyo: Chikuma gakugei bunko.

Takashima, Toshio. 2006. Suikoden *to Nihonjin* [*Water Margin* and the Japanese]. Tokyo: Chikuma shobō.

Tam, Yue Him. 1981. *Riyi Zhongguoshu zonghe mulu* [Combined Catalog of Chinese Books Translated into Japanese]. Hong Kong: Chinese University Press.

Tanaka, Kanako. 2000–. *Sanjūshi* [The Three Beast-men]. Tokyo: Shūeisha.

Tay, William. 1984. "Wang Meng, Stream-of-Consciousness, and the Controversy over Modernism." *Modern Chinese Literature* 1.1: 7–24.

Terada, Katsuya. 1998–2010. *Saiyūkiden daienō* [The Marvelous Adventures of Monkey King]. Tokyo: Shūeisha.

Terrinoni, Enrico. 2012. "Translating *Ulysses* in the Era of Public Joyce: A Return to Interpretation." In *Bridging Cultures: Intercultural Mediation in Literature, Language, and the Arts*. Eds. Ciara Hogan, Nadine Rentel, and Stephanie Schwerter. Stuttgart: Ibidem-Verlag, 113–24.

Thom, Robert, trans. [1840] 1991. *Yishi yuyan* [Aesop's Fables]. In *Zhongguo jindai wenxue daxi: Fanyi wenxue* [A Compendium of Early Modern Chinese Literature: Translated Literature]. Ed. Shi Zhecun. Vol. 3. Shanghai: Shanghai shudian, 225–42.

Thomsett, Kay, and Eve Nickerson. 1993. *Missing Words*. Washington, DC: Gallaudet University Press.

Thornber, Karen L. 2009. *Empire of Texts in Motion: Chinese, Korean and Taiwanese Transculturations of Japanese Literature*. Cambridge, MA: Harvard University Press.

Thornton, Weldon. 2001. *Voices and Values in Joyce's* Ulysses. Gainsville: University Press of Florida.

Tihanov, Galin. 2018. "Bakhtin, Translation, World Literature." *Waiguo yuwen yanjiu* 6. At: https://mp.weixin.qq.com/s/kBUKLN0vYVlpLwZZXCMmOg

Toriyama, Akira. 1984–1995. *Doragon Bōru* [Dragon Ball]. Tokyo: Shūeisha.

Toury, Gideon. 1980. *In Search of a Theory of Translation*. Tel Aviv: Tel Aviv University, The Porter Institute for Poetics and Semiotics.

Tuan, Iris Hsin-chun. 2007. *Alternative Theatre in Taiwan: Feminist and Intercultural Approaches*. Youngstown: Cambria Press.

Tymozcko, Maria. 2007. *Enlarging Translation, Empowering Translators*. Manchester: St. Jerome Publishing.

Tymozcko, Maria. 1999. *Translation in a Postcolonial Context*. Manchester: St. Jerome Publishing.

Van Coillie, Jan, and Walter P. Verschueren, eds. 2006. *Children's Literature in Translation: Challenges and Strategies*. Manchester: St. Jerome Publishing.

Van Doorslaer, Luc. 2018. "Bound to Expand: The Paradigm of Change in Translation Studies." In *Moving Boundaries in Translation Studies*. Eds. Helle V. Dam, Matilde N. Brøgger, and Karen K. Zethsen. New York: Routledge, 220–30.

Van Doorslaer, Luc. 2012. "Eurocentrism." In *Handbook of Translation Studies 3*. Eds. Yves Gambier and Luc van Doorslaer. Amsterdam: John Benjamins, 47–51.

Vanderschelden, Isabelle. 2000. "Why Retranslate the French Classics? The Impact of Retranslation on Quality." In *On Translating French Literature and Film II*. Ed. Miriam Salma-Carr. Amsterdam: Rodopi, 1–18.

Venuti, Lawrence. 2011. "The Poet's Version; or, An Ethics of Translation." *Translation Studies* 4.2: 230–47.

Venuti, Lawrence. 2007. "Adaptation, Translation, Critique." *Journal of Visual Culture* 6.1: 25–43.

Venuti, Lawrence. 1995. *The Translator's Invisibility: A History of Translation*. New York: Routledge.

Venuti, Lawrence, ed. 1992. *Rethinking Translation: Discourse, Subjectivity, Ideology*. New York: Routledge.

Voigts-Virchow, Eckart. 2014. "Anti-Essentialist Versions of Aggregate Alice: A Grin without a Cat." In *Translation and Adaptation in Theatre and Film*. Ed. Katja Krebs. New York: Routledge, 63–79.

Wachtel, Michael. 2017. "Translation, Imitation, Adaptation, or Mutilation? Robert Lowell's Versions of Boris Pasternak's Poetry." In *Novoe o Pasternakakh*. Ed. Lazar Fleishman. Moscow: Leksrus, 591–636.

Wakabayashi, Judy. 2016. "Script as a Factor in Translation." *Journal of World Literature* 1.2: 173–94.

Wakabayashi, Judy. 2005a. "The Reconceptualization of Translation from Chinese in Eighteenth-Century Japan." In *Translation and Cultural Change: Studies in History, Norms and Image-Projection*. Ed. Eva Hung. Amsterdam: John Benjamins, 119–45.

Wakabayashi, Judy. 2005b. "Translation in the East Asia Cultural Sphere: Shared Roots, Divergent Paths?" In *Asian Translation Traditions*. Eds. Judy Wakabayashi and Eva Hung. Manchester: St. Jerome Publishing, 17–65.

Wakabayashi, Judy. 1998. "Marginal Forms of Translation in Japan: Variations from the Norm." In *Unity in Diversity? Current Trends in Translation Studies*. Eds. Lynne Bowker, Michael Cronin, Dorothy Kenny, and Jennifer Pearson. Manchester: St. Jerome Publishing, 57–63.

Wakabayashi, Judy, and Kang Ji-hae, eds. 2019. *Translating and Interpreting in Korean Contexts: Engaging with Asian and Western Others*. New York: Routledge.

Wang, Dahong, trans. [1977] 1993. *Du Liankui* [The Picture of Dorian Gray]. Taipei: Jiuge chubanshe.

Wang, Hailan. 2012. *Murakami Haruki to Chūgoku* [Murakami Haruki and China]. Tokyo: Ātsu ando kurafutsu.

Wang, Hongzhi. 2007. *Chongshi xindaya: Ershi shiji Zhongguo fanyi yanjiu* [Reinterpreting *Xin, Da* and *Ya*: Twentieth-century Chinese Translation Studies]. Beijing: Tsinghua daxue chubanshe.

Wang, Hui. 2008. "Yishi yuyan *kaoshu*" [Researching *Yishi yuyan*]. *Journal of Translation Studies* 11.2: 81–98.

Wang, Zhisong. 2009. "Fanyi, jiedu yu wenhua de yuejing: Yetan Linyi Cunshang wenxue" [Translation, Interpretation, and Cultural Border-crossing: Another View of Lin's Translations of Murakami]. *Riyu xuexi yu yanjiu*, no. 144: 117–22.

Watanabe, Hideo. 1991. *Heianchō bungaku to kanbun sekai* [Heian Literature and the World of Chinese Writing]. Tokyo: Benseisha.

Wei, Xin. 2017. "The Literary Chinese Cosmopolis." PhD thesis, University of Oxford.

Weinbrot, Howard D. 1966. "Translation and Parody: Towards the Genealogy of the Augustan Imitation." *English Literary History* 33: 434–47.

Weiss, Timothy. 2004. *Translating Orients: Between Ideology and Utopia*. Toronto: University of Toronto Press.

Wen, Zhaoxia. 2006. *1980 nian hou Ri Han yingshiju zai Zhongguo de chuanbo* [The Spread of Japanese and Korean Films and TV Drama in China since 1980]. PhD thesis, Jinan University.

Worton, Michael, and Judith Still, eds. 1991. *Intertextuality: Theories and Practice*. Manchester: Manchester University Press.

Wu, Qiulin. 1994. *Shijie yuyanshi* [A History of World Fables]. Shenyang: Liaoning shaonian ertong chubanshe.

Wu, Youshi, and Liu Shoushi, trans. 1968. *Maitian bushou* [The Catcher in the Rye]. Taibei: Shuiniu chubanshe.

Wu, Zhijie. 2009. *Zhongguo chuantong yilun zhuanti yanjiu* [A Specialized Study of Traditional Chinese Translation Theories]. Shanghai: Shanghai yiwen chubanshe.

Xiao, Qian, and Wen Jieruo, trans. 1995. *Youlixisi* [Ulysses]. 3 vols. Taipei: Shibao wenhua.

Xu, Jianzhong. 2000. "Translation Variation: A Future Trend." *Translatio-FIT Newsletter* 4: 384–97.

Xu, Jun. 1996. *Wenzi, wenxue, wenhua*: Hong yu hei *Hanyi yanjiu* [Words, Literature and Culture: A Study of the Chinese Translations of *Le rouge et le noir*]. Nanjing: Nanjing daxue chubanshe.

Ya, Siming. 2006. "Cunshang chunshu yu Linjia puzi" [Haruki Murakami and the Lins' Shop]. At: www.dw-world.de/dw/article/0,2144,225 2159,00.html. Accessed December 3, 2006.

Yamamoto, Atsuji. 1990. *Saiyū shōjotai* [The Maiden Team]. Tokyo: Kadokawa shoten.

Yamashita, Kazuo. 2007. "*Ryūsei hanazono* o furikaeru Karyū būmu no yukue" [The State of the Chinese Wave: Looking back at *Meteor Garden*]. *Ajia yūyaku* 97: 134–43.

Yan, Ming. 2014. "Dongya guobie Hanshi tezheng lun" [On the Characteristics of Literary Sinitic Poetry in Individual Countries in East Asia]. *Anhui shifan daxue xuebao* 42.3: 299–307.

Yan, Ruifang. 2011. *Qingdai Yisuo yuyan Hanyi sanzhong* [Three Translations of Aesop's Fables in the Qing Dynasty]. Taizhong: Wunan tushu.

Yang, Bingjing. 2009. "Wenxue fanyi yu fanyi wenxue; Linyi Cunshang zai Zhongguo dalu" [Literary Translation and Translated Literature: Lin Shaohua's Translations of Murakami in the Mainland]. *Riyu xuexi yu yanjiu* 144: 123–8.

Yang, Yuniang, trans. 1991. *Maitian bushou* [The Catcher in the Rye]. Taipei: Linyu wenhua shiye chubanshe.

Yao, Dadui. 2018. "Shijie wenxue de liutong he zaishengchan: Jindai Yisuo Hanyi de zaiyingyi he fangxie" [The Circulation and Reproduction of World Literature: Aesop's Fables as Imitated & Retranslated into English in Modern China]. *Xiandai Zhongguo yanjiu* 25.2: 166–79.

Yao, Steven G. 2002. *Translation and the Languages of Modernism: Gender, Politics, Language*. New York: Palgrave Macmillan.

Yasumoto, Seiko. 2015. "Cultural Harmonization in East Asia: Adaptation of *Hana yori dango/Boys over Flowers*." *East Asian Journal of Popular Culture* 1.2: 113–31.

Ye, Gongchao, trans. 1932. "Qiangsheng yidian henji" [The Mark on the Wall]. *Xinyue* 4.1 (January): 1–12.

Yip, William. 1998 [1960]. "Youlisaisi zai Taibei" [Ulysses in Taipei]. In *Liushi niandai Xianggang xiaoshuo xuan* [Selected Short Stories from Hong Kong in the Sixties]. Ed. Ye Si. Hong Kong: Tiandi tushu, 39–40.

You, Xiuyun. 2017. "Ruan Yu *Chuanqi manlu* yilei hunlian gushi yanjiu" [A Study of Love and Marriage between Supernatural Beings in Nguyễn Tu's *Truyền Kì Mạn Lục*]. MA thesis, Ming Chuan University, Taiwan.

Zhang, Chishan, trans. [1888] 1961. *Haiguo miaoyu* [Aesop's Fables]. In *Wanqing wenxue congchao: Yuwai wenxue yiwen juan* [A Collectanea of Late Qing Literature: Translations of Foreign Literature]. Ed. Ah Ying. Vol. 4. Beijing: Zhonghua shuju, 1107–34.

Zhang, Yanhong. 2013. "*Nuowei de senlin* zhuyao Zhongyiben yanjiu: Yi Linyi he Laiyi wei zhongxin [The Major Chinese Translations of *Norwegian Wood*: On Lin's and Lai's Translations]." MA thesis, Ocean University, PRC.

Zhang, Zhihu, trans. 1985. *Maitian bushou* [The Catcher in the Rye]. Taipei: Yuanzhi chubanshe.

Zhou, Zuoren. 1982. "Mingyi *Yisuo yuyan*" [Ming Dynasty Translations of Aesop's Fables]. In *Ziji de yuandi* [My Own Garden]. By Zhou Zuoren. Taipei: Wanli shuju, 194–7.

Zhu, Nandu, trans. 1960. "Chubin" [The Funeral Procession]. *Xiandai wenxue*, no. 4: 28–32.

Zolbrod, Leon M. 1967. *Takizawa Bakin*. New York: Twayne Publishers.

Index

accuracy 15, 139, *see also* equivalence
adaptation 1–3, 5, 8, 16–20, 24–34, 56, 75–90, 91–126, 143, 152–4, 157, 158, 184, 189, *see also* tradaptation
  of drama 17–28
  in East Asia 198–201, 204
adaptation studies 1, 18, 34, 75–90, 109, 126
adjustment 28, 93, 94, 102, 153
Aesop's fables 7, 34, 37, 38–55, 105, 201
aesthetics
  aesthetic fidelity 62, 65, 68–9
  aesthetic school 57–60, 69–71, 133
  beautification 59–61, 66, 69
  elegance 41, 57–60, 70
alienation 87, 161
Allen, Joseph 146
allusion 23, 132, 135, 149 n.4
alterity 87
appropriation 21–2, 51, 83, 109, 139, 150, 161, 163, 186, 196
Aristotle 29, 33, 52, 131–3
"Armed Christ" 170–2
Art of Poetry 133
Asai, Ryōi 99
assimilation 17, 45–50, 53, 88
audio description 84
Augustan era 132, 135–7, 175, 179, 183–4, 195
authenticity 20–1, 30, 160
autonomous text 10, 196 n.14

Baer, Brian 12
Bai, Juyi 149, 151
Bakhtin, Mikhail 76, 104

Barthes, Roland 15, 76
Bassnett, Susan 15, 177
Bastin, Georges 22, 83
Baudrillard, Jean 21, 197
Benjamin, Walter 19, 107
Bhabha, Homi 76
Blanchot, Maurice 76
Bloom, Harold 11, 185,
Boase-Beier, Jean 61–2, 68
Borges, Jorge Luis 11, 162, 165 n.3
Boys over Flowers 109–27, 200, 203
Brower, Reuben 140, 185

canonical works 9, 97, 141, 195
caricature 26, 181
Catcher in the Rye, The 70–1
Cathay 33, 139–40, 194
Cattrysse, Patrick 11, 19, 86
censorship 71, 114
Chatman, Seymour 182
Chen, Xiying 59, 60
Chesterman, Andrew 12, 30
children's literature 38, 56, 80–1, 89, 91
Chineseness 116, 150, 159
Clements, Rebekah 99
cloning 184
close translation 12 n.2
coherent 58, 170
colonization 30, 141, 202
communicative function 2, 14, 84, 88, 108, 133, 143 n.11, 145, 199
comprehensibility 57, 60
copying 30, 134, 180, 185, 193, 197, 203, *see also* plagiarism
correspondence 68, 86, 99, 139
creativity 21, 30, 31, 62, 134–6, 139, 141, 160
cultural proximity 102, 109, 120, 124

Daly, Lloyd 39, 48
Darwin, Charles 27, 29, 54, 93
Dawkins, Richard 193
Delabastita, Dirk 6
Denecke, Wiebke 151, 161
derivative texts 6, 10–11, 14, 22, 24, 77, 131, 139, 146–7, 154, 179, 180, 183
Derrida, Jacques 15, 76, 136
deviation 80
Diamond, Catherine 16–17, 21–2, 79–80, 89
disciplinarity 1, 5 n.4, 11, 18, 20, 31, 76–81 n.3, 86–8
distortion 34, 142, 181, 183, 185
Dollerup, Cay 80
domestication 3, 48, 67, 82, 87, 97 n.5, 108, 126, 154, 163, *see also* naturalization
Dragon Ball 187–8, 191, 193
Dream of the Red Chamber 28, 104, 114, 168
Dr. Jin 122, 126
Drunkard, The 172–6
Dryden, John 20, 135–8, 185, 197
Du Liankui 103–5

Eco, Umberto 15, 165
ecology 80, 92–6, 97, 105, *see also* adjustment; environment
Edo period 102 n.11, 122, 152
Eight Dog Warriors 151, 154 n.9, 155–8, 160, 161
emulation 61, 135, 141, 145, 147, 150, 175–6, 179, 182, 184
environment 27–8, 93–4, 96, 106, 117, 126, 162, 166, *see also* ecology
epimythium 43, 52
equivalence 3 n.2, 6, 12–15, 18, 23, 27, 38, 59, 62, 69, 86, 103, 108, 148, *see also* accuracy
Erasmus 135
Eurocentricism 3, 7, 92, 126, 198

Even-Zohar, Itamar 2, 13, 50, 163, 175
evolution 4, 23, 24, 27–31, 53, 82, 93, 94, 150, 152, 179, *see also* Darwin, Charles; genetics; selection
Evolution and Ethics 53, 57, 94, 138
exoticization 43

fable 46, 48–56, 104
faithfulness 12, 15, 17, 18, 53, 57–61, 66, 68–9, 79, 86, 89, 107, 140, 144, 168, 185, *see also* fidelity
fan writings 26 n.11, 186, 194 n.12, 195
fidelity 1, 3, 6, 8, 12–15, 18–19, 27, 31, 38, 53, 57, 59–69, 81, 88, 90, 107, 137, 139–40, 143, 185, 198, *see also* faithfulness
film adaptation 13, 15, 18, 77–8, 82, 84, 88
film remakes 78, 85
Finnegans Wake 164, 174
Flower-like Boys 118–20, 122, 126
Fludernik, Monica 165
folklore 157
forgery 26, 30, 181
For You in Full Bloom 121–3
Fraleigh, Matthew 148
free translation 1, 3, 7, 12–15, 19, 20, 22, 26, 33–4, 37–56, 91, 131, 184, 200
Fu, Lei 60, 61
Fujii, Shōzō 62 n.6, 65, 68, 112

Gambier, Yves 18
genetic criticism 28
genetics 29
Genette, Gérard 34, 76, 179–82, 195
Gentzler, Edwin 16–18, 96
Gillespie, Stuart 137

globalization   79, 87, 88, 109, 123–5
Gottlieb, Henrik   84–6
Greene, Thomas   133–5, 139

Handford, S. A.   39, 48
Henningsen, Lena   21, 30, 175, 197
Hermans, Theo   2, 13, 132, 184
Horace   20, 132, 133, 137
Hu, Gengshen   94
Huang, Zhonglian   13
Hunan Satellite station   114–17
Hutcheon, Linda   81, 182
hybridity   45, 47, 65, 154, 182, 191, 196

ideology   10, 95, 147
idol drama   116
imitatio   33 n.17, 131–44
imitation   1–5, 8–16, 45, 60, 86, 94, 99, 102, 127, 161, 198, 200, 201, 204, *see also imitatio*
  compared with adaptation   24–6
  importance of   20–3
  Joycean imitations   162–78
  manga imitations   179–97
  methodologies of   30–4
  poetry imitations   147–51
  yomihon imitations   152–60
indigenousness   23, 29, 46–7, 50–1, 56, 95, 99, 111, 116, 146, 148–9, 151, 163, 176, 184, 203–4
influence   7, 11, 31, 40, 71, 96, 140, 147, 162–4, 174, 185
Inoue, Yuhiko   121
intercultural studies   87–8
interference   16, 68, 89
intermediality   4, 8, 16, 18, 19, 21, 76, 78, 84, 93, 110–4, 122, 152 n.8, 201
intertextuality   11, 15 n.5, 76, 82, 196
intervention   15, 59, 100, 187, 204
It Started with a Kiss   121–2
Iwabuchi, Koichi   123, 126

Jakobson, Roman   6, 12, 62, 75–6, 84
Japaneseness   149
"Japanese odor"   67, 68, 120, 148–9
Japanese Wave   109, 115 n.9, 124
Japanization   109, 124, 149, 201
Jesuit translators   38–41, 44
Jewel in the Palace   124
Johnson, Samuel   76, 137, 138, 175, 185
Jones, William   138
Jonson, Ben   21, 24, 135–6, 177
Joseon dynasty   122, 147
Journey to the Extreme   179, 186, 189–93
Journey to the West   29, 34, 97, 114, 134, 152, 180, 185–96, 200, 204
Joyce, James   9, 23, 26, 127, 134, 162–78, 201

Kafka on the Shore   63
Kamio, Yōko   110–12, 204
Korean Wave   109, 115 n.9, 124–5
Korkut, Nil   182, 183
Kuhns, Luke   183
kundoku   63, 100, 150, 152, 159–61, 199 n.2, 203
Kyokutei, Bakin   151, 156

Lai, Mingzhu   64–6
Lambert, José   2
Lefevere, André   13, 15, 177, 184
Let's Go Watch the Meteor Shower   115, 118
Lhermitte, Corinne   19, 33, 184
liberalism   19, 38, 44, 56, 69, 107, *see also* free translation
Lin, Shaohua   7, 62–9, 71, 148
Lin, Shu   39, 46, 51–5, 69, 92, 97, 105–7
lingua franca   4, 111, 148
literalism   13, 15, 34, 38, 56, 94, 107, 202–3

literal translation 3, 12, 39, 59, 91, 95, 107, 157, 203, *see also* semantic translation; source-text-bound translation
Liu, Yichang 165, 172–6
localization 5, 95, 109, 111–15, 118–26, 142
Longinus 133
Lowell, Robert 139–41, 194
Lu, Xun 13, 53, 107
Lu, Yin 170–1, 176

McFarland, Thomas 10, 142
Maiden Team 188, 193
Malinowski, Bronislaw 96
manga 8, 9, 29, 34, 109–26, 179, 185–96, 199, 200, 203–4
manipulation 8, 62, 89, 109, 115, 185, 196
Martí-López, Elisa 22, 23, 152, 160, 163
Marvelous Adventures of Monkey King 188
media culture 125
Meiji Japan 92, 148
metaphor 11, 29, 45, 133–5
metaphrase 136, 137
Meteor Garden 111–20, 126
Miller, Scott 107
mimesis 131, 132
Minekura, Kazuya 189, 190, 193
modernism 8, 26, 139–40, 165–74, 176–7, 179
modernity 109, 124, 125, 202
Murakami Haruki Fever 62, 200
mutilation 196
myth 46, 77, 146

Naremore, James 18, 77
narrative style 158, 162, 164–7, 175
  free indirect speech 167–8, 170
  interior monologue 167 n.5, 170–3

narrated monologue 167, 172
  stream of consciousness 9, 23, 163–76
national language 72
Natsume, Soseki 66
naturalization 48, *see also* domestication
New Tales from Mount Kŭmo 98
Nord, Christiane 56
Norwegian Wood 62–6, 71, 112

Ogyū, Sorai 67 n.9, 150, 151
Okajima, Kanzan 152, 155, 156
original(ity) 1, 6–11, 14–23, 25–30, 58–71, 79, 81–4, 86, 88–90, 92, 94, 95, 98, 99–108, 111–24, 131–43, 145, 147, 149–56, 160, 163–4, 168–83, 185–90, 193–9, 201, 203
Orphan of Zhao 92
Ortiz, Fernando 96
Other, the (*vs.* Self) 79, 82, 87, 126, 149–50, 159, 204

paraphrase 105, 135–8
Parks, Tim 166
parody 10, 21, 26, 134, 138, 150, 179–85, 197
pastiche 26, 30 n.14, 149, 154, 176, 179–83, 186, 196–7
Patariro Journey to the West 189
Pavis, Patrice 79, 95
Picture of Dorian Gray, The 96, 103
plagiarism 10, 21, 30, 45, 110, 185, 197, *see also* copying
playfulness 9, 13, 17, 79, 83, 93, 94, 102, 122, 134, 150, 154, 180–96
Pollack, David 97, 148
polysystems 163, *see also* Even-Zohar, Itamar
Pope, Alexander 62, 132, 137–8, 175
popular culture 109, 125
poststructuralism 11, 15, 76

Pound, Ezra   32, 33, 139–40, 175, 194
Pratt, Mary Louise   96
predecessor text   29, 192
"Preface to *Ovid's Epistles*"   136
promythium   52
prototypical translation   12 n.2
Proust, Marcel   169, 176
Pu, Songling   49
Pym, Anthony   95, 111, 178

Qian, Zhongshu   69, 106
Quintilian   133, 137
radical translation   143, 185, 193

Raw, Laurence   78, 82–3
reception   14, 17, 24, 40, 62–9, 80–1, 83, 88, 89, 97, 108, 110–25, 144, 151, 159, 162, 175–7, 191, 201, 204
recontextualization   82, 95–6, 101, 142, 185
re-creation   59, 68, 178
reframing   95–6, 104
regionalization   109
register   49, 71
Reimer, Andrew   185
reinterpretation   26, 57, 60, 95–6, 103–5, 108
rejuvenation   195
relocation   17, 96, 154
Renaissance, the   61, 131, 133–5, 179, 183–4, 186
renewal   94, 162, 195
reproduction   70, 94, 133, 136, 167, 180, 186
resurrection   131, 142, 189
retelling   56, 192
re-version   56
rewriting   68, 75, 76, 79, 80, 86–9, 95, 97–8, 103, 131–41, 146–7, 150, 178–9, 184, 186, 194–5, 198–204
Ricci, Matteo   38, 44

Romance of the Three Kingdoms   97, 98, 99, 102 n.12, 114, 152, 200
Romantic Movement   10, 11, 19, 20, 22, 92, 98, 106–7, 121, 126, 132, 138–9, 145, 149, 160, 179, 195
Rose, Margaret   182

Salinger, J. D.   70, 71
Salmon, Claudine   97, 200, 202, 204
Sanders, Julie   22, 81
Scheiermacher, Friedrich   62
selection   94
Self (*vs*. the Other)   79, 82, 87, 126, 149–50, 161
semantic translation   139, 142, 159
sign interpreting   84
simulacrum   197
Sinicization   8, 48, 65, 201
Sinographic sphere   159–61
Sino-Japanese poetry   147–50
Sino-Vietnamese poetry   147
slash fiction   195
Sound and the Fury, The   173
source-text-bound   12 n.2, 106, 159
Stam, Robert   13, 18, 78
Steiner, George   22, 82, 137, 161
Steininger, Brian   149
Story of Jin Yunqiao   97
Strange Stories from the Leisure Studio   49
Strange Tales of the Bow Moon   157
style   8, 9, 40, 46, 79, 110, 114, 138, 140, 147–8, 154, 157, 158, 162, 185, 201
  of Joycean translations   170–5
  of Lin Shaohua   58–62, 65–72
  of parody   179–82
  of *Ulysses*   164–8
stylistics   61

Takashima, Toshio   155, 157–8
Takebe, Ayatari   153, 156
Takeuchi, Yoshimi   150

Tales of Moonlight and Rain 101
Tanizaki, Jun'ichiro 66
Tempest, The 142–3
text
  hypertext 34, 95, 180 n.1
  hypotext 34, 95, 173, 177, 180–2
  predecessor text 192
  source text 6, 12–17, 22, 25, 27, 34, 37–9, 41, 47, 51, 53, 56, 59–62, 65, 70, 72, 80, 82–3, 86, 90, 96, 101–3, 106–8, 117, 120, 136–7, 139, 141–4, 154, 159, 163, 176–7, 180, 183, 185–6, 188, 192, 194, 199, 203
  successor text 15, 192
  text-types 1, 131
Thom, Robert 39–46, 51–3, 56
Three Beast-men 188–9, 193
Tihanov, Galin 145
Toriyama, Akira 187
Toury, Gideon 2
tradaptation 17, 18, 75, *see also* adaptation
transcreation 3, 5, 59, 61, 62, 72, 108, 131 n.1, 134, 158, 162–78
transcription 40, 146
transculturation 3, 31–2, 81, 95–6
transfer studies 5 n.4
transformation 3, 5, 15, 25, 26, 34, 48, 58, 76, 96, 133, 180, 184, 185, 190
translatability 87, 166
translation, types of
  audiovisual translation 84
  drama translation 70
  interlingual translation 76, 146 n.1, 160, 203 n.4
  intersemiotic translation 16, 75, 76, 84–6, 93
  intralingual translation 6 n.5, 75, 146 n.1, 203 n.4
  intrasemiotic translation 84
  poetry translation 132, 184

translation proper 6, 12 n.2, 27, 76, 84–5, 185, 199
translation studies 1–3, 5–8, 11, 14, 15, 18, 19, 27, 29, 75–6, 78, 80–90, 94, 96, 108, 137, 143, 146, 161, 163, 177, 184, 197–8, 203–4
translinguality 15
transmission 23, 28, 38–40, 80, 95, 97, 98, 112, 146, 164, 193, 200, 204
transmutation 5, 18, 76, 99, 108
transplantation 5, 23, 28, 95, 165, 169, 178
transposition 5, 18, 26, 62, 108, 112, 131 n.1, 135, 142, 145, 163, 181
transtextuality 1–4, 7, 9–34, 63, 75, 86, 89, 94–5, 97–8, 106, 110, 131–5, 143, 145–6, 150, 161, 180, 198–204
travesty 26, 181
trendy drama 110
tribute 183, 194
Trigault, Nicholas 38, 44, 51 n.14
Trimming the Wick 96, 98, 102
Tymozcko, Maria 5

Ueda, Akinari 101
Ulysses 9, 26, 127, 134, 162–79, 201
"Ulysses in Taipei" 168–70, 172
untranslatability 87

Venuti, Lawrence 16, 81–4, 92, 132, 141, 143
verbatim translation 12 n.2, 184
versionings 143–4
Voigts-Virchow, Eckart 192–3

Wachtel, Michael 140
Wakabayashi, Judy 3, 91, 147, 150, 159, 203
Wang, Dahong 96, 103–4

Water Margin 97, 99, 114, 151–9, 188 n.5, 200, 204
Waves, The 173
Weinbrot, Howard 20, 183–4
Westernization 124
Wilde, Oscar 96, 103–5, 201
Wild Sheep Chase, A 62 n.6
Woolf, Virginia 164, 166–7, 176, 177

Xu, Yuanchong 57, 58, 60–2, 68–9, 71

Yan, Fu 51, 53, 57–61, 68, 94, 138, 202
Yao, Steven 19, 139
Yip, William 168–70, 172, 173, 175, 176
yomihon 151–61
Young, Edward 131

Zeng, Xubai 59
Zhang, Chishan 39, 45–8, 55
Zhuangzi 43, 50, 58
Zukofsky, Louis 139–40